SOCIAL TRAPS AND THE PROBLEM OF TRUST

A 'social trap' is a situation where individuals, groups or organisations are unable to cooperate owing to mutual distrust and lack of social capital, even where cooperation would benefit all. Examples include civil strife, pervasive corruption, ethnic discrimination, depletion of natural resources and misuse of social insurance systems. People will cooperate only if they can trust that others will also cooperate. Much has been written attempting to explain the problem, but rather less material is available on how to escape it. In this book, Bo Rothstein explores how social capital and social trust are generated, and what governments can do about it. He argues that it is the existence of universal and impartial political institutions, together with public policies which enhance social and economic equality, that creates social capital. By introducing the theory of collective memory into the discussion, Rothstein makes an empirical and theoretical claim for how universal institutions can be established.

BO ROTHSTEIN is the August Röhss Chair in Political Science at Göteborg University in Sweden. Among his publications in English are *The Social Democratic State: The Swedish Model and The Bureaucratic Problems of Social Reforms* (Pittsburgh, 1996); *Just Institutions Matter: The Moral and Political Logic of the Universal Welfare State* (Cambridge, 1998); *Restructuring the Welfare State* (co-edited with Sven Steinmo, New York, 2002); and *Creating Social Trust in Post-Socialist Societies* (co-edited with Janos Kornai and Susan Rose-Ackerman, New York, 2004).

Series Editor
Robert E. Goodin
Research School of Social Sciences
Australian National University

Advisory Editors
**Brian Barry, Russell Hardin, Carole Pateman, Barry Weingast
Stephen Elkin, Claus Offe, Susan Rose-Ackerman**

Social scientists have rediscovered institutions. They have been increasingly concerned with the myriad ways in which social and political institutions shape the patterns of individual interactions which produce social phenomena. They are equally concerned with the ways in which those institutions emerge from such interactions.

This series is devoted to the exploration of the more normative aspects of these issues. What makes one set of institutions better than another? How, if at all, might we move from the less desirable set of institutions to a more desirable set? Alongside the questions of what institutions we would design, if we were designing them afresh, are pragmatic questions of how we can best get from here to there: from our present institutions to new revitalized ones.

Theories of institutional design is insistently multidisciplinary and interdisciplinary, both in the institutions on which it focuses, and in the methodologies used to study them. There are interesting sociological questions to be asked about legal institutions, interesting legal questions to be asked about economic institutions, and interesting social, economic, and legal questions to be asked about political institutions. By juxtaposing these approaches in print, this series aims to enrich normative discourse surrounding important issues of designing and redesigning, shaping and reshaping the social, political, and economic institutions of contemporary society.

Other books in this series
Robert E. Goodin (editor), *The Theory of Institutional Design*
Brent Fisse and John Braithwaite, *Corporations, Crime, and Accountability*
Itai Sened, *The Political Institution of Private Property*
Bo Rothstein, *Just Institutions Matter*
Jon Elster, Claus Offe, and Ulrich Preuss, *Institutional Design in Post-Communist Societies: Rebuilding the Ship at Sea*
Mark Bovens, *The Quest for Responsibility*
Geoffrey Brennan and Alan Hamlin, *Democratic Devices and Desires*
Adrienne Heritier, *Policy-Making and Diversity in Europe: Escape from Deadlock*
Eric Patashnik, *Putting Trust in the US Budget: Federal Trust Funds and the Politics of Commitment*
Benjamin Reilly, *Democracy in Divided Societies: Electoral Engineering for Conflict Management*
Huib Pellikaan and Robert van der Veen, *Environmental Dilemmas and Policy Design*
John S. Dryzek and Lesue Holmes, *Post-Communist Democratization: Political Discourses across Thirteen Countries*
Jonathan G. S. Koppell, *The Politics of Quasi-Government: Hybrid Organizations and the Dynamics of Bureaucratic Control*
Jürg Steiner, André Bächtiger, Markus Spörndli, and Marcus R. Steenbergen, *Deliberative Politics in Action: Analyzing Parliamentary Discourse*

SOCIAL TRAPS
AND THE PROBLEM
OF TRUST

BO ROTHSTEIN

CAMBRIDGE
UNIVERSITY PRESS

628163199

CAMBRIDGE UNIVERSITY PRESS
Cambridge, New York, Melbourne, Madrid, Cape Town, Singapore, São Paulo

Cambridge University Press
The Edinburgh Building, Cambridge CB2 2RU, UK

Published in the United States of America by Cambridge University Press, New York

www.cambridge.org
Information on this title: www.cambridge.org/9780521848296

First published 2005

Printed in the United Kingdom at the University Press, Cambridge

A catalogue record for this book is available from the British Library

ISBN-13   978-0-521-84829-6 hardback
ISBN-10   0-521-84829-6
ISBN-13   978-0-521-61282-9 paperback
ISBN-10   0-521-61282-9

To AnnChristin

Contents

Tables and figures

Tables

Figures

Acknowledgements

I came to this topic, almost by sheer accident, from the world of welfare and social policy research. It is a very pleasant world, filled with nice things such as equality, justice, liberty, progress, and the development of social rights. Doing research on the problem of social traps has taken me into a very different intellectual landscape. It is filled with things like corruption, ethnic conflicts, distrust, suspicion, treachery, opportunism, deceit, discrimination, and many other forms of misery. There has been more than one night when thinking about all this misery has kept me awake. Seeing things through these conceptual lenses does not bring a lot of sunshine to one's mind.

On a journey into a difficult and dark terrain like this, one needs a lot of supporting and cheerful friends, and, as with many other things in life, I have been spoiled beyond reason. I am especially thankful to two persons: Margaret Levi, who for many years has been like a mentor to me. In this project, she has both inspired me and introduced me to many important things and thoughts. Her generosity and helpfulness is simply extraordinary.

I have been fortunate to have collaborated with Sven Steinmo for almost fifteen years. His good advice, thoughtfulness, and good spirits have been crucial for me in many difficult situations. If I ever needed a really good *consigliori*, Sven would be the one.

I started working on this project when Robert Putnam asked me to join him in a project about the development of social capital and political culture in a number of Western countries. The intense discussions in this project were crucial for my understanding of the problem of social traps. Among the participants in this project, I would especially like to thank Peter Hall,

Claus Offe, and Jean-Pierre Worms for inspiring conversations and many valuable comments on early drafts of what became chapter 4 in this book.

Special thanks are due to Ira Katznelson, Madge Spitaleri, and Eric Wanner at the Russell Sage Foundation in New York where I had the privilege to serve as visiting scholar for ten months during the beginning of this project. The Russell Sage Foundation is simply a marvellous operation, unmatched in its very special combination of generosity and perfection.

János Kornai and Susan Rose-Ackerman invited me to participate in the project "Trust and Honesty: Theory and Evidence in the Light of Post-Socialist Transitions," at the Collegium Budapest Institute for Advanced Study. Few intellectual experiences have been so rewarding for me, and I am truly grateful for the two months I spent in daily discussions with colleagues from fifteen countries and seven different disciplines.

My home base is the Department of Political Science at Göteborg University. It is simply a great place where it is fun to be – a rare thing for academic departments. Many colleagues in the department have contributed to this book. First in line is Sören Holmberg, who deserves a special prize for his splendid combination of enthusiasm for this project and forbearance with me, and for insisting that if you are clever enough there is a way to find a quantitative measure for everything. Peter Esaiasson, Victor Galaz, Mikael Gilljam, Lennart J. Lundqvist, Lennart Nilsson, and Maria Oskarson have given me lots of good advice, often more (and better) than I could handle. Bengt-Ove Boström, Margaretha Hellgren-Glimje, Eva Meuller, and Leena Hiltunen have all in many different ways helped me with the administrative aspects of this project. Rosemary Nordström skilfully made English of my text.

I have had the privilege to work with a number of colleagues from what I now have to admit is the younger generation in political science. Dietlind Stolle and I started to work on the problem of social capital in the mid-1990s and we have collaborated ever since. I have tried very hard, but it is impossible to match Dietlind's energy and inventiveness, and I am truly grateful that I have had the opportunity to work with her. The two articles we published together in 2002 and 2003 have been very important for this book.

Eleonora Pasotti guided me to new insights about the importance of cultural theory for understanding the mysteries of clientilism "Naples style," for which many thanks. Parts of chapter 2 in this book are based on a paper we wrote together. Paola Cesarini was the first to comment on the first draft of what became chapter 1, and afterwards generously shared her insights about theories of collective memories and many other things. For two years, Ylva Norén Bretzer was a very dedicated research assistant when this project started – and we have since worked in parallel on the problem of trust and democracy. Staffan Kumlin's ingenious thinking about ways to test some of the early ideas I had about how social trust is generated has been crucial for the argument presented in chapter 5.

Anders Biel, Arne Bigsten, Hans Blomkvist, Dario Castiglione, Daniel Eek, Kimmo Eriksson, Robert Goodin, Carina Gunnarsson, Donald Granberg, Jörgen Hermansson, Olle Häggstrom, Tim Knudsen, Per Molander, Kenneth Newton, Elinor Ostrom, Göran Rosenberg, Per Selle, John Scheimann, Örjan Sturesjö, Piotr Swistak, Charles Tilly, Eric Uslaner, Mark Warren, and Daniel Wohlgemuth all generously gave me comments and offered valuable advice, for which many thanks. Special thanks also go to Sheri Berman and Susan Rose-Ackerman who read and commented on the whole manuscript.

Financial support for this project has been given from the Swedish Science Council, the former Swedish Council for Research in the Humanities and Social Sciences, the former Swedish Council for Research in Social Policy, and the Bank of Sweden Tercentenary Foundation.

I have made some really smart decisions in my life. The very best was to marry AnnChristin. This book is for the shimmering light in your blue eyes.

1

Reflections after a long day in Moscow

All intellectual journeys have a particular beginning. This one commenced one evening after a long day in Moscow five years ago. In November 1997, I was invited by the Swedish Ministry for Foreign Affairs to speak at the Swedish Embassy in the Russian capital. President Boris Yeltsin was soon to make his first (and only) state visit to Sweden and his entourage of civil servants and politicians was eager for more information about Swedish society. There were many issues upon which they sought enlightenment, according to the Foreign Affairs official who contacted me, and what they wanted from me was a lecture that addressed how the Swedish welfare state worked and how we "controlled the Swedish state." It sounded intriguing, and I accepted the invitation with alacrity. I should add that I had no real personal experience of Russia, and my contacts with the extensive Swedish and international research community concentrated on Eastern Europe were even more limited then than they are now.

The lecture, which was interpreted to Russian, was sadly of a somewhat more mundane sort. Much of it dealt with the sometimes esoteric differences between universal and selective welfare programs, the right of Swedish citizens to occasionally appeal the decisions of government agencies, the mysteries of the principle of public access to official records, and peculiar institutions like the Parliamentary Ombudsman. I cribbed a bit from the basic class I taught in public administration policy and some more from a study of Swedish welfare policy that I had published a few years before (Rothstein 1998a). Still, my Russian listeners seemed enthralled, especially when they grasped the economic magnitude of the Swedish public sector.

Following my talk, and those given by other invited guests from Sweden, the Embassy had arranged the kind of refreshments customary in diplomatic contexts to promote more informal discussions between us and the Russians. One of the people I spoke to introduced himself as the third-ranking official in the Russian tax administration. He let me know that he was exceptionally interested in Sweden and Swedish state administration, for a very particular reason. He had been in touch with his colleagues at the National Tax Board in Stockholm and they had told him something that struck him as highly improbable – that the Swedish National Tax Board collected 98.7 percent of what they billed Swedish taxpayers. Could this be possible, he wondered, or were they pulling his leg? He wondered because his and the Russian tax administration's most pressing problem at that time was that they could not collect more than about 24 percent of the total taxes due from Russian citizens according to their tax returns.

"Oh yes," I said after a few seconds' thought, "That sounds about right." The figure did not count the "black" and "gray" market economy, of course, but that the Swedish National Tax Board probably collected such a percentage of the total amount it actually assessed citizens sounded about right to me. To his next question of how that could be possible, I answered that it was probably owing to two things. For some years in the mid-1980s, I had had the privilege of working closely with Urban Laurin at the Department of Political Science in Uppsala, whose penetrating and skillfully crafted doctoral dissertation had been on the inclination (or disinclination) of Swedes to pay their taxes, so I was not entirely at sea on the subject (Laurin 1986). Through long-standing collaboration with political scientist Margaret Levi at the University of Washington in Seattle, I had also been in touch with certain aspects of American research on this intriguing subject (Levi 1988; Scholz 1998; Scholz and Lubell 1998).

Using the research by Laurin and others that I knew something about at the time, I answered that Swedes' willingness to pay taxes was founded on a widespread belief that the tax administration was reasonably competent and compelled *most other citizens* to pay in one way or another. And since people believed that other people generally paid what they were supposed to, they also paid. Laurin's dissertation in particular supported that hypothesis – i.e. that tax compliance and evasion depended to a great extent on what people believed other people did. This is not unique to Sweden. Two American researchers summarize their findings as follows: "citizens will meet obligations to the collective despite the temptation to free ride as long as they trust other citizens and political leaders to keep up their side of the social contract" (Scholz and Lubell 1998: 411). A large Danish study based on survey data has also shown such a correlation: "the lower the social trust, the lower moral standards when it comes to paying taxes" (Goul Andersen 1998: 246).

But, I went on, research has provided an explanation. Most Swedish citizens understood that all the money was not stashed in Stockholm by the National Tax Board. At the very least, a substantial portion would conceivably come back in the form of child benefit, old age pensions, health care, public schools, the wages of professors of political science, and other purposes of general interest to the public and the individual. According to that research, acceptance of the need to pay taxes cannot be based solely on compulsion or threats of audits, as such an apparatus of compulsion and control would become far too expansive and costly (Levi 1988). It is also unlikely that most people pay taxes for purely altruistic reasons. Some form of *conditional assent* must come into the picture. We understand this to mean that citizens are prepared to pay their taxes under certain conditions (albeit somewhat grudgingly). Those conditions are, I said, first that people believe that "most others" probably pay what they are supposed to, and secondly that most of the money is used for purposes people consider legitimate.

"Fascinating, truly fascinating," said my Russian interlocutor. He explained that there were two reasons most Russians did not pay their taxes, which jibed with my reasoning to a certain extent. Russian citizens believed that since most other people did not pay, it was rather pointless to play the honorable taxpayer. Moreover, they believed that most tax bureaucrats and other civil servants were corrupt to the core. Either they took bribes to let people get out of paying taxes, or else they personally confiscated a considerable portion of the taxes that were, despite everything, actually paid. If, contrary to all expectations, some tax revenues reached the proper addressee in the Russian state administration, the general belief was that those civil servants were also corrupt or that the funds were spent for generally illegitimate purposes.

The Russian bureaucrat then wondered whether it was true that most officials in the Swedish state administration could not be bribed. I answered in the affirmative and then inquired, somewhat discreetly, whether the beliefs of Russian citizens about widespread corruption and bribery in his tax administration were founded. "Oh yes," he answered forthrightly, to my surprise. "It is a large bureaucracy with more than 100,000 civil servants, and sure, many are ready, willing, and able to take bribes. But most of them also realize that the current situation is untenable and are fundamentally opposed to the generally rampant corruption." He said that the problem is actually the same as that of the taxpayers. It is rather pointless to be the only civil servant who does not take bribes if one believes that almost everyone else does. My new Russian friend explained that if he could just find some way to convince the majority of civil servants that most others would stop taking bribes and putting tax revenues in their own pockets, he was sure the overwhelming majority would also be prepared to desist from corruption.

At the time, there was a great deal of coverage in Russian and Swedish newspapers about the non-payment of wages and pensions that was engendering widespread nervousness across Russia. With that in mind, I asked my Russian friend again whether most Russian citizens realized that if they did not pay their taxes, the state would never have provide them with schools, health care, and retirement pensions. He replied that most Russians understood that very well but, again, most also believed there was no point in being the only honest actor in such a rotten game. Why should they loyally cooperate with a state they perceived to be genuinely corrupt, and why should they behave honorably when everyone they knew – neighbors, friends, and coworkers – cheated? Who wants to play the part of the village idiot in rose-colored glasses? Or, as put in the English terminology that dominates the social sciences, "who wants to be a sucker?" I could not come up with a reasonable counter argument. Unadulterated altruism is a rare bird, at least when it comes to paying taxes. Another problem is that in situations like these, no good actually came out of altruistic behavior. Those who loyally kept paying their taxes despite knowing about the general disloyalty in the game fed nothing but the corruption.[1]

Certainly, this insight into the state of affairs is as logical as it is grim, and we cogitated over the issue as we made further judicious use of the delights the Ministry for Foreign Affairs had laid before us that evening. But my increasingly interested Russian interlocutor continued to probe. He wondered whether I, as a political scientist, had any sound theories that could explain the state of his tax bureaucracy and the Russian society. I perked up, and said that indeed was something for which we in the social sciences actually had remarkably good theories. The Russian situation he had outlined was, I was able to say, a brilliant illustration of a phenomenon given the metaphorical designation of *the social trap*, among many other names. Especially in the expanding area of *non-cooperative game theory*, it is one of the central problems –, that is, how to explain the way that cooperation can be established among self-interested utility maximizing actors. Cooperation is based on trust – or, to use another word, *social capital.* Without trust, I explained, societies, groups, and organizations fall into similar social traps.

---

[1] When I wrote this, there were reports in the Swedish newspapers about the problem of police officers in St. Petersburg supplementing their wages by robbing western tourists and businessmen (*Dagens Nyheter*, September 2, 2002). As a Swede engaged in the attempt to increase trade between Sweden and Russia expressed it, it is difficult to achieve anything worthwhile under such circumstances.

The fine art of driving a taxi in Palermo

Diego Gambetta, one of the foremost researchers into the question of how to explain the southern Italian mafia and society, has provided one of the best illustrations of the "social trap." Gambetta's case has to do with taxi drivers in Palermo, Sicily. I am sure they are like all other taxi drivers for the most part, but according to Gambetta they have one rather unique trait: they do not use their two-way radios and have no use for a dispatch center. The reason for this is that when they introduced those new-fangled ideas in the early 1980s, the system degenerated into chaos and universal anarchy (Gambetta 1993: 220ff.).

The utility to taxi owners of a dispatch center that can call taxis over the radio is obvious. Customers need keep track of only one phone number and can be served by the nearest car and thus save time, while taxi owners get more customers and shorter routes. Customers, taxi owners, and the drivers they employ all profit by such a system, which is why taxi owners in most areas of the world have formed alliances and shared the costs of similar dispatch centers, even though they are actually in competition with each other. This simple example of what it needs to create efficient competition among profit maximizing actors in a market shows that competition is not enough. The actors must also agree to establish *institutions* that are not ruled by competition and self-interest, but are rather driven by norms such as impartiality and the public good. In this case, the idea of such an institution is that customers can call a dispatch center that inquires which driver is closest to the address and, when that driver responds, requests them to take the fare.

But, according to Gambetta, it turned out to be impossible to get this rather elementary system to work in Palermo. The reason for this was that that in order to get the most fares, taxi drivers in Palermo frequently lied about how close they were to the places in the city where they were ordered by the dispatch center to pick up fares. Soon everyone knew that everyone else was embroidering the truth, and so everyone added a few more stitches . . . and a few more. The dispatch center concept is based on the fundamental but uncertain principle that taxi drivers can be confident that none of the others will say they are closer than they really are in order to get the fare. Such a *social norm* must be established for the system to work. We can safely say that this is a rational strategy for the collective of taxi drivers as the fares are evenly allocated, for reasons of probability, if all drivers state their locations honestly. But since taxi drivers in Palermo, according to Gambetta, could not trust one another, a snowball of deceit upon deceit started rolling and finally everyone lied, always saying they were "just around the corner" in order to claim the fare. Taxi driver *A* gives his location, *B* waits to hear it and then says that he is a little closer, whereupon *C* calls in and says he is even closer, and so on.

Gambetta says there is no incontrovertible evidence that many taxi drivers cheated this way, but the very belief held by the majority that "most drivers" cheated was enough to break down the system as increasing numbers chose to leave the organization. Gambetta concludes that, without trust, there is no possibility of establishing a cooperative equilibrium (1993: 224). That lack of trust led to the closure of the dispatch center and taxi drivers had instead to wait in line at taxi stands around the city, got substantially fewer fares, and had to drive further every time they picked up a customer. *The social trap* had snapped shut around them. Suspicion had led them all into a lose–lose situation, despite the fact that they all understood that everyone would have profited if they had trusted one another.

But . . . how do you get from Moscow to Stockholm?

I held forth for some time, giving other examples of this fascinating theory, even though it had until then played a somewhat obscure role in my own consciousness, in part because it was frequently presented in an intricately mathematized – and thus, for me, rather inaccessible – form (cf. Scharpf 1997). However, a number of recently published books following that theoretical line but with a distinctly empirical orientation, including those by the American political scientists Gary Miller (1992), Elinor Ostrom (1990), and Robert Putnam (1993), had increasingly roused my interest in the phenomenon. Why did the extent of interpersonal trust and the capacity to establish what some economists call "efficient" institutions (everything from local taxi dispatch centers to all the institutions of states governed by rule of law) vary so widely among different societies, regions, cities, and individual organizations (cf. Myhrman 1994)?

Anyway, for my Russian interlocutor I rolled out large parts of the theoretical and empirical arsenal that social science could contribute towards explaining the situation in which he and all of Russian society then found themselves – one of widespread corruption, lawlessness, mafia control, and crippled public welfare programs. I must admit that I felt rather pleased with myself, especially because the Russian tax official nodded in agreement at many points during my rather lengthy monologue. But then he asked a question that in one blow stripped me of answers and gave me the basic theme of this book. "Tell me, Professor Rothstein," he said, "now that we know all of this and have all of these marvelous theories and intriguing studies, what should I do to make Moscow like Stockholm?"

Instantly, I was at a loss for words.[2] I had never thought along those lines and I immediately realized, not without some embarrassment, that social science can offer no answers on this issue that are in the least reliable and even fewer that are useful in practice. We have excellent models for explaining static situations and systematic corruption as well as various forms of trustful cooperation over time, but there are no useful models for explaining what causes a change from one state of affairs to another. How can you get people who have long harbored deeply rooted mutual suspicion to suddenly begin to trust one another and cooperate loyally for the common good? Why should people with long-standing and extensive experience and memories of the untrustworthiness (evil, duplicity, cruelty, etc.) of "other people" suddenly begin to rely on one another? In a game like this, trust is not just an empty gesture or a personal preference. It is a matter of fundamentally changing a worldview to one that says most other people will also act in solidarity and cooperate – for example, by giving up tangible resources (paying taxes and refraining from taking bribes). It is not simply a matter of changing values, either. People who take bribes or evade taxes may simultaneously hold values by which they actually consider what they do to be morally wrong and harmful, not only to society but also to themselves over the long term. The reason they continue to act treacherously or opportunistically is not necessarily that they (or their culture) suffer from some kind of moral defect, but rather that there is no point in being the only honest player in a rotten game at which everyone else cheats (or is perceived to be a cheater). This is a case when rationality fails because one *cannot rationally decide to forget* treacherous behavior (cf. Elster 1983). The act of trusting people who cannot be trusted can be very risky.

According to the logic of the social trap, even people with clear preferences for "fair play" will continue their disloyal behavior because they believe, and for good reason, that almost all "other people" are going to keep playing dirty. And, again, this is not because most other people are actually evil and fundamentally disloyal, but because they expect that everyone else will cheat. Changing the situation is thus a matter of changing the worldview of large groups of citizens about the kind of society they live in and how people might conceivably act in that society. Therein, we have captured two of the central insights of non-cooperative game theory which will dominate this book. First, that political and economic actions should be understood as "strategic" in the sense that *what we do depends on what we expect "other people" are going to do* (Schiemann 2000). Secondly, that *the end result of individual rationality may very well be collective irrationality* (Lichbach 1997). Any group of agents risks being trapped in a non-cooperative equilibrium,

---

[2] An unusual experience, I must admit.

even though they all realized that a more cooperative equilibrium would bring welfare gains to all of them. As Per Molander has argued, this is in fact a deathblow to every type of idyllic notion that rational agents without coordination can establish efficient equlibria (Molander 1994: 84).

On the difficulty of seeing what does not exist

The following days were full of reflection and contrition. The power of my Russian friend's dilemma was suddenly clear to me. I also realized that the social trap problem certainly did not apply exclusively to Russia, but also to all of the post-socialist societies, not to mention the developing countries with their persistent poverty and corruption (Kornai, Rose-Ackerman and Rothstein 2004; cf. Rodrik 1999). My lecture at the Embassy about such strange phenomena as universal child benefit, active labor market policy, and the parliamentary ombudsman in a public sector that encompassed more than half the gross domestic product (GDP) must have seemed exceedingly odd to my Russian listeners, considering that I devoted not a single word to issues such as bribery and corruption. It was also entirely clear to me that a great deal of the research I had done and been involved in to that point, and which had to do with Swedish social, labor market, and education policy, was based on two tacitly accepted premises – circumstances that I and my colleagues in this type of research had taken for granted, but which we should have analyzed and problematized. First, the existence of fundamental trust in "most" other citizens in Swedish society. Second, the belief that public administration may certainly be both complex and bureaucratic, but that it is not being eroded by corruption to any significant extent.[3] In our defense, it is not easy for the research community to study that which does not exist, but from a comparative perspective it should have been clear to us that these were core issues to be addressed (cf. Blomkvist 1988).

   Much of this welfare state research has involved the attempt to explain differences in the scope and direction of welfare and social policy in the Organization for Economic Cooperation and Development (OECD) countries. The problem may be described as follows: How should we explain the great variations in social and welfare policies among these countries that are otherwise rather similar in terms of socioeconomic conditions? When all is said

---

[3] In his novel *The Red Room* (1989) the Swedish author August Strindberg gives a famously negative depiction of Swedish bureaucracy as "The Civil Service Department for the Payment of Wages to Civil Servants." However, the salient point from the perspective of this book is that bribery and corruption are *not* part of Strindberg's depiction. I believe that if bribery and corruption had been generally accepted, Strindberg would certainly have included it in his description of the civil service bureaucracy that he found so abhorrent.

and done, Sweden, the United States, Italy, Denmark and Belgium, Germany and Japan are all western, capitalistic, industrial, patriarchal, democratic, liberal market economies. Given the structural logic of the market (or that of the class struggle, the gender struggle, etc.), these countries should have developed rather similar social insurance and social service systems, but they have not. On the contrary, national public policies in these areas so critical to the civic welfare have evolved very differently. A battalion of international welfare state and social policy researchers has devoted extraordinary effort since the 1970s to describe and attempt to explain these differences. Researchers in the Scandinavian countries have primarily emphasized the symbiosis between strong unions and social democratic parties. Some have added to the mix the existence of certain unusual political institutions that favored the inception of a general welfare policy. But after my long conversation in Moscow, it became clear to me that we who are engaged in this research have failed to see an important piece of the puzzle in the building of the Scandinavian welfare state – i.e. the lack of significant corruption and the high level of interpersonal trust in Scandinavian societies. It seems utterly unreasonable to think that it would have been possible to shape public opinion in favor of transferring such large economic resources to various public welfare administrations if the people had strongly believed that those administrations were basically corrupt and/or engaged in systematic abuse of power. It seems equally unlikely that it would have been possible to create these comprehensive social insurance systems if citizens were convinced that most other citizens abused or cheated the taxation or distribution systems.

This illustrates one of the difficulties of conducting social scientific research, that of studying what does not exist. In general, this is categorized as counter-factual history, in which questions such as "what would have happened if . . . ?" are asked. These "if . . . so" questions can sometimes be less meaningful (what would have happened if Napoleon had had access to nuclear weapons at Waterloo?) but, properly used, they are an important element of research because they indicate potential lines of development that could have been entirely logical. In particular, counter-factual thinking constitutes one of the cornerstones of comparative policy research. For example, if interpersonal mistrust and widespread popular suspicion of authorities based on corruption or discrimination are much more common around the world than the opposite, it becomes interesting to ask two questions in order to deepen our understanding of Swedish policy. The first is counter-factual: What would have happened if Swedish policy had been characterized by the kind of interpersonal mistrust and corruption illustrated in my conversation in Moscow? Secondly, what is the origin of the relatively high level of trust that Swedes feel in each other and in their public agencies?

A possibly true story set in Rome, some time in the late 1960s

Allow me to give a specific example of this weak spot in our thinking. Along with many other Swedish researchers, I have studied the Swedish active labor market policy for sound reasons, including its large scope from an international perspective. The active labor market policy has also constituted a central component of the Rehn–Meidner model, a unique macroeconomic model that dominated Swedish economic policy from the late 1950s well into the 1980s. It was in many respects a centerpiece in what became known as "the Swedish Model" (Milner and Wadensjö 2001). A great deal has been written about the origin and function of the model, but it can be concisely described as a means of combining the internal need of the Swedish Trade Union Confederation (*Landsorganisationen* – LO) for uniform wage development with the government's interest in applying strong pressure for structurally transforming industry in order to stimulate economic growth. Instead of allowing the financial strength of individual firms or industries to determine local wage demands, the unions' wage demands were made progressively more uniform. The consequence was that less efficient firms and industries that were unable to pay wages at the centrally determined level were eliminated while expansive firms/industries could earn large profits, most of which they were forced by tax policy to use for further expansion. The policy provided several advantages to the unions, primarily with respect to internal wage policy. It also benefited the social democratic governments because they were able to control inflation by pursuing an austere finance policy while at the same time harvesting the fruits of strongly increased economic growth (Lindvall 2004). However, one main problem was how to manage the labor force eliminated by structural rationalization – i.e. the many workers who lost their jobs in firms and industries that could not match the centrally determined uniform wages. For a party and a union movement strongly committed to "full employment," this was a hard problem because the Rehn–Meidner model would create unemployment for those who happened to work in less efficient firms and industries. The idea of the Rehn–Meidner model was that it would be possible to transfer this part of the labor force to the type of expansive industry favored by the prevailing wage policy (mainly the large export oriented firms/industries).

According to the "inventors" of the model (the trade union economists Gösta Rehn and Rudolf Meidner), this required a comprehensive public labor market apparatus supplied with extensive administrative and financial resources. Through various "active" measures (well-equipped employment offices, generous subsidies to workers who relocated, and a large program for vocational training), redundant labor could be transferred to new employment. In his memoirs, former Prime Minister Tage Erlander describes the crucial meeting between the leaders of the Social Democratic Party and the leaders of the (blue collar) LO in 1955, when he became persuaded that the model was feasible:

> For the first time, I declared my support for the Meidner–Rehn labor market policy. Before then, I had been concerned that it would hasten the closure of companies compelled by free market economizing. But if the mobility-creating policy did not only increase mobility in the labor market, but also led to more socially aware use of our capital assets, if, in other words, the labor market policy gained a stronger selective element, then my fears were erased. (Erlander 1976: 41)

The catch was how to gain legitimacy for such a large initiative in such a comprehensive administrative body, which would also have far-reaching power over the employment conditions of many individual wage earners and thus also their living conditions: or, as was put in a report to the 1952 Social Democratic Party Congress: "of delicate nature and far-reaching significance to many population groups" (quoted in Rothstein 1996: 137). For the entire thing to work, an ordinary, rule-bound civil service bureaucracy was out of the question; experience gained from the labor market policy of the 1930s and the massive mobilization and labor shift during the war years made this exceedingly clear to the policy makers in the Social Democratic Party. Instead, what was needed was a body that, relatively liberated from precise rules and regulations, could rapidly intervene in the often highly flexible labor market, both nationally and locally. The problem of legitimacy was to a great extent solved by creating an organizational form based on ideological commitment – i.e. a "cadre administration." This was expressed in several ways, including the abandonment of recruiting based on merit. Personnel in the labor exchanges and various "active" labor market programs were instead recruited directly from the union movement and then trained to understand the logic behind and support the implementation of the model.

To cut a long story short, this active Swedish labor market policy became a success story and sparked widespread international interest from the 1960s (Milner and Wadensjö 2001). One indication of that interest was that Gösta Rehn was appointed head of the OECD's Secretariat for Employment and Social Affairs, a position he held from 1963 to 1973. From that position, he attempted to export Swedish labor market policy, and enjoyed considerable success. Countries such as Austria, France, Great Britain, Norway, and West Germany were inspired to partially restructure their labor market policies according to the Swedish model (Rothstein 1987). He was not equally successful everywhere, however. In the late 1960s, Rehn was invited by the Italian government to come and present the model of how a rational labor market policy should be organized. His Italian hosts thought that everything looked very interesting in the model world, but when he broached the subject of how it should all be organized, they began to smile.[4]

As Rehn expanded on his model in ever greater detail and stressed how important it was that the new and expansive labor market agency should not only have large financial means at its immediate disposal, but also that the agency, subject to no central direction or control, should be able to swiftly allocate funds according to its evaluation of the state of local and regional labor markets in various industries, the smiles of his Italian hosts began turning into grins. Gösta Rehn became perplexed and somewhat irritated, as it seemed to him, at not really being taken seriously. Finally, he was compelled to ask what his Italian hosts thought was so entertaining about his presentation. The answer was immediate. Could he imagine what would happen if such an apparatus was turned loose in places like Naples and Palermo? According to his Italian hosts, it would quickly fall under the control of organized crime, and its vast resources, combined with the discretionary power of the administration, would turn the agency's activities into a cash cow for the mafia. Gösta Rhen's success stopped north of the Alps. No active labor market policy was ever introduced in Italy.

The logic of the social trap

The psychologist John Platt invented the concept of the *social trap*, a metaphor he coined in a paper published in 1973. The *social trap* may be considered an "umbrella term" for a number of strategic situations in which social actors find themselves, in which the central element is that their behavior is determined by their assessments of the future action of others. The logic of the situation may be described as follows:

- The situation is such that "everyone" wins if "everyone" *chooses to cooperate.*
- But – if people cannot trust that "almost everyone else" will cooperate, it is meaningless to choose to cooperate, because the end is contingent on *cooperation by almost everyone else.*
- Thus, non-cooperation may be rational when people *do not trust that others will also cooperate.*
- Conclusion: Efficient cooperation for common purposes can come about only if *people trust that most other people will also choose to cooperate.*
- Lacking that trust, the social trap will slam inexorably shut. That is, we end up in a state of affairs that is worse for everyone, even though everyone realizes that they would profit by *choosing to cooperate.*

---

[4] I was told this story by Ingemar Ståhl, Rehn's then assistant at the OECD office in Paris (and later a well-known professor of Economics).

This illustrates the four central foundations of the theoretical approach that will guide this work. The first is the central difference between *individual and collective rationality*. The second is that we should presume that political and economic actions are strategic, meaning that *what people do depends on what they believe others are going to do*. The third is that the notion so common in social scientific theory, that human action should be understood as the result of rational utility maximization, is of no help whatsoever when it comes to predicting whether or not the jaws of the social trap will close. For the individual, whether or not an action is rational cannot in these types of situations be determined solely by reference to one's individual preferences, but is rather determined by the social context. It may certainly be rational to choose non-cooperation if one has reason to believe that the others are not going to participate. But if one has reason to trust that others are going to contribute (i.e. that they are actually trustworthy), it may be rational to cooperate. This trust or non-trust in *the others* is, as I will show later, often historically and/or politically determined by the collective memory. The fourth important point in the logic of the social trap is that our possibility to get out of such situations is limited by the fact that we *cannot rationally decide to forget*. As a metaphor, the social trap indicates that the memory is simply something we cannot make rational decisions about. It is because of this historical and contextual specificity that social traps are a more serious and difficult social problem than other similar situations. For example, if it was possible for Israelis and Palestinians to say: "Let's forget all the bad things we have caused one another and start all over again in a cooperative spirit," that part of the world would (given my knowledge/prejudices about the entrepreneurial skills among these two groups) be an extremely prosperous region. However, for the human mind it seems impossible to forget treacherous and deceitful behavior. Simply put, this is a "willing that cannot be willed" (Arthur 1999; cf. Elster 1983). For example, taxpayers who have experienced grave corruption in the tax administration are not likely to forget this the next time their tax bill arrives. Citizens who are used to politicians who systematically misuse government resources to enhance their incumbency advantage are not likely to embrace strong support for democratic practices, and so on (Golden 2003). Moreover, according to psychological research on how the memory works, the more one tries to forget traumatic experiences such as deceit and discrimination, the more vivid they become (Baddelely 1999; cf. Frey 2004). One major problem here is that political entrepreneurs often build their power by manufacturing the notion of the other group's treacherous behavior into a collective memory of their own group, which makes collaboration between the groups even more difficult. The impossibility of making rational choices about what we remember is probably the most serious case when rationality fails if measured as the implication for human suffering. To my surprise, I have found very little discussion in the literature of this relation between memory, rationality and social traps.

In sum, the theory about social traps allows us to link two approaches in the social sciences that are usually widely disparate: those which stress the importance of historically established *social and cultural institutions and norms*, and those which emphasize the importance of *human strategic actions and choices*.

Game theory as strategic theory

When social scientists hear the term "game theory," they usually associate it with two things. The first is the use of rather complicatedly mathematical analysis which is difficult to understand. The second is the premise that human action corresponds to the action of the self-interested utility maximizing "*homo economicus*," a starting point which many find highly unreal. However, the approach to game theory in this study differs from these two premises in two important ways. To begin with the mathematical aspect, it is true that a very large part of game theoretic analysis uses mathematics, and consequently is often obscure to those who do not understand this "language". As stated by Fritz Scharpf, most of this literature "written by mathematicians for other mathematicians, not only *seems* forbiddingly technical, but *is* in fact practically inaccessible to the uninitiated" (1997: 6). However, the basis of the approach used in this book is that there are two sides to game theory, one *mathematical* and one *cognitive* (Boudon 1996; Scharpf 1997: 6–10). The mathematical approach to game theory is of course legitimate and some fundamental insights have certainly come out of this research, for example the well-known Nash-equilibrium. However, for reasons that will be spelled out below, I think that it is unlikely that the solution to the problem stated here (how to "get from Moscow to Stockholm") is going to emerge from the mathematical approach. The likelihood of a breakthrough on the mathematical side of the theory (e.g. the equilibrium analysis of the kind for which Nobel laureate John Nash became famous) must be judged negligible. Nevertheless, I believe that research on the *cognitive* side of game theory is only in its infancy. That is, if what people do depends on what they believe others are going to do, the question of how those images and beliefs about *the others* enter human consciousness and how they are reshaped into political actions, becomes the very crux of the matter (Denzau and North 1994; Rothstein 2000b). It could be argued that a more suitable term for this approach would be *strategic theory*. The assumption is that people are engaged in strategic action "in which the outcomes are a joint product of their separate choices," which means that what they do, depends on what they think the other ones are going to do (Scharpf 1997: 4).

From such a perspective, the critical issue in game theoretic analysis becomes a cognitive question, namely, *Who are the others* (the tax bureaucrats, the social workers, the Serbs, the local police, the Hutu, the Palestinians, the loyalists, the Maronites, the white middle-class, middle-aged professors) and what can I (or we) expect of them? Can they be trusted, are they going to respect me and my rights, or should they be regarded with varying levels of mistrust? In the Russian example above, the issue is of course the public opinion about tax officials in particular and the public bureaucracy in general. It is certainly no problem to find cases in which the issue of trust and distrust can be a matter of life and death (Eidelson and Eidelson 2003; Kaufman 2001). However, such drastic examples are not required to illustrate the importance of the cognitive side of game theory. We have all found ourselves in situations within organizations or teams where it was obvious that everyone would have gained if everyone had pitched in and made an effort to contribute. But it is no fun to discover that you are the only one living up to that requirement while the others shirk their obligations. In such cases, personal loyalty depends on how we perceive and anticipate the loyalty of *the others*.

The second and third points have to do with the self-interest and rationality of the actors in game theory. This is a hotly debated subject, but if we go back to the description of the logic of the social trap, we can determine that the presumption that human action is rationally utility maximizing does not help us predict the outcome, because in that kind of situation what people perceive to be rational action is entirely *context dependent*. It can be rational to not cooperate, but it can also be rational to cooperate, and this choice of strategy depends on how the individual perceives and anticipate the likelihood that *the others* will act in one way or the other. This assessment may come from many different sources, such as personal knowledge about the individuals in question, culturally determined stereotypes, or memories of how the actors have acted in similar situations in the past (van Lange *et al.* 2000; Scharpf 1997). There is also a well-known case within the theory (known as the Prisoners' Dilemma) which presumes that the rational action is always to choose non-cooperation in order to free ride on the cooperation of others – that is, the best individual strategy would be for each to defect and implicate the other (Morrow 1994: 78f.). However, as I will show later, this variant of the theory has not been sustained by empirical tests. Or, as has been formulated by Arthur Stinchcombe: "life is not as ruthless as game-theory predicts" (1992: 196f.).

The problem, however, is general and is certainly not solely about using economic resources efficiently. Even those arranging some exceedingly deserving event (e.g. a demonstration or manifestation for an environmental end, support of resource-deprived groups in the Third World or a boycott of chlorine-bleached disposable diapers) will often end up mired in a problem of this nature: that many may be prepared to participate if they believe that a great enough number of others will also participate. This is not due to self-interest alone. The effect of a political demonstration or manifestation that draws only a thin crowd is often counterproductive, a small turnout will be interpreted as a sign that there is no widespread support for the issue (Lichbach 1995). Simply put, the goal to be achieved often requires that a sufficient number support the premise, but most people will jump on the bandwagon only if they believe that most others in their situation are also going to come along for the ride. The relationship is the same when it comes to the ethics of the individual civil servant. In an extensive review of corruption as an economic problem, Pradhan Bardan concluded that corruption represents an example of frequency-dependent equilibria: "our expected gain from corruption depends crucially on the number of other people we expect to be corrupt." (Bardhan 1997: 1331). This also makes it difficult to fight corruption, because the government that airs the issue of a widespread corruption that must be fought also reinforces the belief that the majority of its civil servants are corrupt (Krastev and Ganev 2004).[5]

But when can the game begin?

The theoretical presumption in this study is that people's actions are governed by what they believe their counterparts are going to do in response to their own actions. In many respects, this idea turns upside down much of how social scientists usually go about explaining how human actions should be explained, a lot of which has been based on viewing human beings as determined by structural conditions. If you simply gather enough information about an individual's previous circumstances (occupation, income, sex, education, ethnicity, place of residence), you can predict her actions. Cognitive game theory makes a different prediction, which is that human action cannot be explained only by such "backward mapping." Instead, we need "forward mapping", which is how individuals anticipate the reactions to their actions. *Anticipation* is thus a key concept – i.e. when people decide to act in one way or another, they have often tried in their decision process to predict the various possible reactions of their counterparts. While behavioral science has regarded the human being as steered by the past,

---

[5] There is an abundance of definitions of corruption, as well as a large body of literature that has attempted to classify various forms of it. One common definition is that corruption is "the abuse of public resources for private gain, through a hidden transaction that involves violation of some standards of behavior" (della Porta and Vannucci 1999: 16; cf. Rose-Ackerman 1999). A simpler and maybe more elegant definition is "the exchange of official decision for some payment" (Offe 2004: 78).

cognitive game theory sees human action as controlled by what individuals expect "ahead" in time (cf. Boudon 1996; Turner 2001). Thus, for the "social trap" type of problem, economic theories based on self-interest have very limited value, because what is "self-interest" in situations like these is determined by the social, historical and cultural circumstances that influence our expectations of how "the others" are going to act. If an individual believes that others are also going to reciprocate her initial cooperative behavior, it is usually rational for him to decide to cooperate. But if she is convinced that the opposite is true, it would, once again, be irrational (or even dangerous) to cooperate.

Thus when it comes to the matter of self-interest and utility maximization, the premise here is that this is not a requisite basis for applying a game theory approach. Analysis of social norms and culturally established beliefs has also become increasingly common in this area. (Bates 1997; Boudon 1996; Bowles and Gintis 2002; Denzau and North 1994; Levi 1998; Ostrom 1998, 1999). The reason for this is that a fruitful analysis of the "game" can begin only when the players have been formed in number and, first and foremost, in their values, norms (including prejudices), cognitive maps, memories, and worldviews (Mantzavinos, North, and Shariq 2002). For this kind of analysis, Fritz Scharpf has used the apt designation "games real actors can play." By this, he means that if game theory is going to be used for "real world" problems, the analysis should not start from the unlikely scenario of perfectly informed, strictly rational, memory-free actors upon which a great deal of mathematically oriented game theory is based. Instead, we must consider how real political actors must act when equipped only with incomplete information and limited knowledge about the type of actors and the rules they are dealing with, yet with an understanding that the outcome of their interaction depends on choices made by (almost) all players (Scharpf 1997: 5).

How serious is the problem with social traps?

There may be reason here to try and communicate an understanding of the magnitude of the problem this book will be addressing. One way of illustrating this is to point out that it can also be called the problem with many names. This list is long: *Provision of Public Goods, Problem of Collective Action, Tragedy of the Commons, Prisoners' Dilemma,* and *Social Dilemma* are but a few (Ostrom 1998).

I have chosen the metaphor of the social trap because I believe it expresses two elements of the problem that are especially important. First, that actors in a strategic situation where they can choose cooperation or non-cooperation may end up in a situation that is most disadvantageous to them all – or, to use an even more graphic expression, a pathological situation – without any of them having intended that result (Elster 1989a). This may, for example, happen quite simply by mistake when something that actually is an attempt to cooperate is misunderstood by the counterpart, who perceives the action as deceitful or threatening and answers in the same coin, escalating the situation into a social trap. It may also arise in ethnic conflicts, for example,when there are leading political actors who control the flow of information and who, out of pure self-interest, choose to concentrate only on negative information about the other group's intentions (Hardin 1995; Kaufman 2001). This kind of strategic control and manipulation of the flow of information about *the others* is one of the main features of many of the violent ethnic conflicts that shook the world in the late twentieth century (cf. Bates, de Figueiredo, and Weingast 1998).

Secondly, the term "trap" in this metaphor refers to the sad fact that once a group, an organization, or a society has ended up in such a state, it is usually very difficult to escape. To breach an enduring social trap would require people who (for good or bad reasons) have developed deep mutual mistrust over a long time to suddenly begin to trust one another and thus erase their memories about the untrustworthy and deceitful behavior of the other group (Elster 1989a: 26). As I shall argue below, trust is a very special psychological variable. One of its peculiarities is that (like moral innocence or virginity) it seems very difficult to recover once it has been lost. You cannot simply rationally decide to trust people whom you have mistrusted for a long time, even if you fully understand that the development of mutual trust would be very advantageous. However rational it may seem, it appears impossible to decide to forget a thing like the experience of severe injustice or betrayal of trust. Once a society, an organization, or a group has been caught in a social trap situation, it usually stays there. The argument in this book is that while not impossible, it is very difficult to get out of social traps. However, most mathematically oriented game theorists shake their heads dolefully when asked how people can get out of social traps, or to use their terminology, "suboptimal equilibria" (Bendor and Mookherjee 1987; Bendor and Swistak 1997). Such equilibria are, they say, "extremely robust."[6]

The problem of the *social trap* is a kind of meta-problem under which many important social and organizational problems can be categorized (cf. Ostrom 1998). Take the following example: Most environmental problems

---

[6] My Polish-born friend and mathematically minded colleague in this field, Piotr Swistak, has a habit of saying somewhat provocatively that it is a typically Swedish syndrome to believe that for every social problem there must also exist a working, as well as a normatively appealing, solution. According to him, the rest of the world does not work that way.

related to excessive use of natural resources are of this nature. We all have an interest in clean air and water, but if I do not believe that *the others* will limit their driving or sort their rubbish for recycling, I have no reason to be the only one who behaves in an environmentally sensitive manner. All commercial fishermen working along a coastline know that if they do not limit their catches, the fish – and thus the industry – will die out, but it is rather pointless to be the only commercial fisherman who behaves responsibly if all the others are casting their nets with abandon (Acheson and Knight 2000). Another problem applies to wage increases in a labor market with strong unions. Every union leader knows that everyone gains by wage trends that are not strongly inflationary. But if they cannot get any assurances that other unions will act responsibly, union leaders cannot defend moderate action to the rank and file (Elster 1989a: 19).

In certain respects, Scandinavian-style universal welfare states can be viewed from this theoretical perspective. There may, for instance, be broad acceptance of paying taxes for things such as universal health care and unemployment insurance. But if the belief spreads that many people receiving disability or unemployment benefits are not actually sick or unemployed at all, but rather prefer not to work for purely selfish reasons, there is reason to presume that there is a lack of solidarity spreading within the system. The solidarity upon which the welfare state is built is in all likelihood *conditional* – i.e. based on confidence that the institutions within the system are such that they do not invite widespread cheating. Should this trust in the institutional functions of the system be undermined, they may break down even though a large majority may believe that general social insurance programs of that type should exist (Rothstein 2001).

There are fascinating analyses of the fall of entire civilizations, such as of the fall of the Roman Empire, based on this theme. In his book on the connection between corruption and the fall of Rome, Ramsay MacMullen (1988) emphasized the onset of the purchase and sale of military and other public services. People with little or no competence came to hold important offices and they used them for their own gain instead of acting according to prevailing orders and ensuring the general interests of the state. One result of the privatization of public offices was that military officers became more interested in making illegal profits from their offices instead of engaging in battle. For example, instead of putting military strategic considerations first they positioned their troops where the possibilities for extorting wealth from the civilian populations were most favorable (MacMullen 1988: 192). It became particularly difficult to maintain the provisioning of army camps because the supply lines had become progressively less reliable as a result of burgeoning corruption (MacMullen 1988: 177). The consequences for Rome's military capacity and ability to protect its borders were, according to MacMullen, severe (cf. Molander 1994). Another fascinating example is the recent research about the collapse of the civilization on Easter Island. Biologists and anthropologists working together have found that the people who erected the gigantic stone sculptures once lived from off-shore fishing for which they used large canoes. To build these, they used the giant palm trees that were abundant on the island until the fifteenth century when, because of intense clan conflicts and tribal competition, the islanders cut down the trees until deforestation was complete. The consequences were dire, not only for the possibilities of deep-sea fishing, but also for soil erosion, extinction of eatable land birds, and depletion of fire wood. The end results were starvation followed by a severe population crash and descent into cannibalism. Jared Diamond's reflection on this new research is worth citing:

> Why were Easter Islanders so foolish as to cut down all their trees, when the consequences would have been so obvious to them? This is a key question that nags everyone who wonders about self-inflicted environmental damage. I have often asked myself, "What did the Easter Islander who cut down the last palm tree say while he was doing it?" Like modern loggers, did he shout "Jobs, not trees!"? Or: "Technology will solve our problems, never fear, we'll find a substitute for wood"? Or: "We need more research, your proposed ban on logging is premature"? (Diamond 2004: 23)

The problem is age-old. Aristotle writes about it in *Politics* in the following way: "For that which is common to the greatest number has the least care bestowed upon it. Every one thinks chiefly of his own, hardly at all of the common interest; and only when he is himself concerned as an individual" (sec. 1262a). One of the most prominent historical figures in political philosophy, Niccolò Machiavelli, the secretary of the Florentine Republic, devoted much of his writing to the problem of corruption (see especially *Discorsi*, vol. I, chapters 16–18), taking many of his examples from the fall of the Roman Empire. A central theme in Machiavelli's sixteenth-century thinking of the problem is that the very best of laws and political intentions are worthless if the political culture is tainted by corrupt habits among the governing and the governed (Bonadeo 1973: 19).

Many grave ethnic conflicts can also be described in part within this problem scenario. Both groups have an interest in avoiding conflict, but to do so they must be able to trust that the members of the other ethnic group will not subject their own members to systematic discrimination (e.g. in schools, the health care system, the justice system, and the labor market) or out-and-out persecution. But if one ethnic group cannot rely on the other ethnic group to accord respect to principles of equal treatment and non-discrimination, it is pointless for the first group to do so. To cite an extreme (but sadly not at all unusual) case, it may seem rational to try and ethnically cleanse the neighboring village today if you are entirely convinced that the villagers are waiting only for reinforcements in order to attack your own village the next day (Gross 2001; Peterson 2000).

Another illustration can be taken from Argentina. According to recent reports, leading politicians are financing their political campaigns by incomes from the kidnapping of children of rich industrialists. Together with the police and the prison administration, they have organized a system in which convicted criminals are let loose during the night time in order to carry out the actual kidnapping. The perpetrators cannot be convicted because they have the perfect alibi of being locked up in prison. Judges, police officers, prison guards, and politicians are all reported to be part of this system.[7]

The list could go on at length with cases taken from, for example, organization theory (Kramer and Tyler 1996; Miller 1992), research environments (Bennich-Björkman 1997), fresh water resources (Ostrom 1990), and agricultural environmental initiatives (Lundqvist 2001). There is yet another reason why the problem of social traps is so grave which is that social traps constitute what are called in game theory "stable but inefficient equilibria," i.e. states that are clearly bad for everyone, but where no individual actor has any incentive to change things.[8] Empirical evidence shows that perceptions of *the others* are highly stable and difficult to change. These cognitive or mental maps are often included in enduring cultural socialization processes, where they strongly characterize the worldviews of individual actors with respect to things such as the honesty and competence of state institutions or whether it is reasonable to trust other people in general or specific groups of people (Denzau and North 1994). Yet another problem enters the equation here. It has been shown that the transition from an "efficient" equilibrium to an "inefficient" equilibrium in areas as disparate as organization theoretic research and research on the origins of ethnic conflicts can take place with a kind of catastrophic logic. That is, once confidence and trust in *the others* is destroyed, the transition from cooperation to a social trap can take place very quickly, in what can be most closely likened to an epidemic process – or, more metaphorically, as a snowball effect (Sitkin and Darryl 1996).

---

[7] Nathan Shachar, *Dagens Nyheter* August 8, 2004. On the magnitude of political corruption in Argentina, see Rojas (2004).

[8] In purely technical terms, there are many different types of such equilibria. In this book, the term refers to that which is referred to in the more mathematically oriented game theoretical literature as a "Nash equilibrium," i.e. "a pair of strategies that are best replies to each other on the equilibrium path" (Morrow 1994: 351). The situation is thus one where none of the actors can improve her situation by undertaking a unilateral change of strategy (cf. Hermansson 1990: chapter 4).

Social traps and political institutions

Especially in relation to research on developing countries and their often persistent or even worsening poverty, there seems to have emerged something of a consensus among political scientists, economic historians, and economists that the problem can be explained by the lack of what game theory calls *efficient* institutions – i.e. institutions that enable trust and confidence to be established in organizations and societies (Blomkvist 2001; Gunnarsson and Rojas 1995). An easy way to understand such of institutions may be to look at them as if they were the institution of the referee in sports such as soccer. In this activity, there are naturally conflicting interests between teams, as both teams clearly want to win. But they also have a common interest in establishing an impartial and uncorrupt group of referees, as it is meaningless to play soccer against a team that has "bought" the referee. This can be compared to a market where buyers and sellers have conflicting interests in the outcome of the transaction but a common interest in the existence of legal institutions that can impartially settle disputes. If one party has illicitly usurped advantages *vis-à-vis* these institutions, the other party will in all likelihood be reluctant to enter into contracts in the first place. "Efficient institutions" are institutions that, to use an economic term, reduce transaction costs between parties with a mutual interest in interacting in repeated sequences, even if they have conflicting interests in the specific transactions. Transaction costs are costs that arise outside the actual exchange – e.g. to establish and uphold contracts.

This has to do with the establishment of the institutions that we generally associate with the concept of a state governed by the rule of law and with the general extent of corruption in public administration. One important communicator of this insight is economic historian Douglass C. North, the 1992 winner of the Nobel prize in economics. His theory, like all other pivotal social scientific theories, is rather simple: In a society with non-existent, unreliable, and/or corrupt political institutions, entering into and upholding the kind of agreements that constitute the foundation of transactions in a market economy becomes very costly for individuals (North 1990). For that reason, any number of production and trade agreements advantageous to all parties are simply never made. The quality of political institutions ("quality of government") has increasingly emerged as a central explanatory factor behind economic growth. Or, as said in the conclusions of a research report carried out by a group of prominent economists that encompasses data from almost 160 countries: "Rich countries have better political institutions than poor countries" (La Porta *et al.* 1999: 40). The problem is partly economic, partly about trust. "Efficient institutions" in the sense referred to here are not cheap; it takes fairly hefty tax revenues to establish them. One conclusion in the above-mentioned report is that "better performing goverments are also larger, and collect higher taxes. Poorly performing governments, in contrast, are smaller and collect fewer taxes." (1999: 42). However good its intentions, it is not that easy for a government to persuade the citizenry to pay higher taxes today to an inefficient (corrupt and/or incompetent) state establishment which they (for good reasons) mistrust. Why should they trust that their hard-earned money would be used to create a more competent and efficient public administration? Inducing people to make the transition from mistrust to trust is probably one of the more difficult tricks in the world of politics. As an expert on economic conditions in Latin America expressed it:

> I don't think there is any more vital issue in Latin America right now . . . It's a vicious cycle that is very hard to break. People don't want to pay taxes because they say government doesn't deliver services, but government institutions aren't going to perform any better until they have resources, which they obtain when people pay their taxes. (Rother 1999)

The usual but simplistic answer to this problem (and to my Russian bureaucrat) is that the government needs to introduce "the rule of law" type of institution. Corrupted bureaucrats and tax-cheating citizens would then be caught by the police and punished by the courts. By "fixing the incentives" in this way, standard economic theory tells us that the problem would be solved. It's simple, just increase the negative pay-off for cheating and corruption (including the risk of being caught) to a point where the fear of being caught would be higher than the greed that led agents to engage in tax fraud and corruption. When society is constructed so that fear is larger than greed, things go well. But as has been argued by Pranab Bardhan, Michael Hechter, Mark Lichbach, and Gary Miller, for example, accomplishing this is not easy, because constructing such an institution is in itself a collective action/social trap problem (Bardhan 1997; Miller 1992). Presuming standard utility maximizing self-interested agents, where do you find the uncorrupted judges, bureaucrats, and policemen in a society where corruption is rampant? Most judges and policemen may reason like my Russian tax bureaucrat, perfectly willing to act honestly, but only if they trust most other policemen and judges to do the same (Hechter 1992; Lichbach 1995). Mancur Olson skillfully described the gravity of the problem of poorly working political and legal institutions in his last published paper. He addressed the problem of why the gap between the rich and poor countries in the world is widening instead of narrowing, as predicted by economic equilibrium theory:

> the large differences in per capital [sic] income across countries cannot be explained by differences in access to the world's stock of productive knowledge or to its capital markets, by differences in the ratio of the population to land or

natural resources, or by differences in the quality of marketable human capital or personal culture. Albeit at a high level of aggregation, this eliminates each of the factors of production as possible explanation of most of the international differences in per capita income. The only remaining plausible explanation is that the great differences in the wealth of nations are mainly due to differences in the quality of their institutions and economic policies. (Olson 1996: 16)

If Mancur Olson's thesis is correct, the human cost in terms of poverty and misery in countries with poorly working political and legal institutions is enormous. The latest report from the United Nations Development Program (UNDP) addresses the correlation between political and administrative institutions and poverty. Much of the report is a distressing account of how the differences between the world's countries are growing rather than shrinking. There may be reason to recall that it was not so very long ago that the well-known economic historian Alexander Gerschenkron claimed that the poor countries of the world possessed one great advantage – they could just duplicate the institutions proven to work well in the successful countries and in so doing, avoid the costs incurred by the latter through trial and error (Easterly 2001).

One might believe that these problems of corruption have long since been given great consideration in international aid policies and research but, surprisingly, this is not the case. For example, the highly regarded *Handbook of Development Economics* published in four volumes between 1988 and 1995 never mentions corruption in its more than 3,000 pages. Organizations such as the World Bank and the International Monetary Fund (IMF) have begun addressing this problem only in the last few years (Easterly 2001: 223). In a report to the IMF, Dani Rodrik, another well-known economist in these contexts, discusses the relation between institutions and economic growth. His argument is that the encounter between the neo-classical economy and the developing countries,

> served to reveal the institutional underpinnings of market economies. A clearly delineated system of property rights, a regulatory apparatus curbing the worst forms of fraud, anti-competitive behavior, and moral hazard, a moderately cohesive society exhibiting trust and social cooperation, social and political institutions that mitigate risk and manage social conflicts, the rule of law and clean government – these are social arrangements that economists usually take for granted, but which are conspicuous by their absence in poor countries. (Rodrik 1999: 1)

Thus, not only political scientists and sociologists studying the modern welfare states, but also many economists studying developing countries, for long neglected the importance of functioning political institutions. Naturally, corruption exists to a greater or lesser extent in all countries. What

I mean here are situations when corruption becomes systematic to the point that you can talk about it as part and parcel of the political and administrative culture. These are situations where all or parts of the public machinery are taken over by corrupt networks and where interactions between citizens and civil servants routinely include some form of bribery (Karklins 2002). In a report published in 2002 of the situation in Bosnia-Herzegovina, the UNDP presents the results of a survey study showing that between 60 and 70 percent of the respondents believe that severe corruption exists in the health care system, the justice system, and the media. Slightly more than half believe that corruption also exists in the various UN bodies working within the region. The conclusion made in the report is telling:

> For the average citizen, therefore, it seems that corruption has broken down all barriers and dictates the rules of life. That is not very different from saying that *they interpret life in terms of corruption.* As long as bureaucratic practice remains unreformed and there is a lack of transparency and accountability in public business, this will continue to be the case. People will use whatever mechanism they think will bring them an advantage and those in office will take advantage of that in their turn. (UNDP 2002: 27, emphasis added)

If corrupt public institutions make people "interpret life in terms of corruption", social trust is not likely to develop. As indicated by the economic and political difficulties in Russia, for example, establishing a working market economy solely by privatizing previously state-owned assets has proven fraught with great difficulties. The "economic shock therapy" that some economists prescribed seems to have been based on an assumption that efficient political institutions would by some functional (or magical) means appear by themselves once privatization of the economy had become a fact, or else that they were not necessary (Hedlund 1999, 1997; Rothstein 2004). But history is not "efficient." There is no guarantee or social function by which the institutions needed to solve "the eternal basic problems for every society" will be established (Eisenstadt 1968: 410).

The argument in brief and plan of the book

The argument in this book can be summarized as follows. Social traps are for real and they constitute a serious threat to the well-being of every society and group of people. The main puzzle is the stark variation in how groups, organizations, and whole societies have been able to handle this problem. This variation exists over time – i.e. there are groups, organizations, and societies that have managed to escape the social trap for a very long time and there are those that have quite suddenly fallen victim to its logic. There are also cases (albeit fewer) in which societies have been able to escape the

logic of the social trap. Moreover, as our example from Moscow intends to
show, there is also a great contemporary variation among not only countries,
but also regions and even nearby local communities. Empirical indicators of
social trust, corruption, economic growth, the rule of law, and other similar
measures show a fascinatingly high degree of variation. Just to take one
example. If we compare the percentage of people who respond positively to
the question whether they think that most other people in their society can
be trusted, there is a lot of variation that needs to be explained. In countries
such as Denmark, Sweden, and the Netherlands, the percentage of people
stating that they believe most other people in their societies can be trusted
is around 60 percent, while in countries such as Brazil, the Philippines,
and Turkey, social trust is around a meager 10 percent.[9] Measures of the
quality of political institutions – for example, the widely used corruption
index established by Transparency International (TI) – show an even higher
degree of variation. The central aim of this book is to make a contribution
to how this variation can be explained.

One question to be addressed is if the existence of the social trap problem
should be explained by reference to individual rationality or to cultural traits.
In chapter 2, I shall argue that neither of these two dominant approaches
in the social sciences is sufficient for this problem, and present a theoretical
model that can serve to conceptualize the central variables in this drama.
This chapter is largely geared towards an intensive, yet admittedly somewhat
internal, academic discussion. Chapter 3 explores the discussion about the
concept of "social capital," which has become a central question in research
on the problem of social traps. The aim of the chapter is to present a precise
definition of "social capital" and also to argue that it is an important addition
to the universe of concepts in the social sciences. Chapter 4 is an analysis
of the relation between the welfare state and social capital in which I show
that, contrary to what many have believed, an extensive welfare state is
conducive to the generation of "social capital." This argument comes with
the reservation that this is valid only for social policies of a certain type,
namely those that are universal. Chapter 5 presents empirical evidence for
the first central claim I want to make in this book, namely that "social
capital" is generated by the existence of universal and trustworthy political
institutions. Conversely, it is dysfunctional (corrupt or in other ways grossly
unfair) political institutions that destroy "social capital" in a society. This
argument goes against the dominant view that has seen "social capital" as
a function of a vibrant civil society in which citizens spend a considerable
amount of time in different voluntary associations. The conclusion I make
is that activity in voluntary associations and a vibrant civil society may be

[9] Source: World Value Surveys: http://wvs.isr.umich.edu/.

good for many reasons, but that it has little to do with the generation of "social capital." Increased participation in voluntary associations can thus not be seen as a remedy for societies that have fallen into social traps. I dare to say that the policy implications of this result are of some significance. Instead of blaming the citizens for not being active in voluntary associations and not getting involved in civil society, this shifts the burden for societal malaise to the political system and the political elite. The argument is that it is *governments* that are to blame for low levels of "social capital" because of their failure to establish universal and trustworthy political institutions.

Chapters 6 and 7 analyse what has become a major problem in the social sciences, namely how trustworthy and universal institutions can be created. It is argued that, so far, we lack a plausible theory for this problem (that is, how we can move "from Moscow to Stockholm"). It is argued that within existing approaches, neither the establishment nor the reproduction of universal institutions can be explained. If my theory is correct that it is universal and trustworthy institutions than can make us avoid social traps, this is of course a serious problem. In chapter 8, I present an empirical case study on how such a transition from mistrust to trust has been made, and I draw some preliminary conclusions concerning the circumstances in which universal institutions can be created. In the final chapter 9, I draw a number of conclusions about what we know, and what can be done about, the problem presented to me in Moscow.

2

On the rational choice of culture

Culture, rationality, and social traps

Should the variation in the problem of social traps be understood by reference to inherited cultural traits or by reference to individual rationality?
Do people engage in corrupt practices and become cynical and mistrusting
towards their fellow citizens through established and taken-for-granted cultural norms, or should this be seen as a rational response to dysfunctional
institutions and untrustworthiness? This problem is directly linked to one
of the most intense debates in political science which concerns the value
of theories based on cultural systems versus the approach labeled "rational
choice." According to one important textbook, they stand "as the principal
competing theoretical schools" in the discipline (Dowding and King 1995;
Lichbach and Zuckerman 1998: 5, cf. Elster 2000a). While proponents of
the rational choice approach may often agree that culture is important for
understanding how agents get their preferences, they add that explanations
based on culture "resist systematic analysis" (Johnson 1997: 6). Advocates of
the culturalist approach often similarly agree that the control over symbols,
rituals and identity may be "bitterly contested" in a strategic game of power
(Ross 1998: 45). But they also state that "rational choice scholars are often
drawn to models of individual behavior that are not only very wrong, but
known to be very wrong, as depictions of what political subjects actually do,
think, and feel" (Lustick 1997: 12).

The argument I want to make is that neither of these approaches is sufficient for explaining the great variation in the degree of corruption and
social trust around the world. For example, according to the latest report
from Transparency International (TI, an international organization that

produces an index of levels of corruption), Finland is presently the least corrupt country in the world. But is this because the Finns have a different way of understanding what it means to be a rational human being than, say, Nigerians or Hungarians? Or is it because the Finns have a specific way of being seized by cultural norms that makes their behavior differ from people in Southern Italy or Argentina? Obviously, there is a problem with theories predicting that societies can either end up in hopeless social traps or may for some ad hoc reason avoid them, but there is nothing in the theories that can help us explain what is likely to happen. Simply put, theories predicting that "anything can happen" are not very valuable. As has been stated by Elinor Ostrom: "the really big puzzle in the social sciences is the development of a consistent theory to explain why cooperation levels vary so much and why specific configurations of situational conditions increase or decrease cooperation in first- or second level dilemmas" (Ostrom 1998: 9).

There are, of course, many variants of culturalism, rationalism and those approaches situated in between. Leaning more towards the culturalist approach is historical institutionalism, arguing that institutions do not only change preferences but also belief systems and ideas (Dowdin and King 1995; Rothstein 1996a; Steinmo and Thelen 1992; Thelen 1999). And within the rationalist tradition, some scholars has started to give culture a prominent role in explanation: For example, Bates and Weingast have argued that:

> most game theorists fail to acknowledge that their approach requires a complete political anthropology. It requires detailed knowledge of the values of individuals; of the expectation that individuals have of each other's reaction; and of the ways in which these expectations have been shaped by history. (Bates, de Figueiredo, and Weingast 1996: 30)

The argument in this book is that the problem of social traps cannot be handled solely within either the rationalist or the culturalist approach. Instead, a more unified conceptual map is needed that combines insights from both these perspectives. Such a conceptual map should avoid a number of shortcomings that affect both culture- and interest-based explanations. In their standard form, both rational choice and cultural approaches face two fundamental problems. First, both have a problem of unrealistic basic assumptions about what drives political behavior. Secondly, both approaches are geared towards deterministic reasoning.

The limitations of existing approaches

Rational choice assumptions about decision making are highly problematic. As one scholar in this approach states: rationalists "tend toward a mechanical-behavioral view of subjectivity, and adopt a particularly anemic or thin version of intentionality, rationality, and interests" (Lichbach 1997: 256). There are thus serious problems within the rationalist approach concerning the amount of information that individuals can handle, how they cope with uncertainty, the role that social norms/emotions play in their decisions, their capacity to make complicated strategic decisions, and where motives may come from. Empirically, the situation has been summarized as follows:

> There is no longer any doubt about the weight of the scientific evidence; the expected-utility model of economic and political decision making is not sustainable empirically. From the laboratory comes failure after failure of rational expected utility to account for human behavior. From systematic observation in organizational settings, scant evidence of behavior based on the expected-utility model emerges. (Jones 1999: 297)

The experimental research in particular shows that people cooperate much more than the theory predicts, even in the so called one-shot Prisoners' Dilemma games (Sally 1985). The conclusion to be made is that we cannot build our analysis about how societies fall into (or get out of) social traps on a theory that starts from assumptions that are so obviously wrong. The same type of criticism could, however, be directed towards culturalism. Culture is often described as an overwhelming force making agents look like "cultural dopes" (Giddens 1984). For example, Ian Lustick describes the idea of the agent in cultural analysis as "behaviors performed without those so engaged making any decisions or choices" (Lustick 1997: 12). In the view of social anthropologist Clifford Geertz, culture is to be seen as a unified "system" with overwhelming power (Swidler 2001b). Culture, from this perspective "is a worldview that explains why and how individuals and groups behave as they do" (Ross 1998: 45). Obviously, there is hardly any room for such things as intentions, strategic action, not to say deliberative choice, within this perspective. Once the world has been "culturally constructed" for them, individual agents are no longer "agents" in any meaningful sense of the word (Lustick 1997: 12).

A second objection is that both theories have difficulties handling variation over space and time. Consider for example problems such as patronage and corruption, both showing great variation in time and space (Bardhan 1997). Once a corrupt system is in place, it is easy to explain why agents, even if they have "anti-corruption" norms, engage in corruption and patronage. Simply put, if it is "common knowledge" or "intersubjective understanding" (Schiemann 2000) that everyone takes/gives bribes, there is no point in being the only honest agent, because this will not lead the system towards any form of change. One can explain such "stable equilibria" by both interest-based rationality (few agents want to be "suckers"), and by culture (giving/taking bribes is the "intersubjective understanding"). But how should we explain the enormous variation of corrupt practices that exists in the contemporary world from either one of these approaches?

The problem becomes even more accentuated when we want to explain changes in corrupt practices that do occur. Why did the Swedish state move away from corrupt practices in the nineteenth century? (Rothstein 1998b). What made the system of political patronage in Naples decline in the 1990s? (Pasotti 2001). There is nothing in either the culturalist or the rational choice approach that, without ad hoc reasoning, can explain why such changes should occur. This has, from a rational choice point of view been described as the "once the system gets there, it stays there" problem (Bendor and Mookherjee 1987). The paradox is that there is very little room for agency, strategy, and choice within the rational choice approach once a system of incentives is in place. Why would self-interested agents who dominate institutions by extracting "rents" ever change these institutions? For example, once established, authoritarian rule would never give way to democratization. But such determinism is unwarranted, not only in a rationalist but also in the culturalist approach. The following example from the author Ian Buruma shows why:

> At a literary gathering in San Francisco, I met a distinguished writer from Yugoslavia. In an attempt to break the ice, I asked her whether she was Serb or Croat. She answered me courteously, but with a hint of impatience at my crass ignorance: "I am a Yugoslav. In Yugoslavia, we don't think in those categories anymore." This was in 1990. (Ian Buruma, "The Blood Lust of Identity," *The New York Review of Books*, April 11, 2002)

It should be a fair guess to say that the answer would have been different only a couple of years (or maybe even months) later. But would it have been different because of a change in the "pay-off matrix" (Hardin 1995) or because of a genuine change in the author's cultural belief system of what made her identity (Kaufman 2001)? Obviously, in some situations, even deep-rooted cultural variables such as one's own national identity may change very rapidly. In particular, models for recognition of cultural traits can change very quickly.

Yet, the discipline of political science, and of comparative politics in particular, has hereto been largely unable to study such cultural changes in a cumulative, progressive and effective manner. The reason lies primarily in the current inability of the cultural approach to produce a precise conceptualization of its tenets, and hence a coherent vocabulary. The impact of cultural variables has been hard to operationalize within a discipline-wide approach. The conceptual use of culture in comparative politics is often vague and undefined, leading to contradictory results. Even where defined, there is no consensus over what constitutes "culture": it is present in the literature as cognitive (identities, ideas), as attitudinal (practices, attitudes), and as rule-providing (institutions/rules/norms). Further, there is often a failure to demonstrate a distinct causal role for culture, leaving the argument in a tautological form: cultural aspects of a situation exists, therefore they are causes of the situation (Lichbach 1997: 257).

Taking on the realist challenge in political science

As has been argued by Shapiro and Wendt (1992) and MacDonald (2003), much of the debate between the rational choice and the cultural approaches is based on different "taken-for-granted" epistemological assumptions. From the instrumental empiricist approach to epistemology, there is no problem with theories that are based on unrealistic assumptions about what actually drives human behavior, as long as they produce testable and generalizable hypotheses that make good enough predictions. The epistemological assumption in logical empiricism is that people act "as-if" rational calculations cause them to act in a particular way. In this line of thought, it does not matter if empirical research has refuted again and again the notion that people act according to the template in the expected-utility model, because this is only "useful fiction" for creating testable hypotheses (MacDonald 2003: 553). However, since the 1970s, instrumental (or logical) empiricism has been criticized on many grounds within the philosophy of science. From the approach known as "scientific realism," it has been pointed out that one major problem with this "as-if" approach in logical empiricism is that it it lacks an interest in specifying the actual causal mechanisms that drive behavior. The intention here is not to make an argument in this meta-theoretical debate. Instead, I want to point out that this "as-if" approach in logical empiricism has serious effects for comparative politics in its efforts to explain variation among countries. Simply put, if we want to explain the variation that exists with the problem of social traps, we need to understand how the causal mechanisms between different types of institutions and different types of human behavior work (Hall 2003).

According to this approach, the focus of political science should be on empirically consistent explanations about the actual causal mechanisms that make agents act in different ways (Shapiro and Wendt 1992). In the social sciences, almost all such mechanisms are "unobservables" because they are relations between agents (power, influence, preferences, anticipation, calculations, etc.). However, this plea for turning the focus on theoretical specifications of the actual (realistic) causal mechanisms that are at work, rather than being content with predictions based on statistical correlations, is admittedly a tall order. It implies that we should work with theories that give a realistic picture of what actually causes political behavior. Moreover, if political science aspires to produce theories that are universally applicable to problems such as variation in corruption and social trust, it is self-evident that scientific realism presents a very demanding challenge. What is needed at the present stage is a more unified conceptual space in which the development of such theories can take place through coherent and progressive knowledge accumulation. Such a unified conceptual space should allow the necessary conversation between the two "epistemic camps" described above, and encourage a systematic analysis of political phenomena that take both culture and rationality into the same conceptual map.

A causal mechanisms approach

The central claim of scientific realism is that attention should be directed towards the causal mechanisms that are at work in social practices (Hedström and Swedberg 1998; Sayer 1992). The reason is that covering laws are not an appropriate approach for the social sciences because they cannot explain the enormous variation in practice that exists, not least when it comes to the problem of social traps. A covering law about social traps would either predict their inevitability or the reverse. Deterministic covering laws are thus rare in the social sciences. The type of probabilistic law that comes out of instrumental empiricism does not lead to causal explanations, for two reasons.

First, it is difficult to distinguish *correlation* and *causation* (Elster 1989b: 3). Schelling (1996: 36 ff.) provides an alternative statement of this idea, when he argues that without social mechanisms we can produce only predictions, and not explanations. Schelling consequently argues why explanations are more useful than predictions. A probabilistic law suggests only that a relationship is likely to exist, but it will give no clue as to why it is likely to be so. The covering law model justifies the use of "black-box" explanations, which means that we may know that when one set of variables move, another set of variables also moves, but we lack a theory of why the one set moves the other. Hedström and Swedberg (1998: 9) argues that "What characterizes a black-box explanation is that the link between input and output, or between explanans and explanandum, is assumed to be devoid of structure, or, at least, whatever structure there may be is considered to be of no interest."

Second, the aggregate character of statistical analysis prevents reliable explanation because "the neutral aggregate could mask a homogeneous population of neutral individuals – or a heterogeneous population of individuals who are all strongly affected but in opposite directions" (Elster 1999: 12). This of course does not imply that quantitative analysis is not important.

As Hedström and Swedberg (1998: 17) argue: "Quite the contrary: Quantitative research is essential both for descriptive purposes and for testing . . . theories." However, they continue, "it should not be the dominant tool for generating theories."

Mechanisms thus offer a better basis for social explanation because they address with some generality how a relationship between variables that can somehow be measured was brought about. Yet, they are less stringent than deterministic law-like statements: they are "frequently occurring and easily recognizable causal patterns that are triggered under generally unknown conditions and with indeterminate consequences" (Elster 1999: 1). By getting knowledge about these "unknown conditions" and by trying to find empirical evidence for their consequences, we may approach explanations in cases like this when deterministic covering laws cannot be sustained.

The adoption of causal mechanisms should not thus be understood as simply adding another "intervening variable" to the explanation. Instead, it is geared towards understanding why "one variable changes another" (Hage and Meeker 1988: 1). Mechanisms address the "what makes it happen" question that, again, goes beyond establishing a statistical correlation between variables (Sayer 1992: 104). Since we are dealing with how one type of belief (if other people can be trusted) is affected by and affects other types of beliefs (e.g. the character of political institutions), which in its turn affects action, this is a complicated affair.

Since the focus of political science tends to be on explaining political action, scholars tend to focus on cognitive mechanisms alone. McAdam, Tarrow, and Tilly (2001) extend this argument, to point out that all patterns guiding social phenomena, including social structures, are mechanisms. In other words, for the analysis of social structure we also cannot achieve laws, but only mechanisms. Structural mechanisms include both environmental and relational mechanisms because both environmental resources (physical resources and formal or informal institutional resources) and configurations ("relational" events in McAdam, Tarrow, and Tilly's terms) ultimately constitute structural features.

The argument here is that a mechanism-based approach in the social sciences must take individuals as the basic unit of analysis. Mechanisms may alter relations, but if they link distinct persons into a collective they must ultimately operate through the individual. They can be macro mechanism, but only as long as they are based at least in principle on micro-causal mechanisms that explain individual behavior (Elster 1989b).

New political actions emerge from cognitive mechanisms (although very often not as intended by actors). In other words, political change is actor-based and hence occurs only when agents take notice and act upon structural changes, other people's actions or new opportunities. However, mechanisms need not be coupled only to instrumental rationality. On the contrary, how mechanisms work in different social settings should be an open empirical question. They may equally be based on emotions, problems of information, or ideology. The implication is that a focus on causal mechanisms makes it necessary to specify how we see the relation between rationality and culture and how they are related at the individual (micro-)level.

Rationality as subjective rationality

Two theories of human rationality have found application in political science: procedural, bounded rationality from contemporary cognitive psychology, and global, substantive rationality from neo-classical economics. The principle of "objective" rationality, unless accompanied by extensive empirical research to identify the correct auxiliary assumptions, has little power to make valid predictions about political phenomena. Rather, an explanation that takes the role of individual behavior seriously requires a focus on subjective rationality.

One can conceive of human action that is inherently non-purposeful. However, for the purposes of the empirical analysis of political behavior, non-purposeful ("futile") action can be disregarded as not playing a significant role (rituals have a purpose, as praying and small-talk illustrate). This is separate from saying that an action can have unintended and unpredicted effects. Since most political actors act in a purposeful manner most of the time, subjective rationality is a valid empirically grounded approximation of political behavior. As Elster suggests, subjective rationality takes into account the constraints on knowledge that agents face:

> For some purposes, rational-choice theory can be summarized by saying that people do as well as they can. In general, however, we need to take account of the fact that the full set of objective opportunities available to the agent may not be known to him. Today, for instance, governments do not really know whether it is possible to develop commercially viable fusion power. Or, to take a more mundane example, an automobilist arriving in an unknown city without a map will not know the full set of paths that will take him through it. Applied to this situation, the theory says that people do as well as they believe they can. (Elster 2000b: 16)

Yet, the assumption of subjective rationality should not be limited to interest-based explanations: after all, rational choice cannot claim property rights on the basis that political agents have goals and use their brains to pursue them. Cultural explanations also assume that people have goals and that they may act strategically. Otherwise, they would be indeterminate as explanations. The role of interests in explaining action is inseparable from the individuals' perception of what their interests are, as well as the perception of available strategies and outcomes. Culture as a belief system is therefore necessarily an integral part of any explanation.

This important point is often not made explicitly because both the researcher and his subject share the same cultural reference, and hence do not explicitly explain why it affects actions. In Ann Swidler's terms, in such cases both subject and researcher are part of the same cultural logic (Swidler 2001b). Goldstein and Keohane (1993) concur that for "traditionalist societies, the individualistic and secular scientific premises of this world view remain intellectually and morally alien" (1993: 9). Indeed, the presence of a discrepancy between the researcher's and the subject's perception of interests and strategies is not far-fetched. Researchers with fieldwork experience often report their inability to fully comprehend the logic behind their subject's actions. As stated by Raymond Boudon: "The basic shortcoming of the 'rational choice model' resides in the fact that, except in trivial cases, social action rests on beliefs, and the 'rational choice model' in its current version has little to say about the question of how to explain collective beliefs" (Boudon 1996: 147).

Obviously, we need to know more about the agents than that they will try to maximize power, wealth, and status. They may, for example, maximize the likelihood of realizing an idea about how their society should be organized that has little to do with their own personal power, status, and wealth. They may maximize a certain notion of their own identity or of how others should perceive their identity (Garme 2001; Ringmar 1996). They may even sacrifice power, status and wealth (and maybe their own life) in order to see this identity realized.

This development of giving individuals a broader repertoire than just rational utility maximization is not confined to political science. In economics, the approach has become known as "behavioral economics." The idea is to embrace the insights of other disciplines such as sociology and psychology in the effort to incorporate more realistic assumptions about what drives human behavior. This field has thus documented failures of the rational-actor model – failures of expected utility theory, seemingly irrational cooperation, and time-inconsistent preferences (Fehr and Fischbacher 2002; Loewenstein, Rabin and Camerer 2004).

How do these developments contribute to a more unified conceptual framework for political science? I would argue that they show how keeping a commitment to methodological individualism permits the development of a mechanisms-based micro-foundation combining subjective rationality (thus focusing on descriptive, rather than normative modeling), with accepting agents' limited computational capacity and that emotions influence choice behavior, the importance of networks and social contexts, as well as specific group dynamics and preferences.

Culture-as-a-toolbox

The argument above suggests that a combination of self-interest and self-esteem as the target of optimization is a better assumption for political science, because it reflects the fact that political actors are driven by concerns of the right as well as of the good – that is, they may operate with dual utility structures and they are "conditional cooperators" (Fehr, Fishbacher, and Gachter 2002; Levi 1991). Addressing this concern, H. Peyton-Young, a leading scholar in mathematical evolutionary game theory, starts his analysis with the following assumption about how to understand agency:

> Agents are not perfectly rational and fully informed about the world in which they live. They base their decisions on fragmentary information, they have incomplete models of the process they are engaged in, and they may not be especially forward looking. Still, they are not completely irrational: they adjust their behavior based on what they think other agents are going to do, and these expectations are generated endogenously by information about what other agents have done in the past. (Young 1998: 6)

What people "think other agents are going to do" is of course something they learn (or make inferences about) from the culture in which they live. Similarly, "what other agents have done in the past" must be seen as agents in a society sharing some sort of "collective memory" about each other as individuals and groups (who are the Serbs, the politicians, the police, the Catholics . . . and to what extent can they be trusted?). For example, if public officials expect to be bribed, and if *other people* usually bribe them, that gives agents in that society a certain idea about what they can expect when they come into contact with government bodies. The implication is that if belief systems are as important as stated above for explaining agents' choice of strategy, this makes the "residualist" idea in the culturalist approach far too limited.

If we accept that culture as a belief system is necessarily an integral part of an explanation, how should we perceive the influence of culturally based norms if we do not want to accept the idea that culture overtakes agents rationality and is overwhelmingly powerful? One solution has been presented by Ann Swidler who argues that we need to specify how "culture is actually put to use by social actors." Hers is an argument against seeing culture as a having overwhelming structural power in the manner of anthropologist Clifford Geertz. She states that "To describe how culture works, we need new metaphors. We must think of culture less as a great stream in which we are all immersed, and more as a bag of tricks or an oddly assorted tool kit" (Swidler 2001b: 24).

A starting point in this approach is that people *know much more culture* (signals, stories, symbols, rituals, etc.) than they actually use. Secondly, there is variation in how they make use of the cultural repertoire that is available to them and they "select within that repertoire what works at the moment" (Swidler 2001a: 2). Thirdly, people also differ in "how seriously they take their culture and how richly they deploy it" (Swidler 2001a: 71). Lastly, Swidler argues that people sustain a lot of contradictory or uncoordinated cultural codes in their repertoires. That "a settled matron may still know how to get 'down and dirty'" is one of her many examples (Swidler 2001a: 2).

There are certainly variations in the size and diversity of repertoires that people can select in different societies. Nevertheless, this approach disarms the idea that choice belongs to instrumental rationality, while hegemonic norms solely belong to cultural analysis. Instead, a market may become hegemonic, giving individuals no room for strategic maneuvering, while people can be seen as making choices from a menu of cultural repertoires.

Structure, agency and institutions

This discussion of subjective rationality and culture-as-a-toolbox has reviewed why utility based interest alone cannot provide a motivational foundation for political explanation. It is argued that political behavior must be conceptualized taking into account the human tendency to strive both for utility and for what they believe is right. What is the appropriate level at which to apply this idea? Following the causal mechanism approach, methodological individualism is the logical answer. However, methodological individualism is usually considered to be adverse to structural approaches. As social traps are for real, they are of course social structures that cannot, as we have seen, be changed or overcome by individual actors. But methodological individualism should not be seen as to be at odds with the analysis of structural phenomena since our purpose is to explain how entities on the macro-level (such as pervasively corrupt institutions) affect beliefs and actions of individuals. On the relation between structural and actor-centered explanations, I agree with Little (1991):

> Structures do not plausibly cause outcomes, rather they make some outcomes more likely than others. And in these circumstances it is imperative to have further knowledge about the processes at work at the local level – the level of individual agency and choice – if we hope to say why one outcome occurred rather than another . . . If we want to know how individuals will behave in a particular institutional environment of choice, we need to know what their beliefs and goals are and what choices are available to them through which they can pursue their goals. The incentives and constraints imposed by the social structure will have predictable consequences for the choices that individuals will make. In this light then, there is no contradiction between rational choice theory and structural causation; instead the former describes one important family of mechanisms through which the causal powers of social structures are transmitted. (Little 1991: 105)

Yet "social structures" do not act independently. There can be no systems or processes causing social change that is independent of "regularities of individual action" (Little 1991: 18). This position does not call into question the validity of structural analyses. Rather, it points out that social and political structures are the result of the aggregation of individual behaviors. Consequently, structural explanations can be reduced to problems of aggregation of individual-level explanations. The recognition of the ultimate role of human intention in the study of social outcomes leads to an inevitable call for methodological individualism.

The particular structural position (or configuration) of agents *vis-à-vis* each other affects the resulting individual behavior. Thus, the behavior of individuals in groups is irreducible to the behavior of isolated individuals. The fact that actors are in a group is what fundamentally changes the structure of their interaction, their perception of the chances of success, their perception of their safety, their perceptions of gains and losses and their distribution, their emotions, and their concerns of fairness, etc. Most importantly, what changes is their view (their belief system) about what they can expect of the other agents in that group. Will they cooperate or are they more likely to cheat? Can they be trusted or not?

According to the renowned Hungarian economist János Kornai, a certain practice is customary when doctors and patients meet in the Hungarian public health system. After the treatment, it is customary for patients to hand over an envelope containing a sum of money to the doctor. Such illicit "hidden-in-an-envelope" payment is for the average Hungarian physician about 60 percent of his or her total income. Everyone knows that this is something "outside the books," but still "everyone" plays according to this established custom (Kornai 2000). Many doctors and most patients consider that this is an illegitimate system, but it is reproduced because of established mutual expectations and the lack of a plausible alternative. The question here is how we should explain an institution such as this.

There seems to be a general agreement that, at the core, political institutions are "the rules of the game." The question is, however, what should be included in the concept of "rules." One such classic division is between "formal" and "informal" rules. Most people, most of the time follow predefined rules of behavior, and most of these rules are not formalized as laws or other written regulations. Instead they are "routines," "customs," "compliance procedures," "habits," "decision styles," and other social norms about what is considered appropriate behavior" (Hall 1986; March and Olsen 1989). In a more narrow sense, political institutions has been defined as "formal arrangements for aggregating individuals and regulating their behavior through the use of explicit rules and decision processes enforced by an actor or set of actors formally recognized as possessing such power" (Levi 1990: 405). Obviously, "habits," "norms," etc. are neither explicit, nor formalized.

The problem here is where to draw the line. Are we to understand political institutions as any kind of repetitive behavior that influences political processes or outcomes? Or should we reserve the term "political institutions" for formal rules that have been decided upon in a political process? Including "habits" and "culture" and the like has the advantage of incorporating most of the things that guide individual behavior. The drawback is that institution as a concept risks becoming too watered down. If so, it risks the same fate as has happened to other popular concepts in the social sciences (e.g. planning and rationality): if it means everything, than it means nothing.

If "culture," as Douglass North (1990), for example, claims, is nothing but informal institutional rules, then there is no possibility left to distinguish between the important political institutions and other social facts. There would, for example, be no point in analyzing the role of different legal systems that are put in place to combat corruption, because such a broad conceptualization of "political institutions" would conflate such formal legal rules with the overall culture of society. If every type of repetitive behavior can be explained by institutional rules broadly defined, than there is no chance of singling out what role "political institutions," more narrowly defined, play in social processes because the answer is already given in the definition. Another problem is that reductionism is brought in through the back door, only relabeled as "institutions" (Levi 1990: 404).

On the other hand, if you limit the definition of "institutional rules" to the formal ones, you risk missing a lot of not formalized but still "taken for granted" rules that exist in any political organization and which determine political behavior, such as the "hidden-in-an-envelope" practice mentioned above. The advantage, however, is that you may be able to give an answer to what changes in formal political institutions mean – i.e. if "politics" in the narrow sense of the specific design of political institutions, "matters." Comparing political entities (states, regions, cities) with similar historical and cultural traits, but with differences in formal political institutions (such as laws against corruption, for example) may give important results.

One way out of this dilemma is to acknowledge a third type of rule, namely what in public administration has been called "standard operating procedures" (Hall 1986). Other similar labels for this type of rules are "work rules" (Ostrom 1990). By this, scholars have tried to identify the rules actually agreed upon and followed by the agents involved. The advantage of a definition of this sort is obvious. While "culture" and "social norms" are excluded from the definition, rules that are "political" in the sense that they have been established by either an explicit or a tacit agreement are counted in whether or not they have been written down and decided upon in a formal procedure. Any theory of the importance of political institutions must find a way to conceptualize in what way these differ from the general culture in a society (Levi 1990; Steinmo and Thelen 1992).

The question is: What do institutions do? Let me briefly point to three things that are illustrated by the Kornai "hidden-in-an-envelope" example above. First, most obvious, they influence *incentives*. Patients know that they may get much better treatment if they bribe the doctors, and doctors know that they have no reason to refrain from taking the money. First, because even if they do refuse to take the envelope, this will not change the system; secondly, the likelihood that they will be punished is minuscule. This leads us to the second effect of institutions, namely that they influence *strategic behavior*, because they tell actors what other actors are likely to do. In this case, doctors will know that almost all other doctors accepts this kind of money, and patients will know that almost all other patients pay. Patients thereby have reason to fear that they will be treated less well than other patients if they refuse to pay. Lastly, an institution such as this is likely to influence individuals' ethics and norms, simply because it fosters recurrent behavior that most of the agents involved consider unethical.

Doing comparative research on corruption is difficult, For example, the Swedish Research Council would not allow a field experiment in which we tried to see what would happen in a public health clinic in Sweden if we tried to hand over money in the way that is customary in Hungary (and in many other post-socialist countries). Research on uninformed individuals would in a case like this not pass the ethics committee of the Research Council. However, since I have many friends working in the public health sector in Sweden, I have tried to accumulate information on what they think would happen. Almost without exception, the answer is that the doctors and nurses simply would not understand what was going on – that is, they would not understand that they were being bribed. This, I would argue, is not because Swedes are morally superior or less interested in economic rewards than are Hungarians: it's all in the institutions.

Conclusions

What comes out of this discussion is a couple of theoretical directions for our analysis of the problem of social traps. One is that it is necessary to transcend the division between "rationalist" and "culturalist" approaches in the social sciences. I hope to have shown that both rely on highly misleading and empirically refuted conceptions of what drives people to act in certain ways. Since social traps are "for real," the human sufferings because of corruption and deep social mistrust are of such a magnitude that we should not play silly games in our analyses. Secondly, we need construct a theory about how the causal mechanisms actually operate in this problem. Thirdly, it is necessary to try to figure out ways to test the existence of such causal mechanisms. This will be a difficult task because such mechanisms cannot be easily observed and measured: empirical testing will demand methodological creativity. Fourthly, we should concentrate on *subjective rationality*, which implies that we should include rationality on a continuum from the model based on self-interest and expected utility to "culture-as-a-toolbox," in other words, we should not prescribe what type of motivations individuals use, but leave this to the empirical investigation. Lastly, the explanatory force is likely to be centered on variation in institutions, because they can serve as a link between overall structures and individual agency. Institutions as defined above do three things: They present incentives, they induce strategy because they make it plausible to calculate what the other agents are likely to do and, in some cases, they influence ethics and norms. These are at least three good reasons to have variations in institutions as a first hypothesis for why social traps may, or may not, occur.

3

On the theory and practice of social capital

Few books have had an impact on the international debate on political science and policy issues equal to that of *Making Democracy Work*, published in 1993 by Robert D. Putnam. In the flood of books, scholarly papers, and reports from the political and social scientific field in the 1990s, Putnam's book is one of the few that can now be said to have attained the status of a modern classic. This statement does not imply that the theories, methods, and results related to the importance of social capital presented in the book are undisputed. In fact, the opposite is closer to the truth, but it is nonetheless apparent that through this work, Robert Putnam set a new agenda for much of research on politics and society. Not least, his theses have sparked a number of intriguing controversies within the research community (Durlauf 2002; Encarnación 2003; Krishna 2002; cf. Levi 1996; Portes 2000; Stolle 2000a, 2003; Tarrow 1996; Uslaner 2002). The theory has also inspired widespread public discussion and engaged the interest of many people outside the field of social scientific research.

International organizations have also noted the meaning of social capital, especially in the area of development and humanitarian aid (Krishna 2002; Woolcock and Narayan 2000). On its website, the World Bank has posted comprehensive documentation of research and case studies illustrating the importance of social capital to the development of democracy and the struggle to eliminate poverty, indicating that the World Bank supports the building of volunteer organizations as a means of creating economic growth in developing countries.

The impact of a new theoretical model may be assessed in many different ways. One is to see whether its central concepts have caught the interest of the international research community, something that can now

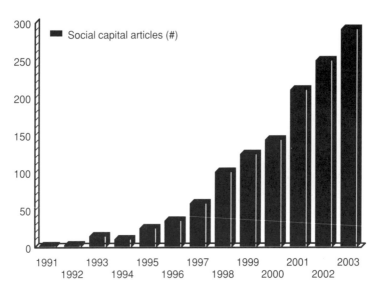

Figure 3.1. Number of published scholarly papers on social capital, 1991–2003
Source: Institute for Scientific Information: Database, Social Science Citation Index;
for more information, see http://wos.isiglobalnet.com/CIW.cgi.

be measured in purely quantitative terms via the International Science
Information (ISI) database, which maintains a searchable database of
articles published in some 3,000 scholarly journals in the social sciences and
humanities. A search for instances of the term "social capital" in the titles,
abstracts, or key words (usually three–five) provided by authors returns the
results shown in figure 3.1.

As shown by the graph in figure 3.1, there has been a very strong increase
in the number of scholarly papers on social capital since *Making Democracy
Work* was published in 1993. From barely a handful early in the decade,
the number for 2002 grew to almost 300. Interestingly, even though Robert
Putnam's disciplinary territory is political science, a check of the ISI database
shows that many other social scientific disciplines have begun delving into
the theory of social capital. If one adds the term "growth" to "social capital"
and executes another search, it emerges that the number of papers demon-
strates a corresponding relative increase during the same period, which
should indicate that many growth economists have also referred to the theory on the importance of social capital (cf. Knack and Keefer 1997; Paldam
and Svendsen 2000; Temple and Johnson 1998).

Naturally, only time will tell whether the theory on social capital, like
so many other social scientific theories, is a dead-end street, a fad, or is of

enduring scientific value. One of my first teachers in political science, the now legendary Lund Professor Hans F. Petersson, was wont to liken social scientific theories to the vine-covered temples that can be found in South American jungles – beautiful, impressive structures, but abandoned. Even so, it seems clear that the theory of social capital deserves serious consideration as a significant potential in the social sciences. It may prove to be wrong, yet nevertheless to have contributed to the advancement of research.[1] A parallel may perhaps be drawn with human capital, a concept introduced in the early 1960s to explain differences in growth between different countries. Human capital was at first also a disputed concept, but is now part of the standard repertoire of many social sciences.

I believe that research on social capital and social trust is promising because it seems to have engendered an unusual effort towards cumulativity in policy and social science research surrounding the problem of the social trap. This can be seen in the two circumstances mentioned above – i.e. in the amount of research energy devoted to the problem and in the distinct increase in communication among researchers working in different disciplines and with different methodological approaches. Studies of the relationship between confidence, trust, and social networks have a vigorous multidisciplinary direction and are becoming an intersection at which not only political scientists from various theoretical points of departure, but also historians, economists, sociologists, philosophers, and many others, meet. Methodological pluralism is another distinct element of this research industry. Scholars from very disparate fields such as evolutionary game theory, opinion and survey research, policy studies, history and political philosophy are studying social capital. One might say that, even if the theory proves to be a dead-end, Putnam has managed to create what in game theory is called a *focal point* in the social sciences (cf. Schelling 1960).

Administration Italian-style

The odd thing about the huge impact of Putnam's book is that it is about something as prosaic as the effects of an administrative decentralization

---

[1] Like scientific theorist and winner of the Nobel Prize in Physics, Steven Weinberg, I do not share Thomas Kuhn's opinion on the importance of the paradigm shift in science insofar as a new paradigm entails complete abandonment of the accumulation of knowledge that took place in the old one. His example is that even though the theory of relativity replaced Newtonian mechanics, the study of physics still begins with Newtonian mechanics. That is, in order to understand the point of a new paradigm, we must first have grasped its precedent. This would imply that political scientists should still begin their studies with the attempt to understand what Plato and Aristotle said about the opportunities and problems of various forms of government. See: "The Revolution That Didn't Happen," *The New York Review of Books*, October 8, 1998.

reform carried out in Italy in the early 1970s. The outcome of the reform was that a great deal of that formerly decided by the central government in Rome (and, not least importantly, by its vast bureaucracy) was delegated to twenty-seven regional parliaments and regional governments. The substance of the reform was responsibility for diverse matters of civic importance such as health care, childcare, economic policy, school issues, elder care, agricultural policy, etc. Putnam and his research team were in the unique position of being able to track the outcomes of this political reform – i.e. how well the regional governments and the administrative machinery they created were able to get the democratic process to work over a period of almost twenty years. Methodologically, the Italian decentralization reform of the early 1970s gave Putnam's project something social scientists often lack in their empirical arsenals: a situation resembling a natural experiment. In a single country under a common constitutional and political structure, there was suddenly a laboratory of how democracy worked available through the opportunity to compare developments in the various regions.

Naturally, what constitutes a "working democracy" is a matter of theoretical and political debate. As with many other core concepts in the social sciences, there is no generally accepted definition of "democracy." However, that which made Putnam's study interesting, and which I believe contributed to its widespread impact, was that he did not stop at a narrow, formal definition of democracy (equal suffrage, equal rights to run for office, etc.), nor did he limit his definition to the representative aspects (such as measurements of voter turnout and social or opinion-related representativity in the regional parliaments). Instead, Putnam chose a much broader definition of what constitutes a working democracy by including aspects of policy implementation. According to Putnam, democracy was not just a matter of formal political rights, nor was it restricted to how well the composition of the regional parliaments reflected the social (or gender, sexual, ethnic, religious, etc.) identities of the electorate, or their opinions on sundry issues. Instead, Putnam and his research team added to the equation that which had actually been accomplished by means of the democratic process in relation to concrete measures in the policy areas for which responsibility had been delegated to the regional parliaments through the decentralization reform. Were any new daycare centers or pediatric clinics built? Did roads and health care centers work? Was agriculture successfully reformed? How were the schools performing and were citizens being informed? Were the regions able to get the machinery of democratic decision making to work all the way down to the level of the everyday lives of citizens?

Putnam's operational index of a working democracy contained no fewer than twelve different variables, half of which actually dealt with policy implementation. According to that view, whether a society may be considered a working democracy is not solely a matter of the degree of democratic legitimacy in the decisions made by parliamentary assemblies and governments, but also whether the society has successfully *implemented* those decisions in fairly reasonable agreement with the intentions of the reform programs. This broader definition of democracy takes into account that citizens actually have a stake in what comes out of the democratic machinery, i.e., that people do not evaluate only the *input* side of the policy (i.e. how well they believe they – their group, their gender, their opinions – are represented, cf. Esaiasson and Holmberg 1996). Putnam added the *output* side of the democratic machinery (i.e. how well the political system implemented various reform programs, cf. Kumlin and Rothstein 2005). The underlying idea in this more comprehensive view of democracy can be described approximately as follows: To vote a parliamentary assembly into office, however representative, in an election, however free and fair, is all very well and good. But if that body cannot make decisions of sufficient quality to enable their implementation, or if the body loses control over the administrative machinery, the democracy in question is not worth much. Putnam pinpointed a neglected point in studies of democracy: the *efficiency* of the democratic government (Mettler and Soss 2004; cf. Rothstein 1996b).

One of the central results of the research project on Italian regional politics was that large, if not dramatic, differences quickly arose between how well the different regions managed their responsibility for these policy areas and their ability to get the democratic process in the region to work. With few exceptions, this proved to be a north/south story – i.e. democracy worked significantly better in the northern regions than in the south. As is customary in the social sciences, Putnam and his research team examined accepted theories for explanations of the influences that make democracy work. They investigated whether the differences in the quality of democracy could be the fruits of economic or social conditions, or whether the explanation lay simply in the different political majorities. The results were meager indeed. None of the "usual suspects" among the factors could satisfactorily contribute to the explanation of variations in democracy in the different regions.

Instead, Putnam's study returned a surprising result. There was a clear correlation between the density and weight of local associativeness and how democracy worked. In a nutshell, the more people were organized in voluntary associations and groups such as choral societies, bird watching clubs, and sports clubs, the better democracy worked. The analysis went one step further, in that Putnam's study showed that the extent of associativeness did not only explain why democracy worked better in certain regions, but also why those regions had experienced superior economic growth. Through analysis of historical economic data and associativeness, Putnam was able to argue that it was not economic growth that stimulated strong voluntary associations but the reverse, that *associativeness triggered economic growth*. Putnam's explanation is that participation in voluntary associations produces *social capital* through which civil transactions can be based upon *trust* in other people in the society – i.e. that people have the courage to cooperate because they trust that others are also going to cooperate. Voluntary organizations create a "binding cement" in the form of strong social norms of trust and reciprocity that enable or facilitate the kind of cooperation upon which democracy is based and which constitutes a cornerstone that makes it possible to sidestep social traps.

The tragedy of the commons

In addition to Robert Putnam's 1993 study, another formative work within this discourse should be mentioned, Elinor Ostrom's *Governing the Commons* (1990). Many decisions in a democracy concern things that can be called "commons," a special kind of shared resource distinguished by the condition that everyone is allowed to use them freely, yet every individual has a strong interest in the resource not being depleted. In this context, one often thinks of various kinds of natural resources such as fishing waters, forests, clean air, or water resources. If all individuals act according to self-interest, they will make maximum use of the resource for their own advantage, as no user can shut the others out. However, this also means that no single individual has an interest in conserving the resource or making efforts to improve it. Depletion of ocean fisheries and the problem of global warming are perhaps the most topical examples of the problem (cf. Acheson and Knight 2000).

The problem of the commons is that, in the short term, non-cooperation provides a better pay-off to the individual than cooperation, while in the long term everyone loses by non-cooperation. This was the problem that inspired Garrett Hardin to introduce the notion of the "tragedy of the commons" in his famous essay (Hardin 1968). Hardin's future scenario for the pastoral grazing land – which can easily be applied to the earth's biosphere (the air, the oceans, the climate) – is unremittingly dark and pessimistic: Human nature's striving for individual resource maximization inexorably leads to overutilization, devastation, and depletion. Everyone loses in the long term when they try to maximize personal utility in the short term.

Research has advanced two solutions to the tragedy of the commons. The first has been state regulation and inspection: because the local population will inevitably overuse the resource, central governments must assume responsibility. However, the inherent problem with this solution has manifested itself in the implementation phase. Systems that involve central regulation have often failed, either because the authorities have been unable to cooperate with the local population in a way that makes it possible for them to obtain the necessary information about how the resource in question might be reproduced, or else they have been corrupted by the local interests they were ordered to monitor.

The second recommended solution stands in diametric opposition to the first. Rather than being put under state control, the resource should be converted to private rights of ownership, giving individual owners an interest in the sustainability of the resources and making it possible to create an efficient market. The problem here has been partly technical – it is not easy to determine who owns the air, the fish in the sea, or grazing lands – and partly to do with the difficulty of efficiently restricting the use of the resource – e.g. groundwater or grazing land. It has thus not been possible to establish either the market or the state as universal solutions to the tragedy of the commons.

As implied above, there is an extensive discussion of Hardin's problem among the research community, but a great deal of the research has either been purely theoretical or else been occupied with trying to verify these models. Usually, researchers have deliberately chosen cases that they knew in advance confirmed the theory that local cooperation to solve the problem is not feasible. Elinor Ostrom empirically analyzed cases in which actors successfully solved the problem. In her book, she showed that a primary issue was whether individual users could be persuaded to participate in the production and maintenance of a number of common ordinances that regulated usage of the common resource. It turned out that whether this could be done depended on whether users perceived *other users'* readiness to contribute to joint action as *credible*. For the regulations to be perceived as credible, users had to submit to supervision and control, but they are hardly likely to be willing to do so if the *social trust* within the group is low from the outset. In short – without supervision, stable cooperation to preserve the commons will be impossible. But lacking mutual assurance of the trustworthiness and predictability of each other's behavior, no one will voluntarily attempt to build stable regulations that will also apply to others. The problem seemed just as unsolvable as Garret Hardin's theory had said.

However, Ostrom showed that in many places, and in many kinds of societies all over the globe, self-governing institutions established for the care and utilization of common resources did in fact exist, institutions that had resolved the dilemma and which had worked for a long time. In one case, she was able to document that people had successfully maintained the resource for several centuries by means of a single type of local regulation. How could it be that something considered impossible in theory was actually feasible in practice? After reviewing a large number of such existing solutions,

Ostrom found that there are several factors critical to bringing about stable institutional solutions to the problem of the commons. She pointed out, for instance, that the actors affected by the rules for the use and care of resources must have the right to participate in decisions to change the rules. For that reason, the people who monitor and control the behavior of users should also be users and/or have been given a mandate by all users. This is a significant insight, as it shows that prospects are dim for a centrally directed solution to the problem of the commons emanating from a state power in comparison with a local solution for which users assume personal responsibility. Ostrom also emphasizes the importance of democratic decision processes and that all users must be given access to local arenas for solving problems and conflicts among themselves. Political institutions at central, regional, and local levels must allow users to devise their own regulations and independently ensure compliance.

How can actors generate the trust required for all of this to work? In her analysis of how farmers in California made the transition from a water-usage situation in which everyone was pitted against everyone else and resources were fast being devastated to the establishment of a self-governing institution that efficiently regulated the use of finite water resources, she writes:

> In each basin, a voluntary association was established to provide a forum for face-to-face discussions about joint problems and potential strategies . . . The provision of a forum for discussion transformed the structure of the situation from one in which decisions were made independently without knowing what others were doing to a situation in which individuals discussed their options with one another. (1990: 138)

How decisions are made is thus the critical factor in changing the views of individuals about what is in their own best interests. Based solely on personal short-term interests, people have reason to act in a non-solidaristic manner, but when put into a situation where they must argue publicly and be held morally accountable for their actions, the significance of social norms becomes crucial to finding a solution to the tragedy of the commons. This does not make people into altruists. It redefines their self-interest so that it harmonizes with the collective interest found in not draining the common resource. Ostrom's finding that the open, democratic nature of the decision process changes behavior from short-sighted egoism to cooperation is pivotal, because it disproves the central postulate of the "public choice" school (as formulated by Nobel laureate James Buchanan) – i.e. that elected representatives behave similarly when they make decisions about public programs and when they act in a market (cf. Granqvist 1987).

Ostrom's work also supports the thesis that there is a correlation between social trust and the phenomenon known as "deliberate democracy"

(Mackie 1998; cf. Mulhberger 2001; Warren 1999). The thought is that we may be prepared to seriously listen to and accept opinions and arguments from those whose interests or ideas are different from our own, but only provided that we can trust that the other side is equally ready to do so. The deliberative democracy model is based on the notion that participants should not enter a democratic decision process bearing pre-set opinions just to find out later, through the taking of a vote, where the majority ends up. Instead, this model of democracy proposes that it is the dialog and arguments of the decision process that should help reshape preferences and that it should be possible after such a discussion to arrive at cooperative solutions that embrace broad majorities. Such broad majorities are important to instill confidence in the long-term stability of the regulations, especially with respect to the design of institutions (e.g. fundamental laws or rules on how commons may be used). Outside of Ostrom, there is significant support in the research for the idea that *trust in the counterpart* is essential for such a democratic process to work (Kollock 1997). As so elegantly formulated by Jan Teorell, deliberative democracy is not about the equal rights of citizens to be involved in decision making, but rather about their equal rights to be involved in making up their own minds (Teorell 1998: 357). Willingness to seriously consider others' arguments is predicated on believing that the others will reciprocate. It is equally meaningless for an actor to carefully compose a serious argument if she is convinced that her counterpart has no interest in considering her opinions.

Those who have chosen to criticize Ostrom's conclusions have pointed out that most of her successful examples apply to small commons used mainly for a single purpose, such as fishing and irrigation systems, to which users are bound by long-term, similar interests. Such a monocultural social environment creates favorable conditions for mutual understanding and trust. However, the magnitude of her contribution is its validity and applicability to most scales and levels with which social science is concerned. National governments trying to handle global warming are basically in the same situation as poor peasants in developing countries – they cannot turn to a central authority for solving their problem of collective action.

We can thus conclude three things from Putnam and Ostrom's research. One is that possible solutions to the problem of the social trap do exist. Secondly, that this does not imply that they will automatically come about. Solutions will not necessarily be employed just because they are possible. Problems of social traps are endemic to all forms of economic and democratic development. The third conclusion is the relative importance that both studies give to the political institutions that are responsible for implementing public policies.

The theory of social capital: a critical perspective

There are substantive reasons for the keen interest aroused by the theory of social capital within and outside the research community. The first is that problems of the nature of social capital are by no means merely theoretical constructs. They constitute all too real barriers to survival for a great many people (Ostrom 1998). The theory has proven unusually accurate at the aggregated level. Where there is a country, region, or city with a large stock of social capital, one is also likely to find a well-functioning and stable democracy, a high level of economic development, and little corruption and other crime (Inglehart 1999, 1997; Woolcock and Narayan 2001). There are also several confirmed statistical correlations at the individual level between social capital and conditions regarded as desirable. Individuals who are strongly involved in social networks and believe they can generally trust other people are healthier, richer, happier, and more optimistic about the future, and better educated than those who have few social contacts and believe that they generally cannot be too careful when dealing with other people (Helliwell 2003; Holmberg and Weibull 1997; Norén 2000; Uslaner 2002; Wollebæck, Selle, and Lorentzen 2001).

However, these are statistical correlations and they say nothing about whether the causal relationship indicated by the theory is true, as the precise nature of the causal mechanisms has yet to be investigated. This book is based on, is a criticism of, and suggests an alternative to, Putnam's theory on the source and significance of social capital. Let us address each in order. I believe that the theory of the significance of social capital is of great value when applied to our ability to solve problems concerning the nature of the social trap. Although not initially constructed by Putnam, he deserves the credit for having conducted empirical research on a large scale to show how the theory might work, and especially its impact on democratic and economic development (cf. Baron, Field, and Schuller 2000). The sort of trust that people who are in danger of falling into a social trap need is specifically of the type defined by the theory of social capital. However, I am critical of the accepted understanding of the theory on two points. The first has to do with one of the core points of the inner logic of the theory – i.e. that it is far from certain that all or even the majority of social networks and voluntary associations have a positive effect on creating a "working democracy." Secondly, research has thus far failed to find any credible evidence on the individual level that engagement in voluntary associations is the source of social capital in the currency of interpersonal trust. My alternative is based on my belief that interpersonal trust and confidence are created by other mechanisms of a more political nature than the sociological variables Putnam advances. In these respects, I think the theory of social capital launched by Putnam is wrong, but it is wrong in a very interesting and productive way.

I believe there are a number of reasons why Putnam's study has attracted so much interest. One is the attention given to the dependent variable. Putnam and his research team expended a considerable amount of effort to create their dependent variable, clearly showing that democracy really worked better in some Italian regions than in others. As far as I have been able to see, no one has criticized the study on this point – i.e. the notion that Putnam found something that was important to explain. A second reason why the study has attracted such interest is probably due to its methodological pluralism. Putnam and his research team used quantitative survey data, in-depth interviews, historical archives, participant observation, and several other methods. They were thus not tied to any specific method but instead allowed the stated *research problem* to govern the choice of method. A third reason for the study's widespread impact is that the book does something rare in the social sciences, namely to connect a historical–cultural explanatory model with a model that also encompasses a rational actor explanation. As stated in chapter 2, the social sciences have long been plagued by this difficulty – i.e. that of regarding human action as influenced by history and culture, on the one hand, and as the product of (more or less) rationally calculating actors who make deliberate choices, on the other. On one side of the equation, Putnam traces the differences between the supply of social capital in southern and northern Italy back through several centuries, comparing the strong status of the civil society in the independent city-states of fifteenth-century northern Italy to the hierarchical political culture of the feudal, autocratic south. To a great extent, this is a study of differences in political culture established over a very long time that determined the different path-dependent traits of the country. However, Putnam connects this analysis to models from rational choice and game theory, giving a plausible explanation for why agents in the different parts of Italy use different strategies. A plethora of historical examples (and a few well-chosen anecdotes) make his account very persuasive – some would say seductive – on this point.

Putnam is by no means the first to cite the specific culture of interpersonal mistrust that dominates southern Italy (cf. Banfield 1958), but the manner in which he successfully linked culture and the rational actor model is unusual, at least in empirical studies. In this context, the critical issue is not whether Putnam's factual analysis and explanation are correct; he has been the target of significant criticism on that point as well (cf. Tarrow 1996). I would instead like to draw attention to the boldness of his approach in making the connection between the two schools of thought that, as shown in chapter 2, are usually presumed to be in critical conflict with one another.

But what is social capital?

In his study of Italy, Putnam defines social capital as "features of social organization, such as trust, norms, and networks, that can improve the efficiency of society by facilitating coordinated actions" (Putnam 1993: 167). He also includes the norm of "generalized reciprocity" as a component of his definition of social capital (1993: 172). This definition is problematic, first because it contains so many different aspects that, secondly, probably all have causal correlations with one another (Newton 1999b: 3). Thirdly, what is to be explained by having social capital (the facilitation of coordinated action) is built into the definition, thereby making it tautological (Durlauf 2002).

It may, for instance, be a social norm to have *faith* in others' trustworthiness. An individual may hold a general subjective norm that she should be able to trust other people and that he should behave in a manner that inspires the trust of others. However, the trust people have in other people or social institutions may also be based on a conviction in the sense of a personal worldview – i.e. individuals have gradually gathered information from various sources about what kind of behavior they can expect of others or of, various government agencies and organizations (Dasgupta 1988: 50f.), for example. Because social norms, worldviews, and belief systems are causally related, it is unfortunate that all these phenomena are included in Putnam's definition of social capital.

Activity and participation in social networks is another thing – that is, each is a *behavior or an act*. As Kenneth Newton has said, there is reason to keep these things separate, because individuals may participate in voluntary associations and networks because they have come to embrace a norm or a worldview that makes them generally prepared to trust other people. But the reverse may also be true: that trust in others is created through regular participation in voluntary associations (Newton 1999b: 4). The readiness to help others to whom one is not directly connected (generalized reciprocity) may also increase if individuals trust from the outset that they will be able to count on others. That trust might very well be greater if the people know one another because they sing in the same choir or play in the same football team. However, all of these are empirical questions that should be kept separate from the definition of the concept. There may also be two connected dimensions of the concept.

Precision in the formation of concepts is a scholarly virtue for many reasons (Bjereld, Demker, and Hinnfors 1999: 93). There is a dilemma here that applies not least to political scientists, because a popular concept such as social capital, that tends to be correlated with many felicitous conditions, becomes a banner eagerly taken up by political actors and interest groups who want to make themselves look good by including their own activities (or that which they otherwise stand for and advocate) within the sphere of the concept. Such politically induced "concept stretching" is problematic because it leads to a situation when the concept can stand for (almost) everything and thus (almost) nothing. There is considerable risk that this kind of conceptual distortion will occur in social capital research.

The definition of social capital Putnam uses in *Making Democracy Work* includes a behavior (active participation in voluntary networks/associations), a function (that facilitates), a belief (that other people can be trusted), and a social norm (reciprocity). The definition is far too broad and there are probably also correlations among the components. A central question is if it is possible to construct a more precise definition. First, the functional component should be excluded. It builds that which is to be explained into the definition itself, making the theory tautological (Baron, Field, and Schuller 2000: 6ff.). The supply of social capital in a group of individuals cannot at once be the explanation behind their cooperation and constitute the cooperation that is to be explained. Likewise, the lack of social capital in a group would then be the same as lack of cooperation, which was the thing that was to be explained.

In part, the same criticism can be directed at building the social norm of reciprocity into the concept of social capital. If on the one hand we understand "reciprocity" to mean that the actors are inclined to follow a social norm to act in solidarity for common purposes, this is also what we are trying to explain and thus something that does not belong in the definition of the phenomenon we believe may constitute the cause of this reciprocity. If instead we understand "reciprocity" to mean that people are willing to cooperate if they believe that others are also going to cooperate, the concept becomes synonymous with trust and therefore superfluous.

What then remains of Putnam's definition is a behavior (activity in voluntary social networks) and a belief about whether or not other people are generally trustworthy. As I will argue later, both of these should be included in the definition of social capital, but they should nevertheless be kept analytically separate because they may be causally linked. That is, the belief that other people in the society in which one lives are generally trustworthy may be created through extensive participation in voluntary associations, but the reverse may also be true. It is possible that people who for various reasons (upbringing, reading of edifying literature) have been imbued with a worldview that most people are trustworthy are those who choose to be active in voluntary associations, and for that very reason. Both of those categories (interpersonal/social trust and participation in social networks) should be included in the definition of social capital, but they should not be accorded the same importance. I believe the "Hell's Angels Syndrome"

constitutes a critical reason to rank social trust as the more fundamental
ingredient, as it shows that all types of social networks do not produce this
type of generalized trust in society. Quite the opposite, the main function of
many interpersonal networks is to produce the antithesis – i.e. mistrust or
even hatred of "most other people" (Portes 2000). Naturally, that applies to
many criminal organizations, but also some ethnic, religious, political, and
economic associations. A society dominated by this type of network does
not have a large supply of social capital.

Not just morals. . . .

Many definitions of social trust abound and I shall touch upon two of
them here because they represent two opposite ends of this discussion. Eric
Uslaner defines social trust as a moral compass or moral norm – i.e. a
decree the individual chooses or is socialized to follow. The propensity to
believe that most other people can be trusted is mostly independent of the
experience of the actual trustworthiness of other actors (2002: 17). In this
type of moralistic trust, *A* does not trust other people in general because *A*
has specific information about these people. Nor does *A* trust individuals
in group *B* because *A* has information that makes this a reasonable belief. *A*
is, quite simply, a person who believes in the moral good of trusting others.
This type of trust is linked to optimism about the future and about the
possibilities to have control over things that are important in life (Uslaner
2002: 33). According to Uslaner, "trust in other people is based upon a
fundamental ethical assumption that other people share your fundamental
values." This does not imply that they share one's political or religious values.
Instead, this moral trust is related to more basic notions that even if others
are different, "you share some common bonds that make cooperation vital"
(2002: 2). Uslaner makes an important distinction between this type of
generalized moral trust, and those whom he labels "particularized trusters,"
whom you find among groups such as "outlaw" bikers and members of hate
groups. Particularized trusters see the world as a dangerous place, they are
prone to believe in conspiracies, they have a negative view about the future
and especially their own ability to influence matters that are important in
their own life. While people with generalized trust see a stranger as someone
with whom they could have a mutually beneficial exchange, particularized
trusters view strangers as hostile people who are likely to exploit or hurt
them.

   The definition of generalized (or social) trust as a moral orientation
and/or world- view that differs from particularized trust is of great value. Yet,
there is a risk that such a definition becomes too detached from things such
as learning and experience. It seems strange to argue that people would think

that most other people can be trusted independently of their experiences about their *trustworthiness*. The day your neighbors suddenly decide to join a militia engaged in ethnic cleansing against your group is likely to have a profound impact on your belief that "most people can be trusted."

Another example is what happens with agents who usually presume that others in their association or society can be trusted when they move to another society where trustworthiness is much less common. A typical high-trusting Norwegian who moved to the Sicily of organized crime and social mistrust or the Albania of eternal blood feuds is likely to learn some bitter lessons. He will learn to be less gullible and become less inclined to trust other people, but that does not imply that his basic moral orientation will change. For example, most Swedes presume that they can be confident in turning to the police for help. Certainly, most of them know that unacceptable things can happen within the police force but if they are the victim of a crime, Swedish citizens do not generally hesitate to call the police. That one should be able to trust the police is probably also a strong norm in Swedish society, but it may also be based on a worldview that the police are generally *trustworthy* (Holmberg and Weibull 2002).

Suppose, however, that the Swedish citizen who has such high trust in the police is considering going on vacation, say to Mexico. There are many good reasons to go there, such as the extraordinary Mayan temples on the enchantingly beautiful Yucatan peninsula. The guidebooks tell her that the best way to get around is by rental car, but the same books also warn tourists against having anything to do with the Mexican police, who are said to be extremely corrupt and involved in various kinds of organized crime. If not absolutely necessary (e.g. for insurance purposes), the guidebooks encourage tourists to refrain from reporting thefts to the police. If a tourist needs a statement from the police that she has been robbed, she must be prepared to pay bribes. The guidebooks also tell our prospective Swedish tourist that if she rents a car, she can count on being stopped by the police who will falsely claim she was speeding and demand that she pay a fine, which will go straight into the officer's own pocket.[2] The Mexican police are poorly paid and that is their way of increasing their income. However, she is warned in no uncertain terms not to protest or demand a receipt, because the police will then quickly "find" all kinds of illegal drugs in her car and she will be in danger of getting into serious trouble and spending a few of her vacation days in a Mexican jail. Then the scenario gets really scary: Women who are sexually assaulted are warned not to contact the police at

[2] In his book *The Elusive Quest for Growth: Economists' Adventures and Misadventures in the Tropics* economist William Easterly recounts a number of fascinating glimpses into his experiences with the gravely corrupt police in Mexico City (Easterly 2001: 242–244).

all, because it is not unusual for women who have been victimized to catch sight of one of the perpetrators at the police station – in uniform![3]

My point *vis-à-vis* Eric Uslaner is that after having been given the scenario described above, even a Scandinavian individual who may hold a moral norm that people should be able to trust the police and "most people in general," will probably not turn to the police when she is in a country like Mexico. Moreover, not only will her trust in the police decline, but also her trust in other people. This is because she has reason to believe that in a country with such a thoroughly corrupt police corps, most people get away with treacherous behavior, and thus they cannot be trusted. My point is that her moral norm concerning trust has not changed. Instead, based on available information, she has formed a different set of beliefs of the extent to which the police force and "other people" in Mexico can be *trusted*.[4] My premise is that this type of information (which of course does not need to have anything to do with reality) is the basis for the extent of social trust. There is some empirical ground for this conclusion. For example, Delhey and Newton came to the same result in their study based on survey data from six European countries and South Korea: social trust is based on *acquired information*, through either direct, personal experience or other means (Delhey and Newton 2003).

Few people are prepared to trust all other people in all instances. That would be "blind faith," which is not the same as trust. Instead, we use a number of *information devices* when we decide if we should trust other people and with what we can trust them. Confidence and trust should be regarded more as the actor's general assessment of reality based on available information, in this case what can be expected of the other actors in our society or association. The conclusion is that trust cannot be defined as mainly a moral orientation.

... and not just utility

An alternative definition has been presented by Russell Hardin, in which trust should be understood as the outcome of rational utility-based expectations. His reasoning is founded on several assumptions. The first is that individual *A* does not trust individual *B* in general, but rather that *A* trusts *B* with a view to something specific (*Y*). That is, I do not generally trust

---

[3] The information was taken from two best-selling guides to the Yucatan peninsula in Mexico, *Lonely Planet* and *First Guides*, both published in 2001.

[4] In the most recently published report (2002) on corruption from Transparency International (CTI) (Corruption Perception Index), Mexico scored 3.6 on a scale of 0–10, with 10 being best. In the same measurement, Sweden's score was 9.3. See www.transparency.org.

the mechanic who fixes my car, I trust him only to handle my car insofar as I have information about his abilities as a mechanic. In other respects, he may be utterly untrustworthy. Secondly, Russell Hardin asserts that there is no such thing as "generalized trust" as it is usually measured in the World Values Surveys, for example. The question does not measure trust because, according to Hardin, it is impossible to trust most other people in one's society, community or association because one cannot have information about all of those people that would make such trust rational. The conclusion according to Hardin's rationalist premise is that I trust people if I have reason to "believe that it will be in her interest to be trustworthy" (Hardin 2002: 13).

The consequence is that people in general cannot be trusted because we have no recurring relationships with these people in general in our societies, and thus we cannot judge their trustworthiness (Hardin 2001). Thus, we cannot know if they operate under an incentive structure that makes it rational for them to be trustworthy. I do not trust my dentist in general, but only because I assume it is in the dentist's own *interest* to behave in a way that does not shake my trust in him. This is motivated by the knowledge that if he did, he would not only lose me as a customer in the future, he might also lose other customers because I would spread damaging information about him. Hardin calls this *encapsulated trust*, meaning that I, in my decision to trust or not trust another person, judge whether the individual's actions are "encapsulated" in an incentive structure by which it is in her interest to behave in a trustworthy way.

Hardin does argue that there may by instances of trust that are not based on interest based expected utility. *A* may trust *B* because *A* knows that *B* is governed by strong moral norms and obligations that prevent *B* from behaving treacherously. But he adds that these kinds of moral norms are very rare, and that they cannot have any impact on the overarching social order or how most human relationships work (Hardin 2001: 4).

Hardin makes the important point that we should differentiate between *trust* and *trustworthiness*. Trust cannot be a moral virtue, because it is simply foolish (or dangerous) to trust people whom you know are not trustworthy (Hardin 2002: 29). Being trustworthy is a moral virtue, while trusting other people in general is not. However, I think that Hardin is too quick to dismiss the moral implications of trust. The reason is that it makes sense to say that when people give an answer to the question if they believe that most other people can be trusted, they make an assessment of their trustworthiness and thereby of the general civic morality of other people in their society. It may not be a moral good to trust other people in general, but the decision to give people the benefit of the doubt may be seen as a moral virtue. Simply put, faced with a social trap problem, and all things equal, it is a moral virtue to start off in a cooperative and trusting spirit than to start off with mistrust. Working from a rationalist game theoretic approach, Andrew Kydd has presented a formal model that shows the possibility of avoiding social traps if actors start building mutual trust by sending "costly signals" that reassures their trustworthiness to the other agents (Kydd 2000: 415). The problem is that without an initial willingness to trust, such spirals of costly signals are not likely to occur. If trustworthiness begets trust, the reverse is also true (cf. Hardin 2002: 32). This has also been shown in experimental work where respondents' answers to the attitudinal trust question ("Do you think most other people can be trusted?") did show a significant correlation with trustworthy behavior in the experimental situation. The conclusion is that, contrary to what is argued by Hardin, the general trust survey question "may be good at predicting the overall trustworthiness in society" (Glaeser *et al.* 2000: 813).

The reason that Hardin believes that generalized trust based on ethics plays no role at the societal level is that people cannot give an adequate answer to such a question because it does not specify "the matters on which one might trust" other people (2002: 201). Hardin argues that instead of trust, answers to the question if "other people can be trusted" measures at the very best some kind of optimism (2001: 14). The question is how we shall understand the difference between having optimism in general about other people's trustworthiness, and believing that other people in general can be trusted. It is difficult to get away from the notion that Hardin's desperate (and to some extent heroic) struggle to keep the concept of trust strictly within the rational choice paradigm has led him to play with words.

Hardin's rationalist analysis of trust also has implications for whether it is possible to trust social and political institutions. His first standpoint is normative – i.e. to underline that the construction of western democracies is in many ways based on the principle that people should not trust the state and its agencies. This is an important point often forgotten in the social capital approach. Institutions such as independent courts, independent audits of government spending, independent universities, principles of freedom of information, and guarantees that the shaping of opinion will not be restricted are all conceived as mechanisms for controlling governmental power. However, Hardin also claims that it is essentially impossible to talk about people having trust in public authorities and official bodies because, in practice, we cannot have information about whether the incentive structure according to which civil servants work meets the requirements embraced in the concept of *encapsulated trust* (Hardin 1999: 23). We simply cannot know whether the control mechanisms that should exist to ensure that civil servants do not behave treacherously towards us are effective or applicable in our particular case. Therefore, we should not, if we are behaving "sensibly" or "intelligently," entrust anything that is valuable to us to public institutions (Hardin 1999: 23). The control and incentive systems are too large and too complex, which Hardin feels "makes it highly unlikely that trust is an underlying factor in the views and expectations of most citizens" of authorities and other public institutions (Hardin 1999: 35). On that basis, Hardin states that it is unintelligent for people to hand over anything of value to public authorities that is not absolutely necessary and which can be produced by private organizations. For that reason, Hardin also asserts that the public sphere should be limited to things such as upholding law and order and economic measures that can be characterized as collective utilities (Hardin 1998).

I believe there are two reasons to criticize Hardin's strictly rationalist definition of trust. The first is that encapsulated trust will make trusting relationships something very rare and will, taken to its logical end point, destroy trust. The reason is that the best strategy for the rational, self-interested A in a relation with B is to feign trustworthiness in a number of transactions of minor value. In so doing, A hopes that B will eventually entrust him with something that is really valuable. At that point, it becomes rational for A to show his true colors and betray B's trust. To quote Fritz Scharpf: "the ability to trust is of course the crucial problem. If one party acts from a solidaristic orientation while the other is motivated by competitive preferences, then the trusting party would be left with its own worst-case outcome . . . In other words, being able to trust, and being trusted, is an advantage – but exploiting trust may be even more advantageous" (Scharpf 1997: 86f.).

Hardin's presumption is that "one of the strongest expectations we must have of people is that in the long run, they will defy our expectations" (Hardin 1998: 23). The problem that arises with this view is that if B assumes from the outset that A's moral compass is such that A will deceive B as soon as the right opportunity comes along, it becomes rational for B never to enter into any kind of relationship with A. According to Hardin, A acts in a trustworthy manner only as long as A gains by it (*ibid.*). But if B assumes that A is such a person, it is not rational for B to ever start a trusting relationship with A. In game theory, this problem is known as "backwards induction": Assume that we have two actors who continually interact. They trust each other because they know their relationship is continuous. But in their final interaction, A, who has been entrusted with something valuable, profits by choosing to stop cooperating with B (e.g. A refuses to pay for the goods B has delivered). If B then assumes that A is going to act treacherously in their last possible interaction, B will choose non-cooperation in their penultimate possible interaction, after which A will naturally choose non-cooperation in the interaction preceding the penultimate possible reaction, and so on (Turner 2001). The rational utility-seeking *A* makes this assumption about *B* because she would have done the same thing as *B* – i.e. exploited the other party's trust for her own gain at an opportune moment.

Therewith, the social trap has slammed shut around them – i.e. mutual mistrust has precluded cooperation for mutual benefit. The problem is easily recognizable to anyone who has seen John Houston's classic movie *Treasure of the Sierra Madre* starring Humphrey Bogart as the unforgettable paranoid gold miner. In this story, three gold miners have expended Herculean effort to pan large amounts of gold in a remote mountain area somewhere in Mexico. When the time comes to take the gold down to the city to cash it, they begin to suspect each other of wanting to steal the others' shares. It is obvious that if they could trust each other and cooperate, their chances of reaching the city with the gold still in hand would greatly increase. But the problem is that they only have the Hardin type of "encapsulated trust" in each other, and since they know that there is no incentive structure available that makes it rational for the others to cooperate, they end up in a classic social trap – i.e. all three lose their gold. They seem to mistrust each other because they have come to know each other a bit too well after all the lonely months together in the mountains. That is, they all know that they did not choose to cooperate in the beginning because they trusted each other, but rather for solely egotistical reasons – the work could not be done without at least three men. Mark Granovetter has expressed this problem well by stating that if one has "a perception by others that one's interests in them is mainly a matter of 'investment', this will make this investment less likely to pay off; we are all on the outlook for those who only want to use us" (Granovetter 1988: 115).

This kind of infinite analytical regression is actually an important element in game theory assumptions on why cooperation among rational self-interested actors is precluded (cf. Kydd 2000). Working from within the rationalist game theoretic approach Ziegler expressed this as, "in a strategic trust game there usually is an incentive for the trustee to misuse trust. The defective outcome is a subgame perfect Nash equilibrium," that is, a situation in which none of the actors has any motive to change strategy and begin cooperating. What this means is that Hardin's rationalist view of trust relationships makes the social trap the most likely result of the actors' transactions (Ziegler 1998: 430). We are all lucky that in reality, the world is not such a grim place as game theory gives us reason to believe. According to Ziegler, the reason we do not always fall into the social traps are moral things such as "honor," "guilt," or other types of social extra-instrumental norms derived from social interaction. The conclusion is thus that if the definition of trust is limited to the rationalist theory suggested by Hardin, then trust will be something exceedingly rare, at least outside the close family and equivalent relationships. And if trust is rare, social traps will prevail.

Another reason to criticize Hardin's definition of trust is empirical. There are actually a great many empirical studies that show that trust is not reducible to interest based instrumental calculation, the results of which are derived from field studies (Ostrom 1998), historical case studies (Rothstein 2000b), experimental approaches (Sally 1995), and survey research (Inglehart 1999; Torpe 2000; Uslaner 2002). To cite one of the most comprehensive analyses done in the latter field: "For most people, trust is not simply a matter of making rational calculations about the possibility of benefiting by cooperating with someone else. Social scientists who reduce the study of trust to questions about rational choice, and who argue that it has nothing to do with moral discourse, miss that point" (Wuthnow 1998: 18). Based on comprehensive panel data studies from the United States, Eric Uslaner has shown that a high degree of trust in other people cannot be explained as an effect of "payback" for help or support provided by others earlier in life (Uslaner 1999).

A third point upon which Hardin may be criticized is his view on trust in public institutions. There is definitively much to be said in favor of his argument that liberal democracy is in many respects constructed on the premise that people should not unquestioningly trust the state and its agencies. But Hardin's view that it is generally unintelligent of people to feel that trust in the state and its agencies conflicts with the idea, with which even he agrees, that people can sometimes trust the legal system and the government's economic policy. It is difficult to understand why it should be possible to induce civil servants in those particular, often extraordinarily complex systems, to act impartially according to some kind of incentive structures, especially considering that if the legal system is abused it can cause us harm on a level unmatched by few other public institutions.

Another cause for criticism is that Hardin struggles with empirical knowledge on this point as well. Survey studies show that popular trust in the state and its agencies varies widely from country to country (Svallfors 1997). This is evident not only in survey studies but also very concretely in the expanse of public agencies in different democratic countries and the types of tasks that have been entrusted to them. This cannot be reasonably explained by saying that the citizens of different countries possess varying degrees of "intelligence" on this point. It can hardly be true that the citizens of the Nordic countries are much less intelligent than people in Brazil or Romania. It is much more likely that Scandinavians entrust their government with more because they have a different experience of what government agencies do (Kumlin 2004; Rothstein and Steinmo 2002).

Social capital: an attempt at definition

The conclusion of the preceding discussion is that neither the one-sided, normative, moral approach nor the one-sided, rationalist, calculating approach can be used to arrive at a definition of social capital or social trust. Instead, the definition of social capital must, in accordance with my arguments in chapter 2, contain elements of both subjective rationality and ethics. This is based on a line of thought introduced by Howard Margolis (Margolis 1982) and later developed by Margaret Levi. The main idea is that most people in most cases do not act out of a single utility function. They do not want only to maximize their utility – i.e. "*homo economicus*" is a simplistic and, as stated in chapter 2, empirically indefensible basis for understanding political action. However, the opposite assumption – i.e. that people are always ready to act morally regardless of circumstances – is not a reasonable basis, either. There are very few Mother Theresas in this world. Few people would continue to act in a cooperative spirit if this was constantly rewarded with other people taking advantage of them. As to the question of whether people act only in pursuit of selfish interests or whether they act morally to ensure the common good, Margaret Levi asserts:

> there is both a normative and an instrumental element in the decision to comply (or not) or to volunteer (or not). Certainly, there are segments of the citizenry whose utility function is unitary; they are purely income maximizers or purely moral. A large proportion, however, appear to have *dual utilities*. They wish to contribute to the social good, at least as long as they believe a social good is being produced. They also want to ensure that their individualistic interests are being satisfied as far as possible. (Levi 1991: 133)

Translated to the problem of the social trap, this means something like the following. Given that actor *A* has sufficient trust in actors *B, C, D* . . . she is prepared to act according to norms of reciprocity even if a strict utility calculation would not give a clear indication that she would personally gain by doing so. When it comes to "repeated games," this is a familiar behavior in game theory that can be explained using the utility model. We are, for example, prepared to help coworkers and colleagues provided that we know that our interaction will continue over the foreseeable future (Axelrod 1987). The problem with many social traps is that we usually have no such direct relation with the others. My willingness to pay taxes, preserve the environment and obey the law does not as such necessarily induce others to do the same.

Thus, criticism of definitions of social capital and trust unilaterally based on the notion that social capital is a phenomenon that can be encapsulated in either the rationalist or culturalist model is justified. In common with Piotr Sztompka, I define trust as a "bet on the future contingent actions of others" (Sztompka 1998: 21). Whether or not I decide to place this bet depends on my own moral outlook, how I estimated the virtues of the ones I'm betting on, and if I think it will be in my rational interest to cooperate, and how I estimate the risks of entrusting other people with something of value. Thus, if there ever was a case where the notion of "imperfect information" was useful, trust is the one. It should be underlined that trust is not just a prediction. This is obvious, because one does not say: "I trust that she is going to hurt me." This shows that there is some *positive morality* connected to trust, or at least that to trust someone implies that we believe that this person will not deliberately cause us harm (Warren 1999: 311).

It seems appropriate to begin the definition of social capital by stating that the concept is a compound of two different terms. "Social" indicates that it has something to do with relationships among individuals and "capital" that it constitutes some kind of asset for the people who possess it. Another starting point is that if social capital really is some type of *capital* (and not just another term for social relations), it must imply that if individuals, organizations, and societies possess this asset, they can accomplish things they could not accomplish if they lacked (enough amounts of) the particular asset. Thus, I think that in the definition we should pay more attention to the capital side of social capital.

Capital can be possessed by both individuals and by aggregates of individuals. Since this goes for physical, financial, and human capital, it should also characterize social capital. On the individual level, I suggest that social capital exists in two dimensions – one *qualitative* and one *quantitative*. The quantitative dimension is simply the number of social contacts an individual has. The more social networks to which an individual has access, and the more extensive those social networks are, the more social capital she has. It is easy to see that this is an asset. Most people get the things they need in life through personal contacts. Examples abound. Most people find jobs through their personal contacts. It is also common to find partners through personal contacts. Information about reliable investments, plumbers, restaurants, and nice places for vacationing very often come through personal contacts. In academia, as in many other professions, it is well known that doing good work it not enough. You also need to have a good network to get invitations to important conferences, hints about job-opportunities, etc. Extensive and varied networks are an asset in all situations where we need help, advice, support, information, encouragement, or care. Such social contacts need not be strong or deep on the personal level. As sociologist Mark Granovetter has asserted, there is also strength in organizations and societies distinguished by extensive "weak ties" (Granovetter 1985).

However, the quantitative dimension alone is inadequate to define social capital. In addition to the sheer number of social contacts, we need to add the qualitative nature of those contacts. The reason for this is obvious: It cannot be an asset to know a lot of people whom you cannot trust, or to be known by many people as a person who cannot be trusted. On the contrary, the latter especially is a liability. To be known by a lot of people but generally regarded as untrustworthy, selfish, treacherous, or unhelpful is no asset. Nor it is an asset to the individual who is trustworthy and helpful if she is involved in a lot of networks where people are the opposite. It is easy to imagine such social networks – e.g. criminal organizations, prisons, local communities with low trust and lots of envy, work teams where the individuals step on each other in order to be promoted, and greedy networks of competitors in a market. To be part of such networks cannot be considered an asset because they are more of a hindrance than an asset. Networks alone thus do not have value. Instead, the value of contacts and networks depends on the *quality of the relations* within these networks. Likewise, it is an asset for the individual to have a reputation as being trustworthy and to be able to trust the people she knows, but if she has only a few and isolated social contacts, it does not add up to much social capital.

To conclude, on the individual level, social capital is the *sum of the number of social contacts multiplied by the quality of trust in these relationships*. Naturally, opportunities to identify simple quantitative measurements of this definition of social capital are limited. How, for instance, should we compare the social capital between individual A who has five social contacts whom she completely trusts and individual B, who has fifty social contacts whom she partially trusts? Nonetheless, I believe that much of the problem with finding any generally accepted definition of social capital is rooted in the failure to understand that the concept has both a quantitative and a qualitative dimension.

This definition of social capital applies also at the aggregate level. The amount of social capital in a society or organizations is determined by (a) the extent of social contacts and networks that the people have on average and (b) the extent to which people generally believe that they can trust most of those contacts. The more people in a society (or an organization) who have many and widespread social relationships with people they believe are trustworthy, the greater the social capital in that society (or organization).

The idea that social capital is an asset at the aggregate level implies that it has value and thereby that it is "good." Against this, many have argued that social capital can also have a dark side, that it can be used for bad things like any other type of capital. Trusting networks, organizations and communities can be racist, sexist, ethnofobic, etc. (Putnam 2000: chapter 22). In one respect, this is certainly true. There is no guarantee that a society and/or organization that has been able to escape social traps will use its public goods for purposes that are morally virtuous. However, for the single organization or society, I would argue that, all else equal, social capital is always an asset because they can achieve things (i.e. create public goods) that they could not have done without it. This has to do with the connection between capital and its "owner." Few would say that societies such as Northern Ireland or Bosnia have a lot of social capital. On the contrary, these are societies plagued by very low levels of generalized trust and extensive contacts among its population. On the other hand, it seems reasonable to say that the warring factions have a high level of social capital internally. Otherwise, they would not have been able to create the resources necessary to start the fighting in the first place.

Social capital and other capital

Finally, there may be reason to stop and consider a few points that differentiate social capital from human and physical capital (cf. Ostrom and Ahn 2001). At first glance, it may seem as if social capital is a vaguer, more mysterious concept than physical capital, for example. As Hernando de Soto showed in his much-quoted book *The Mystery of Capital* (2001), physical capital is, in terms of definition, a substantially more complex phenomenon than is generally believed in the western world. According to de Soto, physical assets can be converted to capital only after the society has created legal terminology to describe them. A piece of land, for instance, does not become physical capital until the society has instituted the legal term "real property" and created institutions in which the size, location, and ownership of the asset are recorded and acknowledged. Only when ownership of a piece of land (or a fishing boat, a firm, etc.) can be legally established can the asset be mortgaged or sold so that the owners can convert it to capital. According to de Soto, much of the poverty rife in the Third World does not exist because those areas lack assets. Instead, the source of poverty is either the lack of any form of conceptualization of capital in the culture or the lack of functioning legal institutions wherein the assets that the people actually possess can be recorded in the form of legal concepts and thus converted to capital (de Soto 2001). With respect to the concept of physical capital, these two problems – the cultural and the legal – may naturally be connected. My intention here is to point out that *social capital* is not necessarily more conceptually difficult to pinpoint than the other two accepted concepts of capital.

More obvious is the fact that, unlike physical capital, social capital does not get progressively worn down with use. On the contrary, it grows with use. The more often we have dealings with people whom it has proven we can trust, the more likely it becomes that we will have further interaction with them and our trust in them will grow. Another difference, primarily in relation to physical capital but also applicable to human capital, is that social capital cannot be bought, especially when it comes to trust in other people. As immortalized in Shakespeare's King Lear, attempts to buy trust ironically destroy it. Trust can be promised and it can be earned, but it cannot be ordered or purchased (Misztal 1996: 21).

As with physical and human capital, investments in social capital are conceivable. On the individual level this involves two things – participating in various kinds of networks and, in the course of those contacts, appearing to be a trustworthy person. As I will show in chapter 5, there is experimental research that shows that individuals can train their ability to assess the trustworthiness of others, but I am uncertain as to whether that would be categorized as an "investment," since the concept is predicated on a deliberate action. On the aggregated level, an organization or society could, for example, facilitate opportunities for building networks within the organization. One can also invest in institutions that increase the likelihood that other actors will behave in a trustworthy manner.

Unlike physical and human capital, particularly the former, it is relatively difficult to measure the supply of social capital, especially its qualitative dimension of trust. It is also more difficult, although not entirely impossible, for governments to invest in social capital, as I will attempt to show later. However, there are also a number of similarities between these three kinds of capital. One is that actors do not invest only in physical and human capital, but also in social capital. Being regarded as credible and trustworthy is an asset for individuals, organizations, firms, and states. As I write this (August 2004), there is considerable discussion in the media concerning what companies can do to recreate the trust capital that has gone to waste through the discovery of a number of instances of what could reasonably be called "corporate corruption" (manipulated accounts and audits, concealed and extravagant executive perks). Business analysts and executives are not alone in discussing this; even the powerful head of the Federal Reserve Bank in the United States is talking about how widespread corporate greed has become more common among big company executives and that it constitutes a threat to trust in the market economy as such (Ekman 2002).

Back to Adam Smith

Adam Smith, perhaps the most prominent figure in economics, is most famous for his thesis on the *invisible hand*, according to which everything would work out for the best if all economic actors behaved only as rational utility maximizers. This most-favored thesis of neo-classical economics was taken from Smith's book *The Wealth of Nations*, which was published in 1776. What has been forgotten, or perhaps repressed, in the version of Smith's ideas usually trotted out for inspection is that Smith actually published *two* comprehensive books. In 1759, Smith published his first book, *A Theory of Moral Sentiments*, which addresses the importance of social norms, morals, and civic virtues. Unfortunately, the book is rarely or never mentioned in economics textbooks. However, new and comprehensive scientific history studies of Smith's ideas show that his two seemingly utterly disparate works should be explained in a theoretical context. When that is done, a Smith emerges who is very different from the neo-liberal *homo economicus* that many have wanted to make him. As Patricia Werhane has shown, Smith did not confuse economic efficiency with egoism. Instead, a thinker emerges who sees that an efficient economy created through the self-interest of market actors is impossible without careful public regulation and the existence of established social norms such as justice, the will to ensure public interests, and other non-egotistical moral virtues (Werhane 1994). Another book by Adam Griswold places Smith in the discussion of social virtues that was the basic theme of the philosophy of enlightenment (Griswold 1999). Vivienne Brown and Stephen Darwall (Brown 1994; Darwall 1999) also assert that we must acknowledge the connection between the two books and that Smith was aware of the particular importance of the "dual utility functions" I mentioned above.

Francis Fukuyama has provided an interesting metaphor concerning how we should view these issues. In his book on the economic significance of trust, he denies the thesis of neo-classical economists that their model of the rational utility maximizer explains about 80 percent of all human behavior and their consequent belief that they have gotten "almost all the way there" (Fukuyama 1995: 13ff.). There are other kinds of behavior, of course, but we should certainly be content with a model that can manage as much as 80 percent. That line of reasoning is also found on Swedish soil in Eklund's best-selling textbook in economics, in which he says that non-self-interested behavior can be ignored as a kind of interfering "noise" (Eklund 1992).

The question Fukuyama asks is how we should actually regard this 80 percent. From one angle, theories that explain as many as eight out of ten human acts are quite impressive. However, Fukuyama provides a metaphor of a bridge that exists to connect two land masses. The metaphor is rather apt – theories exist to connect (at least two) variables. What happens, he asks, if the 80 percent constitutes only a reasonable assumption about the construction of the span itself, but is entirely wrong when it comes to how we should explain why the bridge abutments work? A bridge without working abutments is not only entirely worthless, it is also dangerous. The point, of course, is that the missing 20 percent cannot only be something qualitatively different, but is also central to understanding, on any level, the existence of the remaining 80 percent. This elegant metaphor may also be expressed by saying that the neo-classical model lacks the capacity to analyze the kind of human action that constitutes the social cement that holds societies (and organizations) together (cf. Elster 1989a; Engwall 1998; Miller 1992).

4

Social capital in the social democratic welfare state

In no other western country has social democracy had such a political influence as in Sweden. Having been in government for sixty-three of the last seventy-two years, the party is not only the most successful among social democratic parties but one of the most hegemonic democratic political parties ever. As a consequence of this unique power of the political left, Sweden stands out as extreme on many standard measures used in comparative politics such as public spending, degree of unionization, and voting turnout (Scharpf 2000; Swank 2002). Apart from such purely quantitative measures, it has also been argued that the political and economic system in Sweden has been characterized by a more qualitative difference from comparable countries. From the 1950s until the late 1980s, Swedish society in general and its system of industrial relations in particular was, by many observers, branded with the name of: "the Swedish Model" (Katzenstein 1985; Lindvall 2004; Milner and Wadensjö 2001; Steinmo 2002). One of the more important features of this "model" was an unusually close collaboration between the state and major interest organizations in the preparation as well as in the implementation of public policies (Lewin 1992; Rothstein 1992a, 1992c).

There are thus several reasons why Sweden as well as the other Scandinavian countries should be seen as a critical case for the current discussions about the importance of social capital, civil society, and trust. One is the relationship between, on the one hand, the high level of public spending and ambitious welfare state programs and, on the other, the amount of social capital. Have, as many have argued, the numerous and encompassing welfare programs made not only voluntary organizations but also other forms of informal social relations and networks between individuals unnecessary and thereby fostered social isolation and anomie? Is there something like a "carving out" effect so that more public social programs mean less civil society and thereby less social capital? As stated by Herreros, "scholars working within the social capital paradigm have often assigned that State a negative role in the creation of this form of capital" (2004: 72). According to one large-scale project about the Swedish welfare state, the twentieth century in Sweden has been a "lost century" for civil society because the welfare state has colonized it. The problem, however, is that the project did not present any data to support such a conclusion (Zetterberg and Ljungberg 1997).

Second, what has been the effect on the vitality of civil society of the close collaboration between the government and the major national interest organizations? During the 1970s, political scientists labeled this political system "neo-corporatism," and it was argued that it would take voluntarism out of the voluntary sector because the organizations were getting most of their money and their tasks from the government, thus making them more like government agencies than parts of civil society (Streeck and Schmitter 1985). A standard assumption in the research on neo-corporatism has been that the government's support for, and collaboration with, interest organizations would make the organizations' elite become more professional and less responsible towards their members and that the members' activity would then drop (Micheletti 1995). The Swedish case should provide us with an answer to the question of whether neo-corporatism creates or destroys social capital.

Third, what has been the long-term trend in social capital in this social democratic polity? Robert Putnam has reported a surprisingly sharp decline in almost all major forms of social capital in the United States during the last two decades (Putnam 2000). The differences not only in size and demography but also in many political and economic aspects make a comparison between Sweden and the United States what in comparative methodology is called a "most different design" approach. Especially in political matters, it is difficult to find two western countries that are more different than Sweden and the United States (Granberg and Holmberg 1988). This means that if the trends in social capital in the United States and Sweden were the same, then we could assume that politics at the national level would be of little importance in explaining this phenomenon. Instead we should examine hypotheses such as that the changes in international ideological trends (e.g. postmaterialism) would be the important variables (Inglehart 1997). However, if we were to find significant differences in the forms and trends of social capital in these two countries, then it might very well be the case that politics could explain social capital as much as social capital could explain politics.

The organizational landscape: an overview

In a comparative perspective, Scandinavians are very organized (Goul Andersen and Hoff 1996). Survey data show that of all Swedish adult citizens, 92 percent belong to a voluntary organization. The average number of memberships per person, depending upon the measure, is between 2.9 and 4. More than half of the population (52 percent) consider themselves active, and 29 percent serve as an elected representative in a voluntary organization. Only 8 percent of the adult population stands outside the world of organizations. The degree of unionization is the highest in the world among capitalist economies: around 85 percent of the workforce is unionized, equivalent to 62 percent of the adult population. The sports movement is second to the unions in the number of memberships, with 33 percent, followed by the consumers' cooperatives (32 percent), tenants' organizations (27 percent), and cultural organizations (12 percent) (SCB 1997).

When it comes to activity, the sports movement is the most successful in being able to get one out of five citizens to actually do something. Other organizations with high levels of mobilization (defined as active members in relation to the whole population) are the union movement (10 percent), cultural organizations (6.9 percent), tenants' organizations (5.9 percent) and recreational organizations (5.4 percent). Below 1 percent are the environmental, women's, and temperance organizations, along with the free churches. The Church of Sweden, in which all citizens born in Sweden until recently became members unless their parents stated otherwise, scores 1.8 percent.

"Trust, by keeping our mind open to all evidence, secures communication and dialog," writes Barbara Misztal (Misztal 1996). If this is true, there may be one specifically Swedish (and Scandinavian) way of organizing people that should be of special interest for establishing social capital. This is the so-called "study circles," which have been the preferred educational method, especially in the popular mass movements. Study circles are small groups of adults, usually meeting one evening a week to educate themselves on a special subject. The average number of participants is 8.6 and the average number of hours spent in each study circle is 35.6 (SOU 1996). Study circles are organized by the associations for popular education (which are often part of a popular movement) on topics ranging from the study of foreign languages, to cooking, to computer knowledge, to the EU question, to rock music. Of course, many participate out of an instrumental interest, but as many as 40 percent report that they participate for social reasons. A study shows that 75 percent of the adult population has attended a study circle at some point and that around 10 percent participate on a regular basis. The importance of this type of activity is shown by the fact that each year about 40 percent of the adult population attends a study circle of some sort (Rothstein 1999, 2000a).

As could be expected, there is a positive relationship between participating in study circles and activity in voluntary organizations, voting, and having a more civic-minded attitude in general (SOU 1996: 37, 123). An evaluation based on extensive qualitative and quantitative research concluded that "the study circles have an important societal function besides the learning that is going on and also besides what the participants say about the value of their social functions. It is quite clear that the study circles maintain a civic network right across all social borders" (SOU 1996: 132). In Sweden, this activity is seen as one of the cornerstones of a viable democracy, and consequently about half of the costs are covered by government funds. The government's economic support for the study circles and the educational associations may thus be seen as an example of "creating social capital from above."

Changes in the organizational landscape

Despite the great political differences between them, Sweden is one of the European countries in which cultural and lifestyle trends from the United States are quickly adapted. There would thus be good reasons to believe that the decline in organizational life in the United States that has been reported by Robert Putnam would also occur in Sweden. The data show that, during the post-war period, voluntary organizations have been growing in size, level of activity, and financial resources. Of course, this growth has not been evenly distributed. Women's organizations, the free churches, and the temperance movement have lost members, while the sports, retired citizens', union, cultural and environmental organizations have grown. The growth of the sports movement has been especially impressive – from about 200,000 members in the 1930s to almost 3 million in the 1990s. Two studies of a typical Swedish "middle-town," Katrineholm, conducted in 1950 and in 1988, tell an interesting story on this point. First, there is an increase in memberships and more people are members of many (i.e. more than five) organizations in 1988 than in 1950. Second, although men are members of more organizations, the gender gap is closing. The "Katrineholm study" reports very little change in the membership of different types of organizations, except for the temperance movement, which has lost most of its members, but growth of other organizations has more than compensated for this loss (Perlinski 1990). Thirdly, the overall picture remains that hardly any Swedes fall outside the organizational world and that no decline in membership has occurred since the early 1950s. Other data tell the same story. The Swedish section of the World Value Studies from 1981, 1990, and

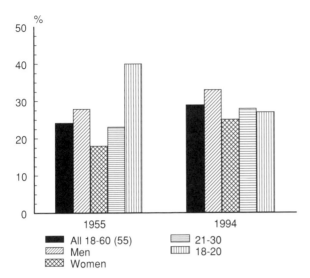

Figure 4.1. Interest in working in voluntary organizations, 1955 and 1994
Source: Data from Forskningsgruppen för samhälls – och informationsstudier
(FSI), Stockholm (*n* 1955 = 2050, *n* 1994 = 650).

1996 shows a considerable increase in membership in charities, sport clubs
and environmental organizations and no decline in membership in political
parties.[1]

Some consider the problem with voluntary organizations not to be with
formal membership or with resources but with activity level. Many traditional popular mass movements have been accused of having mostly "paper"
members. Some organizations, such as the unions, have made membership,
at least to some extent, an instrument of economic rationality rather than
of civic engagement by using various selective incentives to increase membership (Rothstein 1992c). But, as shown in figure 4.1, from the 1950s to
the 1990s there has been no general decline in the willingness to engage
in voluntary organizations; if anything, people are more willing now than
they were four decades ago. The major changes are that women's interest
in voluntary work has gone up, while the interest among the very young
(18–20 years) has gone down.

In the Swedish section of the World Value Study, people were also asked if
they had done any unpaid work in voluntary organizations.[2] Again, there is

---

[1] World Value Studies, data from 1981, 1991, and 1996, own computation.
[2] Source: World Value Studies, 1981, 1990. The question posed was: "Have you done any
unpaid, voluntary work for any of these groups and organizations?" Sixteen different types
of organizations/groups were represented.

no general decline between 1981 and 1996 in this respect. On the contrary, human rights organizations, environmental groups, and, especially, sports organizations seemed to attract more people to voluntary work in 1996 than they did in 1981. This result is supported by Swedish Standard of Living surveys from 1968, 1981, and 1991, showing that the number of Swedes who live outside the world of voluntary associations did not increase between 1968 and 1991 (Fritzell and Lundberg 1994). As for the study circles mentioned above, there has been a considerable growth. The number of adults who participate each year increased from 15 percent in 1960 to around 40 percent in 1975, a level which was pretty stable until the mid-1990s (Rothstein 2000a).

A different result is shown by survey studies conducted in 1987 and 1992 which report a weakening of "affinity" ("*samhörighet*" in Swedish) for the major types of organizations and popular movements (Häll 1994). These results have been taken by several scholars as a clear sign of a major crisis for the voluntary organizations in Sweden (Micheletti 1995). I believe, however, that one can give a different interpretation to this result about organizational "affinity." What has changed may be not so much the willingness to participate in voluntary organizations as it is the Swedish population's notion of collective identity in general and the collectivization of identity that traditionally has been the trademark of the popular movements in particular. This argument is based on interpretations of several different empirical studies. First, the "middle-town" study reported an interesting shift among blue-collar workers. In the 1950s, workers saw themselves as members of the working class and a labor movement committed to changing society. In the late 1980s, workers saw themselves as members of the middle class but not of a labor movement with a common goal. The study reported a sense of mass-elite cleavage within the labor movement. Second, a major survey report published in 1990 claimed that a new type of citizen, endowed with greater knowledge and resources, has emerged and that the educational level of these citizens makes it possible for them to question expert judgments. The virtue cherished most highly by Swedish citizens, according to this study, was the ability to form one's own views independently of others (Petersson, Westholm, and Blomkvist 1987).

It thus seems that the notion of individual autonomy has gained popularity among Swedish citizens, a change over time that can be confirmed. The proportion of citizens deeming themselves able to write a letter appealing an authority's decision increased from 45.1 percent to 68.5 percent between 1968 and 1987. Third, work by Thorlief Pettersson within the framework of a larger study of European values supplies evidence that the citizen of 1990 was substantially more individualistic than his counterpart of ten years earlier and resented impositions and restrictions on individual means of expression. (Pettersson 1992: 51). According to this investigation, which used an index to measure values associated with individualism, an increase in this individualization index from −23 to +23 took place between 1981 and 1990 (Pettersson and Geyer 1992).

One might expect this change in value patterns to be limited to the highly educated middle class, and it is true that individualistic attitudes are most marked in that social group. Interestingly, however, it was only among blue-collar workers that any palpable change took place between 1981 and 1990; both high- and low-level white-collar employees, in contrast, remained largely at their earlier high levels when it came to embracing individualistic values (Petterson and Geyer 1992: 13).[3] Accordingly, the proportion of workers with an individualistic viewpoint in general increased from 39 percent to 53 percent between 1981 and 1990, and those expressing an individualistic outlook toward their working life rose from 17 percent to 43 percent (Pettersson and Geyer 1992).

One might assume that this new individualism would undermine forms of collective action (and for the universal welfare state); however, an individualistically minded citizen is not necessarily an egoistic citizen. On the contrary, in Sweden it appears that collectivism/individualism and altruism/egoism represent distinct and largely independent ranges of values. Accordingly, Pettersson and Geyer argue that the new individualists do not hold the values assumed by neo-liberals:

> Compared with the less individualistically-inclined, moreover, they do *not* show any stronger interest in increasing today's wage differentials, they do *not* evidence any greater tendency to view the poor with a "they-just-have-themselves-to-blame" attitude, they do *not* show any stronger tendency to regard their fellow beings in less of a spirit of trust and fellowship. . . . They are neither the irrepressible entrepreneurs imagined by the Neo-liberals, nor the selfish egoists supposed by the Social Democrats. (Petterson and Geyer 1992: 28–31, emphasis in the last sentence removed, other emphasis in the original)[4]

---

[3] The investigation defines a generally individualistic attitude as one marked by the possession of at least three of the following four characteristics: (1) recommending personal freedom over economic equality, (2) being inclined to hold firm and try to convince others, (3) desiring a stronger emphasis on individual development, and (4) wishing no greater respect for authorities.

[4] That these are two different dimensions among Scandinavian citizens is also demonstrated by Jørgen Goul Andersen (1995). See also Dietlind Stolle and Christian Welzel, "Social Capital, Communitarianism and Human Development: How Threatening is Rising Individual Self-Expression to Social Capital?" (paper presented at the Annual Meeting of the American Political Science Association, Washington, DC, August 29–September 3, 2000).

These largely younger and highly educated citizens are, for example, no more critical of universal welfare programs than were their more collectivistically minded brothers and sisters. One reasonable interpretation of these findings is that a solidaristic rather than an egoistic individualism has appeared. A concept such as "solidaristic individualism" may seem to be a contradiction in terms, but the meaning of this concept is that solidarity does not necessarily imply collectivism – that is, that people have more or less the same values and share the same lifestyles and may be interested in and engaged in the same organizations. By "solidaristic individualism," I mean that individuals are willing to give support to other individuals but also accept that they have other, different values and want to engage themselves in different causes. This support, however, is given on the condition that they can trust their fellow citizens to give the same support for their own different lifestyles and organizational efforts. There is some empirical evidence from other sources that shows that individual autonomy and social responsibility go together. One such source is the analysis from the group behind the European Value Study, which argues that while individualism is increasing, "individualism may involve identification with, and action on behalf of others" (Barker 1992: 5).

One way to understand the diminishing affinity of Swedes for most movements/organizations is thus not as a declining interest in voluntary organizations but as an increasing demand for individual autonomy and a willingness to construct lifestyles and worldviews independently of large collectivities such as the old popular movements. The Society Opinion Media (SOM) surveys, with annual data from 1986 to 2003, show no decrease in the number of people who report being active in organizations. On the contrary, there seems to be a small increase in the percentage who report having some kind of assignment in a voluntary organization (Rothstein 1999). Another survey asking respondents about the amount of work they have done in voluntary organizations during the last month shows a slight increase between 1992 and 1998 (Jeppsson, Grassman, and Svedberg 1999). My conclusion is thus that the decreasing level of affinity for the major organizations/movements should not necessarily be taken as a sign of decreasing willingness to engage in voluntary organizations, thereby diminishing the amount of social capital in Sweden. It may instead reflect the problems the old and established organizations face in creating the type of collective loyalty that existed in the past. If there is a crisis in the production of social capital, it must be manifest in changed patterns of activity, not just in changed attitudes of this sort.

In sum, I think there is something strange in the way that the affinity question has been interpreted, and that it is not a very good indicator of activity in or support for the voluntary organizations. The available data seem to show that when old and established popular movements, such as the free churches and the temperance movement, have a declining stock of members, it reflects a changed composition of organizational life in Sweden more than a general decline in voluntarism.

How should this new organizational landscape be described? Based on their extensive study of voluntary organizations in Norway (which show the same general tendencies as in Sweden), Per Selle and Bjarne Øymyr (1995) have argued that the composition of the voluntary sector in the Nordic countries has changed dramatically since the 1940s. First, the organizations have become less hierarchical; that is, the local clubs act more independently of the national organization, what organizational theorists call "loose coupling." Second, there has been a change from religious, temperance, and purely women's organizations to leisure and cultural organizations, while the economic organizations (unions and cooperatives) have largely stayed at their initially high level. Third, both the diversity and density of the organizational landscape have increased. There are many more organizations and many more different types of organizations in the 1990s than there were during the 1940s. Fourth, the 1990s are characterized by an increasing dynamism in the organizational world – that is, many organizations die but even more new ones are created. Lastly, nowadays, more people get organized in order to fulfill their own individual interests, while collective ideological movements, such as the temperance movement and the free church movement and probably also the labor movement, have become weaker. One way to describe this change is to say that the Scandinavian countries have gone from collective mass movements to "organized individualism" (Selle and Øymyr 1995, cf. Selle 1998). There are good reasons to believe that this change in the organizational landscape has a connection to the type of individualism mentioned above. Choosing an organization may nowadays have more to do with the individual's deliberate creation of a specific lifestyle than with adherence to an established organized ideological collective.

Swedish unions: a special case

Of all Swedish organizations, the union movement is the one with the most members and which is, next only to the sports movement, activating the most people. If there is a general crisis in the idea of popular movements in Sweden, we should be able to detect it here. As stated above, the degree of unionization in Sweden is unusually high: more than 85 percent. The variation in degree of unionization is, in fact, one of the most peculiar differences between western capitalist countries, for two reasons. First, hardly any other important political variable shows such a variation, with France at the bottom with less than 10 percent in unions and Sweden at the top. If it is rational, in any sense, to be a member of a union, then why are there more than eight times as many rational employees in Sweden than in France? Or, to follow the standard theory of collective action, if it is individually irrational to be a union member, then why should Swedes in particular be the most irrational people? Second, the level of unionization has changed dramatically during the whole post-war period. For example, the difference between the level of unionization in Sweden and in the United States, which today is more than five times, was much smaller during the 1950s. The effects of the recent and much-discussed globalization and internationalization of capitalism have come at the same time as the differences in degrees of unionization have continued to increase (Oskarsson 2003).

The answer to this puzzle is, to a large extent, the existence of "selective incentives." It pays more in some countries for the individual to be a member of the union. As I have shown elsewhere, one such selective incentive seems to be of special importance in this case, namely, the degree of control unions have over unemployment funds. Figures from the late 1980s from eighteen OECD countries showed that the five countries with the highest degrees of unionization (Sweden, Denmark, Finland, Iceland and Belgium) all had unemployment systems in which the unions had control over the admin-istration of the unemployment insurance scheme whereas, in the rest, this was handled by governmental agencies. The results from multiple regression analysis showed that this explained 18 percent of the variation in the degree of unionization (Rothstein 1992c).

The idea of giving the unions control over the unemployment insurance scheme is a very good illustration of the relationship in Sweden between voluntary organizations and the state. On the one hand, the unions get a very powerful selective incentive to help them recruit members. On the other hand, the unions also handle the very difficult question of deciding who is really to be considered "unemployed" – that is, what type of work one has to accept or else risk losing the benefits. The government is thereby relieved of having to take responsibility for these very difficult decisions, and this is something that probably increases the legitimacy of the scheme. First, because it is the union officials and not the governmental bureaucrats who take these decisions and, second, because the union officials probably know more about each segment of the labor market and thus the opportunities their members have for finding suitable jobs (Rothstein 1992c).

It should be added that this is not the only type of selective incentives the Swedish unions have been granted by the government. A vast number of industrial laws and regulations give the local unions a say over working conditions, the implementation of work safety regulations, and who has to go first when there is a shortage of jobs. In sum, this means that for many, if not most, employees, membership in the union is only formally a voluntary decision (Rothstein 1992c).

On the other hand, this does not mean that instrumental motives are the only reason for becoming a union member. Surveys from both the late 1970s and from more recent years show that instrumental and solidaristic motives are equally strong when union members are asked why they have decided to join (Lewin 1980; Nelander and Lindgren 1994). Even so, an instrumental motive for joining a union may translate into activity in the next stage and thereby produce social capital. From the standpoint of producing social capital, there is nothing intrinsically bad in combining instrumental and non-instrumental reasons for organizational activity. After all, most people join choral societies in order to pursue a very instrumental and individual preference for singing, not to create interpersonal trust or to make democracy work.

What, then, has happened to union activity since the 1980s? Do the unions in Sweden consist of only passive paper members who see the union as something like a public insurance company controlled by professional bureaucrats, or do unions engage their members in activities that are likely to produce interpersonal trust? Before I try to answer this question, I would like to underline the diversity of the Swedish union movement. Although the blue-collar trade unions organized nationally in the LO are the largest unions, unions for salaried employees organized in the Swedish Confederation of Salaried Employees (TCO) and unions for professionals with academic educations organized in the Swedish Confederation of Professional Associations (SACO) have an almost equally high degree of unionization. Second, the Swedish union movement is both more centralized and more decentralized than is the case in most other OECD countries. The central organizations are very strong, but so, in most cases, are the local clubs in each workplace. By tradition, but also because of the laws regulating industrial relations, Swedish unions have a more direct presence in the workplace. The laws securing the rights of local union officials and the co-determination law have been especially important in this case.

A survey from 1993 shows that 36 percent of all employees had participated in at least one union meeting during the previous twelve months and that 19 percent had also made some sort of statement. A similar study from 1988 shows a slight decrease in this type of union activity (45 percent and 20 percent, respectively). This report also shows that 14 percent of all LO members served as an elected representative, the figures for the two other national union organizations being slightly higher. Given the extremely high degree of unionization in Sweden, this means that a considerable part of the population as a whole (13 percent) is active or serves as an elected representative in the union movement (Nelander and Lindgren 1994, 1999a, 1999b).

The "Swedish Living Conditions" report, which has survey data from 1995, shows similar results. Of the adult population, 36 percent had been in a union meeting during the previous twelve months, and 11 percent reported that they were active as union officials. However, the difference between 1976 and 1995 is significantly negative, –7.6 percent (SCB 1997: 335–339). One explanation for this may be that during the mid 1970s, an unusually high number of new and important industrial relations laws that implied increased local activity had just been launched, such as the co-determination law and the work safety law. Another important factor that may explain the decrease in union activity is the rapid increase in unemployment since 1992.

In sum, it would not be correct to describe the Swedish union movement as a group of vibrant organizations successfully activating a majority of their members, but it would be equally wrong to ignore the fact that 36 percent of the adult population go to a union meeting once a year and that 11 percent go to more than four meetings a year. The percentage reporting active participation went down during the late 1970s, but it has been pretty stable (10–12 percent) since 1980 (SCB 1997: 335–339).

Informal social networks

It has generally been thought that Swedes, either because of their national character or because of the "cradle-to-the-grave" welfare state, had rather weak social ties. I will, for various reasons, leave the question of national character and concentrate on the latter problem, namely, what does a universal welfare state do to informal social networks? Interestingly enough, there are arguments from both the left and the right saying that there is an inverse relationship between these two. The argument from the political right is that when altruism and social problems are taken over by the government, people will stop caring; compassion will be shown only by paying taxes, and informal social networks will be weakened. A major research project about the Swedish welfare state (financed by the employers' federation) concludes, among other things, that "the twentieth century has been a lost century for the civil society" (Zetterberg and Ljungberg 1997).

The argument from the left is, in fact, very similar. According to Jürgen Habermas, the welfare state has "colonized" civil society and undermines what he calls "natural" forms of solidarity. Alan Wolfe argues that the Scandinavian type of welfare state "squeezes families, communities, and social networks" (Wolfe 1989: 22). Wolfe has further argued that an historical irony may exist here – when social obligations become public, intimate ties will weaken and "so will distant ones, thus undermining the very moral strengths the welfare state has shown." (1989: 144). What is somewhat peculiar with these arguments is that they are hardly ever substantiated by any empirical evidence.

If it is true that the universal welfare state has been detrimental to informal social relations, then we should see a weakening of such relations since the 1950s. However, the data show that there has been a strengthening of informal social ties during this period. The Katrineholm "middle-town" study with data from 1950 and 1988 concludes that "the people in Katrineholm have become more socially active. They are members of more organizations and socialize more frequently with their fellow workers, neighbors and friends" (Perlinski 1990: 231ff.). The "Swedish Living Conditions" report conducted by Statistics Sweden (which was based on data from about 7,000 interviews from 1975 and 1995) gave the same type of result. Over this period, there was an increase of 12 percentage points in the number of people who got together with friends each week (from 45.5 to 57.5). The positive changes were statistically significant ($p < 0.05$) for all age groups, except those from 55 to 64 years of age, where the increase was only 3 percentage points, but there was another significant 12 percent increase among those from 65 to 74 years of age. The greatest increase took place among those from 25 to 34 years of age (23.5 percent). Interestingly enough, the figure for women who are homemakers was lower (51 percent) than for women in general (56 percent), and this figure was also lower than for women who worked full time (56 percent). It can be added that the number of people who reported not having a close friend was down from 26 percent in 1979 to 19 percent in 1985; these changes are statistically significant ($p < 0.05$) for all age groups (SCB 1997: 287–301).

This result is confirmed by data from two similar FSI studies conducted in 1955 and 1995, asking if people were "interested in socializing with friends."[5] These studies show that both men and women, young and not so young, seem to be more interested in socializing with friends in the 1990s than was the case in the mid-1950s. In the 1990s, hardly anyone reports being uninterested in socializing with friends.

However, the heart of the matter in the criticism of the welfare state mentioned above is not that people socialize too little but that they do not care enough for others who are in some form of distress and need their help. People in a universal welfare state, according to its critics, turn away from others in need and cold-heartedly refer them to the welfare authorities. Paying high taxes morally relieves them from more traditional social obligations. There are, unfortunately, no data over time to test such an hypothesis; however, in a study, Karin Busch Zetterberg reports from a survey of 2,749 Swedish

---

[5] FSI surveys 1955 ($n = 1509$) and 1995 ($n = 1388$).

adult citizens (aged from 16 to 89) conducted in 1994 (Busch Zetterberg 1996) that more than every fifth adult (22 percent) is voluntarily regularly taking care of someone who is sick, handicapped, or elderly. Of these 22 percent, 5 percent were taking care of persons in their own household and 18 percent were caring for people who lived outside their household. The difference between men and women was surprisingly small: 23 percent of Swedish women and 20 percent of men were voluntarily helping out. Age also had a small effect, varying from 20 to 25 percent between different cohorts. Social class, however, made a difference, with 31 percent caregivers in the upper class and 20 percent in the working class. The type of care given varies, of course, but sometimes included rather demanding tasks such as lifting and helping out with personal hygiene and medication.

"Still, when all is said and done, there is not and can never be any guarantee that stronger relations in civil society will create the practices that enable people to take personal responsibility for the fate of abstract others," Alan Wolfe writes (Wolfe 1989: 258). I tend to agree, but I would add that Wolfe's fear that the strength of the Scandinavian welfare states would destroy such moral obligations seems unwarranted. Whether the amount of voluntary care in Sweden is high or low is, of course, difficult to say from this study, but it seems fair to conclude that the universal welfare state has not wiped out this sort of activity.

For various reasons, there is no equivalent to the British pub, the German *kneipe*, or the French bistro in Sweden. Historically, the severe restrictions on the selling of alcohol made such neighborhood places for socializing very rare. There has, however, been a rather remarkable change in this respect as well. In 1967, the number of fully licensed restaurants was a mere 1,249, which is about one per 6,400 individuals. Twenty-five years later, this has increased eleven times; that is, there are now close to 12,000 fully licensed restaurants in Sweden, which is about one per 650 individuals.[6] This huge increase in the number of fully licensed restaurants is not caused by increased total consumption of alcohol. Instead, it must reflect a change in social habits; that is, consumption of alcohol has gone from private to public. Survey data also show that going to restaurants has now become one of the favorite leisure time activities in Sweden. In fact, it is the leisure time activity with the highest increase between 1982 and 1995; from 25 to 41 percent of Swedes say that they have gone to a restaurant more than five times during the previous year (while only 9 percent report going to a religious service more than five times a year). Although the young are the most frequently

---

[6] Figures from Swedish National Board for Social Affairs, Alkoholstatistik (Stockholm, 1997) and from the National Institute for Public Health, *Försälningsstatistik för alkohol 2003* (Stockholm, 2003).

in restaurants, the increase is significant ($p < 00.5$) in all age groups and highest among those from 45 to 54 years of age, among whom it went from 16 to 34 percent (SCB 1997: 119).

However, the effect of this type of activity on social capital remains unknown. There seems to be a strong connection over time between the decreasing activity in the temperance movement reported above and the increasing interest among Swedes in consuming alcohol in public places, but I dare say not the cause of this change. I leave it to the reader to determine whether this type of change is good or bad for the creation of trust and social capital, but it is surely an indicator of an increased number of informal social contacts in Sweden. However, in the SOM survey data collected for this study, we found (to our dismay, we confess) no relationship at all between high levels of trust and high frequency of visits to restaurants (whether fully licensed or not). We can, however, conclude that much of the criticism of modern society and of the expansion of the welfare state for creating passive and socially isolated citizens seems inconsistent with these empirical findings.

Swedish civil society in a comparative perspective

So far, we have tried to see what has happened over time with the voluntary sector and with more informal social relations in Sweden, and the conclusion is that, although there has been a change in the composition and direction of this sector, we cannot detect a general decline. But time-series data on this question must be supplemented with comparative data. How does the voluntary sector in Sweden fare compared to countries with different and/or less developed welfare states and a more pluralistic political system?

Thanks to two different comparative projects on the non-profit sector and volunteering, we now have data with which to address this question. One of the most common ideas in the debate about civil society is that an encompassing welfare state will make people less willing to do unpaid work in voluntary organizations. If so, voluntary work will be very low in countries with large welfare states, but such a hypothesis is not validated in a survey comparing eight European countries (Gaskin and Smith 1995). The two countries with the most extensive welfare policies, the Netherlands and Sweden, also have the highest scores for the amount of unpaid work in voluntary associations.[7] In response to the question: "In the past year, have you carried out *any* unpaid work or activity for or with an organization which has nothing to do with your paid work and is not solely for

[7] The other countries were Belgium, Bulgaria, Germany, Ireland, the Netherlands, Slovakia, and the United Kingdom.

your own benefit or the benefit of your family?" 36 percent of the Swedish population answered "yes," as compared to an average of 27 percent across other European countries.[8] This says something about frequency but nothing about the *volume* of voluntary work. It may be that people do voluntary work every year but that the total amount is very small. According to this study, however, the Swedish population did not spend fewer hours a month in voluntary work than those of the other seven countries. In considering the type of organization in which the work was done, Swedes scored comparatively high on sports and recreation, trade union/professional organization, civil defense, international development/human rights and peace and, as could be expected, low on health, social services, child education, and community development.

Considering the general theory of the importance of social capital, the Swedish population also seems to volunteer for the right (i.e., non-instrumental) reasons. Of those Swedes who volunteered, 62 percent said they did so to "meet people and make friends," as compared to an average of 36 percent, while only 6 percent said they did so because "it gives me social recognition and a position in the community," as compared to an average of 18 percent (Gaskin and Smith 1995: 50). At the same time, only 11 percent of the Swedish population agreed with the statement: "If the government fulfilled all of its responsibilities, there should be no need for people to do unpaid work," as compared to an average of 37 percent. And finally, in Sweden, 74 percent agreed that "engaging in unpaid work helps people take an active role in a democratic society," compared to the average of 62 percent. These results are confirmed by another comparative study that found that the *per capita* amount of voluntary work in Sweden is considerably higher than in France, Germany, or Italy (Lundström and Wijkström 1997).

This research project also provides data about the way voluntary organizations are financed. Although the size of the non-profit sector in 1990, measured in terms of expenditures as a percentage of GDP, was 4.1 percent in Sweden, the average of the eight countries in the study was 3.6 percent. By this economic measure, the non-profit sector in Sweden is smaller than that of the United States and the United Kingdom, but it is larger than that of Germany, France, or Italy (Salamon and Anheier 1994: 35). Even more surprisingly, although the average revenue from public payments was 42 percent for the countries compared, the Swedish non-profit sector received only 29 percent of its funds from the government (Lundström and Wijkström

---

[8] The interviewers prompted those who answered "no" to the question by showing them a list of the types of unpaid work that people do and checking whether they had done any of them. The "unprompted" figure for Sweden was 32 percent and the average was 23 percent.

1997).[9] Accordingly, the Swedish non-profits obtained 62 percent of their funds through earned income, the highest percentage among the eight countries (the average was 47 percent). The explanation for this is not that Swedes are more altruistic (they are not) or that Swedish non-profit organizations are more successful in generating income on their own. Rather, as Lundström and Wijkström (1997) have pointed out, the non-profit sectors in other countries are more dependent on public money to fund social services, health, and elementary education which, because of the universal welfare state, are relatively small concerns for Swedish non-profits.

Considering informal social relations, the study by Busch Zetterberg (1996) mentioned above on the number of people who voluntarily help others in need makes a comparison with Great Britain possible. Figures from a comparable study in Great Britain based on a survey from 1990 show that this type of voluntary activity is higher in Sweden (22 percent) than in Britain (15 percent). If we compare the number of people who helped people outside their own household, the Swedish figure is 18 percent, while for Great Britain, it is 12 percent.[10]

Comparing surveys from different countries is always difficult because the wording of the question can be interpreted differently. In this case (Zetterberg 1996), there is also a four-year time span between the surveys. On the other hand, this is not a question about attitudes but of actual behavior, which means that the methodological problems should be fewer. Great Britain's welfare system is, moreover, far less universal than Sweden's, and Great Britain is also known for its many charitable organizations. We should thus expect higher figures from Britain, but the data show the opposite. It

---

[9] The study included France, Germany, Hungary, Italy, Japan, Sweden, the United Kingdom and the United States. The "non-profit sector" in this project was defined as formal, private, self-governing and voluntary organizations in the following areas: culture, recreation, education, health, social services, environment, development and housing, civic and advocacy, philanthropy, business, professional, and "other." Religious congregations, political parties, cooperatives, mutual savings banks, mutual insurance companies and government agencies were excluded. Cf. Salamon and Anheier (1994: 13–16). One problem with the economic measures from this study is that unions have been included. In Sweden, the state has given unions a great deal of power over working conditions for employees, such as choosing who loses their jobs first when there are lay-offs. In practice, local unions have this power over employees whether or not they are union members. In many cases, this makes membership voluntary only from a rather formal point of view. As the unions' share of the economic size of the voluntary sector in Sweden is, according to this study, 17.6 percent, the Swedish figures may be exaggerated to some extent. But even if unions were not counted, the relative economic size of the Swedish non-profit sector would still be as large or larger than in, for example, France, Germany, or Italy.

[10] British data from OPCS, General Household Survey: Careers in 1990, *Monitor 17*, Office of Population Census and Surveys. London: The Government Statistical Service, 1992; quoted here from Busch Zetterberg (1996: 197).

thus seems safe to conclude that these results from Sweden and Great Britain do not substantiate the claim that the more extensive and universal the welfare state, the less we will see of voluntary activity based on feelings of moral obligation.

To summarize, in terms of membership, activity, and finances, the voluntary sector in Sweden is as large or larger than those in most other western industrialized democracies. Moreover, the non-profit sector in Sweden is less dependent on governmental funding and is better able to raise money on its own than are many comparable countries. What differentiates the voluntary sector in Sweden, as well as in the other Scandinavian countries, is its *structure*. While historical and political factors have made it weak in areas such as social service, health care, and elementary education, it is strong in the fields of sports, recreation, culture, adult education, and the labor market (Kuhnle and Selle 1992).

The trust scene

Being an active member of voluntary organizations and having lots of informal social contacts will, according to the general theory on social capital, serve to increase the level of trust in society. From the very first World Value Study in 1981 to the latest one carried out in 1999/2000, we know that Sweden, together with the other Scandinavian countries, are the most high-trust societies. More people than elsewhere, around 60 percent, say "yes" to the question "Most people can be trusted" and "no" to the statement that you "can't be too careful when dealing with other people." (Inglehart 1997; Rothstein and Stolle 2003). The low-trust countries such as Turkey, Brazil, and Peru score below 10 percent, while countries like Hungary, Estonia, and Portugal are between 20 and 30 percent trusting (figure 4.2).[11] Recent Swedish survey data do not show a decline in the opinion about whether "most people can be trusted."

On the contrary, generalized trust measured in this way has increased between 1981 and 1997. In the yearly SOM surveys carried out at Göteborg University,[12] we have since 1996 asked not only the dichotomous "trust"

---

[11] Other examples: Venezuela, 10 percent; Romania, 16 percent; France, 21 percent; Bosnia-Herzegovina, 27 percent; Ukraine, 29 percent; Mexico, 30 percent; Italy, 34 percent; Japan, 38 percent; United Kingdom, 42 percent; United States, 49 percent. The percentages are the mean for the 1981, 1992, and 1996 World Value Study survey question on trust.

[12] The SOM studies are conducted by the SOM Institute, which is operated jointly by the Department of Journalism and Mass Communications (JMG), the Department of Political Science, and the School of Management at Göteborg University. Each year since 1986 the SOM Institute has conducted a nationally representative questionnaire on the topic of Society, Opinion, and Mass Media (hence the name SOM). The nationwide study,

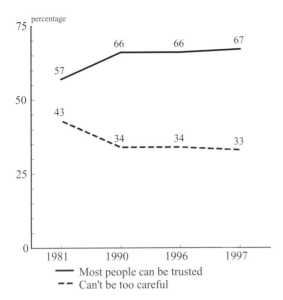

Figure 4.2. Opinions about trust in other people, 1981–1997
Sources: Data for 1981 and 1990 taken from the Swedish section of the World Value Study (*n* = 876 and 994, respectively). In 1996, two different surveys were conducted in Sweden with this question, the third World Value Study (*n* = 957) and one made for this report by the SOM Institute at Göteborg University (*n* = 1,707). The figures shown are the means from these two studies. The data for 1997 are from an FSI survey (*n* = 1,640).

question as stated above, but also a question for which respondents were asked to mark their opinion about whether or not other people could be trusted on a scale of 0 to 10. The result is shown in figure 4.3.

Conclusion: the universal welfare state, social capital, and civil society

To summarize, the overall picture of Sweden is that of a rather vital, growing, and changing civil society in combination with a unusually high level of social trust. In most respects, the amount of social capital seems to have increased since the 1950s. The survey measures of trust show a remarkable stability over time. We can thus tentatively conclude that whatever the problems that may be created by an encompassing and universal welfare state, it

Riks-SOM, has included 6,000 people since 1999. The study is conducted in the form of a questionnaire distributed by mail. For more information, see Holmberg and Weibull (2002), and visit the institute's home page at www.som.gu.se.

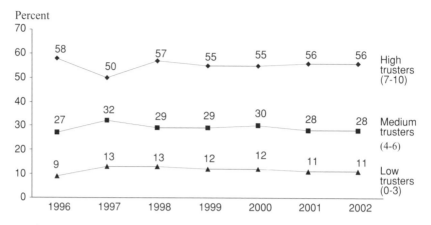

Figure 4.3. Interpersonal trust in Sweden, 1996–2002
Question (translated from Swedish): "In your opinion, to what extent can people in general be trusted?" Please answer on the scale below.
Notes: Data taken from the yearly national SOM surveys, 1996–2002. The scale goes from 0 to 10, where 0 indicates "you can not trust people in general" and 10 "you can trust people in general." "No responses" varies between 1 and 6 percent.

does not cause a decline in social capital. On the contrary, it seems as if the sharp decline in social capital that Putnam reports for the United States, has not occurred in other industrialized countries (Putnam 2002).

Why, then, has the encompassing Swedish welfare state not destroyed trust and social capital? One reason may be in the way that the Swedish welfare state system has been institutionalized. Its main architects sought a social policy based on the idea of a "people's insurance" that would supply all citizens (or in some cases, all but the very rich) with basic resources without incurring the stigmatization associated with poor relief. They not only shunned the means-tested poor-relief system but also the class-segregated Bismarkian type of social insurance (Rothstein and Stolle 2003). The universal character of the welfare state may have three important implications for social trust. One is that people receiving support from the government cannot be portrayed as "the others." Second, compared to means-tested programs, universal ones are far less likely to create suspicion that people are cheating the system (Kumlin and Rothstein 2005). Thirdly, comparing nations, one of the strongest predictors of high levels of social trust is economic equality, something that universal social policies do create (Rothstein 1998a; Uslaner 2002). Lastly, at the individual level, social trust is clearly related to things such as optimism for the future and a sense of being able to have control over one's life. The existence of high-quality universal programs, especially when it comes to areas such as education and health care, may increase feelings of "optimism" and "equal opportunity" among large segments of the population. When people fear for the future and see rising inequality, they are certainly less likely to be optimistic (Uslaner 2002).

Language is, I believe, a problem here. The term "welfare state" is not an adequate description of social programs in Sweden. The word "welfare" – at least in the United States – implies targeted means-tested programs and connotes stigma for the persons receiving it. For Sweden, a "social insurance state" would be a more accurate term.

This is not to deny that there are parts of the Swedish welfare system that have been detrimental to social capital. As in other western countries, a strong planning and managerial optimism, which could indeed take a rather paternalistic form, characterized welfare policy, especially in the late 1960s. High unemployment during the 1990s increased the number of people who depended on means-tested social assistance. I argue, however, that the major bulk of the programs, precisely because they are universal, are not likely to have a negative effect on civil society. In fact, if one looks very closely, leading theorists of civil society agree that general welfare programs cannot be seen as subversive of civil society. In their voluminous book on the political theory of civil society, for example, Jean L. Cohen and Andrew Arato (1993) write (in a well-hidden endnote!):

> We fail to see how social security, health insurance, job training programs for the unemployed, unemployment insurance, and family supports such as day care or parental leave create dependency rather than autonomy, even if the particular administration of such programs as AFDC (such as the man-in-house-rule) do create dependency and are humiliating.[13] But these are empirical questions. The theoretical issue behind such questions is the extent to which social services and social supports are symbolically constituted as welfare for "failures" or as supports for all members of the community. (1993: 664)

Although it is given only footnote status, Cohen and Arato (1993) perceive the fundamental distinction between general and means-tested social policies for civil society. There may be other negative (and positive) effects of a universal welfare state, but it does not keep people from participating in voluntary organizations or helping others in distress.

---

[13] AFDC stands for "Aid to Families with Dependent Children," which has been a major means-tested social assistance program in the United States. The "man-in-house-rule" is a provision in the program that states that if an able-bodied, grown man lives in the household (as husband or cohabitant), then no assistance shall be rendered to that family. This rule has, according to critics of the program, created an incentive for the man to abandon the family and has contributed to a very sharp increase in the rate of family break-up in socially disadvantaged groups.

5

How is social capital produced?

If social capital really has all the advantages evinced by the theory and the by now rather extensive empirical research, the question of how it can be produced logically follows. If social capital really is *capital*, how do we bring about investments? With respect to human and physical capital, the answers to the questions are rather obvious (albeit not always easy to achieve in practice), but the question is considerably more difficult to answer when it comes to social capital. For example, the response to self-proclamations of trustworthiness is to ask what is wrong with a person or an organization that feels compelled to emphasize that particular trait. Instead of producing trust, such messages usually make the recipient suspicious of the sender's intentions. We are prone to think that there is something intrinsically wrong with individuals or organizations that explicitly tell us to trust them. Unlike acquiring knowledge and making tools, the production of trust is based on complex psychological processes (Misztal 1996: 20–26).

The qualitative dimension of social capital – i.e., social trust – is according to our definition a matter of convictions (personal beliefs based partly on acquired knowledge and partly on a moral worldview). Beliefs are not easy to manufacture and they cannot be compelled into existence. Available research shows that opinions on social trust are often rooted in deep-seated personal beliefs that may have been instilled in early childhood or resulted from formative (and when it comes to mistrust, traumatic) experiences (Delhey and Newton 2003; Uslaner 2002). Persuading a misanthropic and cynical individual who deeply mistrusts his fellow human beings to change his mind would probably not be counted among the easier projects in life. When it comes to groups that mistrust or even hate one another, it would in all likelihood be even more difficult. Extensive research findings indicate that, for example, ethnically based hatred and mistrust between groups has a *self-reinforcing effect* on the opinions and beliefs of individuals, becoming therewith part and parcel of group identity and the logic behind its mobilization (Arthur 1999; Hardin 1995; Kaufman 2001).

The situation may be easier when it comes to the more quantitative dimension, but only slightly. An individual may of course be persuaded to become more or less socially available to contacts with "people in general," but in all likelihood this is also a personality factor that is difficult to change. Political means can be employed to make it easier or more difficult for people to encounter other people – e.g. by creating or facilitating public spaces where encounters can take place in ways that do not invite violence or other forms of criminality. State subsidization of popular movements and youth organizations has long been a prominent feature of Swedish policy, although its effectiveness is uncertain. Subsidies to voluntary organizations may even be counterproductive. One example is the very generous subsidization of, for example, the temperance movement in Sweden. It is probably safe to say that the outcome has been a popular perception of these organizations as extensions of the long arm of state authority, which has constrained civic engagement rather than expanded it (Öberg 1994, Rothstein 1992a). On the international level, aid organizations including the World Bank are highly involved in policies for increasing social capital in many developing countries through germinating social networks and voluntary organizations, but so far the results are uncertain. As stated in a summary report from the World Bank, social capital researches "have been more successful in documenting the beneficial impact of social capital than at deriving a policy prescription and providing guidelines about how to invest in it" (Grootaert and van Bastelaer 2001: 25).

The connection between variations in institutional formation at various political levels (e.g. state, region, local community) and the system of beliefs of individuals is the crux of the problem. The causal traffic may go in both directions here – i.e. individuals with a particular orientation may create particular institutional conditions that either advance or hinder the generation of social capital, or certain structural conditions, through their institutional design, may produce individuals with greater or lesser social capital. The connection I will be making here follows the model introduced in chapter 2 for which it is particularly important to specify the causal mechanisms in order to connect institutional conditions to the beliefs and behavior of actors.

Social capital at the individual level

Studies of social capital at the individual level have yielded rather surprising results. From a specific Swedish perspective, which may perhaps be extended to all of northern Europe, we might have assumed that social capital would be especially plentiful within the working classes. The highly developed sense of social solidarity and the historically understood importance of organizing in unions and other class-based organizations (tenant associations, study circles, senior citizens' associations, etc.) could be explained by a high level of social trust (Olofsson 1979). Alternatively, observations of the success of those types of organizations may have brought insight into the importance of solidarity and cooperation among members, making it reasonable to expect that the highest extent of trust would be found in social groups with relatively low income and little education. Likewise, it would seem reasonable to assume that financial success is rooted in a strong orientation towards self-interest and the capacity to exploit others in a competitive situation. The "economic man" assumed to stimulate individual and collective financial success is not known for his devotion to solidaristic cooperation in order to attain common goals in which personal utility takes a back seat. As Ben-Ner and Putterman (1998) said, the human being of the neo-classical economic models is "bereft of concern for friend and foe as well as for right or wrong, and caring only about his own well-being" and cannot therefore "be at the center of a meaningful theory of how and when behavior is influenced by ethics, values, concern for others" (Ben-Ner and Putterman 1998: xvi). If we were to align with the theory of neo-classical economics, we should expect low levels of social trust and civic engagement among the economically successful.

However, the results of current and rather extensive research in the field indicate precisely the opposite. We find high social trust and extensive, expansive social networks among people who are highly educated and have relatively high incomes. Society's "winners" are the people who exhibit a high degree of trust in other people, while the "losers" are the opposite. This appears to apply to all western countries, but as Delhey and Newton have shown, also to countries such as Slovenia, South Korea, and Hungary (Delhey and Newton, 2003, cf. Wuthnow 1998; Newton 1999b; Norén 2000; Patterson 1999; Stolle 2000a, 2000b; Torpe 2000; Whiteley 1999). As Robert Putnam asserted, the "haves" are high trusters and the "have-nots" are low trusters. High social status, optimism, a favorable attitude towards democracy, and general happiness is positively connected to high levels of social trust (Delhey and Newton 2003; van Deth *et al.* 1999; Hall 1999; Putnam 2000; Rothstein 2002; Uslaner 2002). The intricate question is then whether social capital makes people rich and happy or whether successful lives make people into "high trusters." There may also be a substantial degree of feedback over time among these variables. People who enjoy large financial assets are more likely to be able to survive isolated instances of treacherous behavior by people or organizations they initially trusted.

Socio-psychological studies of the causes of social trust make fascinating reading. The research is divided mainly into two camps. The first, advocated by Eric Uslaner among others, asserts that social trust is generated in childhood through the socialization process that takes place within the family. Access to extensive survey data material from the United States has allowed Uslaner to show that there are systematic differences in opinions and values among people who feel what he calls *particularized* trust and those who feel *generalized* trust in other people. The former trust only a very small circle of individuals (e.g. the family and very close friends) or, if they identify with an ethnic or social minority, their peer group. Conversely, they mistrust people in general (i.e. all people outside their immediate circle of peers). They also feel pessimistic about the future and especially about their opportunities to shape their own lives. They mistrust most social institutions and believe that institutions are structured in a way that disfavors them personally. Their misanthropy leads them to believe that the outside world is dangerous and threatening and thus something they cannot control (Uslaner 2002: chapter 2). Using the terminology popular among my students, one could say that particularized trusters believe that the "deck is stacked against them." To them, a stranger is a competitor for the small resources for which they must struggle and thus someone to be avoided and with whom dealings call for extreme caution (cf. Banfield 1958).

In all of these areas, generalized trusters are the opposites of particularized trusters. Uslaner's extensive survey data shows that generalized trusters are optimistic about the future and their capacity to shape their own lives. They believe, and hold as a moral norm, that people should trust other people in general, and not only those within their own small circle of family, clan, group, or tribe. They look favorably upon their societies and believe that if people "play by the rules" they will be reasonably well rewarded. They do not believe that trusting other people is a risky proposition, and they are tolerant of people who are different from themselves. A stranger is a person from whom they might learn something or someone with whom they might enter into a mutually beneficial cooperative relationship. They believe that most civil servants whom they encounter in various contexts are honest and will treat them well (Uslaner 2002: chapter 2).

Experimental socio-psychological research on trust and the social dilemma is very extensive. It is usually based on putting the experiment subjects into small groups and then presenting them with one version or another of the famous Prisoners' Dilemma game. Because experiments such as these may be designed in an almost infinite variety of ways, the established methodological rule is that one should not draw conclusions from single experiments. However, meta-analyses of these experiments have been conducted in which the results of multiple studies were combined. In one such metastudy, Sally (1995) included about 160 experiments with a total of about 5,000 experiment subjects. The overall results of that research in the context of this work may be summarized in four points (Dawes and Messick 2000; Dawes and Thaler 1988; Kollock 1998; van Lange *et al.* 2000; Ledyard 1995; Sally 1995):

1. Self-interested action is not as widespread as assumed by rationalist theory. Even in "rigidly" structured social dilemma experiments, 25–30 percent choose a cooperative strategy.
2. Opportunities for communication dramatically increase the percentage who choose to cooperate. If experiment subjects are allowed to socialize before or during the experiment, the percentage of "trusters" usually rises above 50 percent. Communication serves to induce trust and group identity.
3. It is very easy to induce "tribalism" – i.e. suspicion and conflicts between groups of experiment subjects. This is a very common result when the researcher divides the subjects into groups that are allowed to communicate only internally and not with members of other groups.
4. In series of experiments, the infinite regression mentioned above occurs to the extent that cooperation declines as the subjects approach the end of a number of serial interactions.

A somewhat special result is noteworthy in this context, which is that the values subjects bring with them into the experiment affect whether they will choose to cooperate or not (cf. van Lange *et al.* 2000). That is, their personal cultural or normative values, according to the division proposed by Uslaner, for example, matter (cf. Biel and Gärling 1995; Gärling 1999). One experiment shows that Vietnamese people are much more inclined towards cooperativeness than are people from the United States (Parks and Vu 1994). But perhaps the most interesting for our purposes are the differences among students with different academic majors. Several experiments have indicated that economics students choose to cooperate significantly less often than other students and in so doing end up in social traps more often (Frank, Gilovich, and Regan 1996; Marwell and Dawes 1981).

In experiments where students with different majors were given the opportunity to accept a bribe, economics students chose to do so significantly more often than students with other majors (Frank and Schulze 2000). This begs the question of whether economics students behave as they do because their early childhood socialization processes made them into low trusters or whether it is actually their studies of the subject that create the "mental map" that leads them to choose non-cooperation, based on low generalized trust in others. The results of the cited studies varied. The most persuasive study is the one carried out by Frank, Gilovich, and Regan (1996), which indicates that the behavior is acquired through the course of studies and is not a result of early socialization. The study by Frank, Gilovich, and Regan (1993, 1996) shows that if economics instruction combines the traditional neo-classical message with elements of ethics, the difference between economics students and other students evaporates (Frank, Gilovich, and Regan 1996, 1993). Other studies have challenged Frank's results (cf. Frank and Schulze 2000), but if they should prove sustainable, there is reason to ask whether a society that invests a great deal in studies of traditional neoclassic economics thereby also creates economic efficiency (Rothstein 1996c). From the perspective of gender equality, the last is rather hopeful, as it means that neither men nor women seem to have any inherent psychological disposition to discriminate on the grounds of sex when deciding whom they should trust or not trust. This area of research does not support the occasionally heard claim that the psychological construction of the male subconscious makes men prefer to cooperate with other men, leading them, for instance, to discriminate against women on the job. Nor does experimental research on corruption find any gender differences. In the experiment conducted by Frank and Schulze (2000) cited above, it was shown that the individuals who were the most corruptible were male economics students, while male students of other subjects were the least corruptible. As the authors point out, it is difficult to identify the underlying causal mechanisms for these differences.

Social trust and social intelligence

Finally, there is a need to refer to the results of Toshio Yamagishi's (2001) experimental research on the linkage between social intelligence and social trust. Yamagishi's proposition is that we might presume that people with low social trust are less easily fooled and gullible, and, as a result, more successful, smarter, and more likely to belong to the elite than those with high trust in other people. The naïve souls in the second group would thus be easily duped victims of unscrupulous, egotistical actors and destined to be society's losers. Interestingly enough, Yamagishi's many different experiments (the subjects were mainly Japanese university students) show the opposite to be true.

Social intelligence, according to Yamagishi, refers to the ability to detect and interpret signals from the people one encounters that tell us whether or not they can be trusted. According to Steven Pinker, this skill is highly developed in many people – e.g. those who can discern whether other people's emotions are real or feigned (Pinker 1997: 405).

Yamagishi shows that most Japanese people believe that high social trust is evidence of gullibility, while low trust in others is proof of acumen and quick-wittedness. However, Yamagishi's analysis shows exactly the opposite to be true, offering the explanation that low social trust and lack of social intelligence constitute a vicious circle in individual personality development. Low social trust is a barrier that keeps individuals from entering into social interactions, especially those that involve taking a risk, but can also be very fruitful. This consequently undermines their social intelligence because they are deprived of the opportunity to hone their skills at interpreting the signals that tell them whom they can trust.

Those signals may be of diverse kinds. Yamagishi reports a number of experiments that he and his colleagues performed, which all indicate that high trusters are more receptive to information that signals untrustworthiness and that they are better than low trusters at determining whether others can be trusted (Yamagishi 2001: 139). Because of their lack of social intelligence, low trusters often err once they take the risk of trusting another person, which makes them less likely to seek out productive cooperation with other people. Quite simply, they are wrong more often than others in their judgments of whether other individuals can be trusted. This creates a vicious circle of mistrust and insufficient social intelligence as they become even more disinclined to enter into relationships with others that may entail a risk that they will be deceived. This compels them into a situation where they are damned if they do and damned if they don't. If they initiate relationships, their lack of social intelligence leads to frequent disappointment, which ratchets up their mistrust of other people. If they isolate themselves, their ability to learn to differentiate between people who can be trusted and people who cannot be trusted declines, reducing their chances for positive transactions with others.

Yamagishi has performed several intriguing experiments that show how this relationship works. One shows that students who have high social trust when they begin their academic careers perform better than those with low social trust, controlled for their intellectual capacity (i.e. grades) when the studies began. Yamagishi's explanation is that "high trust students" have a more fully developed capacity to identify other students with whom they can fruitfully cooperate (in organized study groups, etc.) in the learning process, which leads to better academic performance. His point is that mistrust leads to greater mistrust, while trust combined with social intelligence, engenders more trust. Students at the elite Japanese universities, for instance, have higher social trust than students at the lower-ranked universities. This general result on the linkage between social trust, social intelligence, and increased efficiency agrees with results from research on the significance of trust in working life – i.e. in groups within firms and public administrations (Bennich-Björkman 1997; Kramer and Tyler 1996; Miller 1992).

The results arrived at by Yamagishi and his colleagues have certain noteworthy implications at the political level. Social intelligence is something people learn through extensive interactions with other people, especially others who are not of the "same kind" as they. This implies that if we want to "invest" in social capital, we should create conditions that ensure that they will, early in their lives, interact frequently with people who are not of the "same kind" as they. This result suggests at least two institutional conditions at the societal level. The first is a society that creates multifaceted social meeting places. Such societies should have educational systems, from pre-school to university level, that do not segregate on the basis of, for example, ethnicity and social class. We are wise to be cautious about directly applying knowledge gained through experimental research to public policy, but the results indicate the perils of establishing schools, academic programs, or other social systems that recruit only people of a single "kind." This should also support integrated rather than segregated housing, cultural, and employment policies. Society should instead give individuals powerful incentives to step outside their ingrained social patterns and seek new opportunities in new social networks.

The second political condition that I believe Yamagishi's research implies is that social institutions should exist that effectively penalize individuals who engage in opportunistic and treacherous behavior. If individuals are to be persuaded to leave their established local environments and try interacting with other people who are different from themselves, it is reasonable to presume that the chances will be greater that this will happen if they know that trustworthy public institutions exist to which they can turn if they are deceived or cheated. This would imply that an established system that upholds the rule of law is critical. The problem is that all forms of deceptive conduct are not illegal. For instance, courts are of no use against betrayal in matters of love or friendship. The often cruelly abortive attempts to settle custody disputes in courts exemplify this problem.

In short, in a society that for these and other reasons gives individuals opportunities to seek contacts outside their routine and ingrained frameworks, the likelihood increases that overall social intelligence and social trust will rise. According to Yamagishi, individuals in such a society will invest in the cognitive resources that enable them to learn to interpret signals that will tell them whether or not others can be trusted – i.e. they will invest not only in physical and human capital, but also in social capital. Or, in Yamagishi's words:

> Those who have invested a great many cognitive resources in developing such skills can afford to maintain high default expectations of other people's trustworthiness. By maintaining these high expectations, they can enjoy the advantage of being able to fully explore the opportunities that lie outside the established relations. (Yamagishi 2001: 142)

As already said, the question is why people in certain societies have invested more in these kinds of skills. A question like this is based on our conviction that social trust and social intelligence are not genetic or otherwise biologically determined. The important thing is that the research done by Yamagishi and his colleagues takes us logically to the political and social level in our search for the fountain of social trust. If we want to know how to invest in social capital, we need to know what type of society is most likely to generate Yamagishi's high social intelligence individuals. Putnam (2002), and many others, have pointed at the importance of civil society. Inglehart (1999) has emphasized the importance of democracy without specifying what it is in a democracy that increases social trust (or if it is social trust that generates democracy). Uslaner has suggested that one of the strongest predictors of social trust is economic equality and he also specify how the causal mechanism may operate. First, equality of opportunity increases feelings of optimism because individuals will feel they have a fair chance for improving their situation. Secondly, in societies with high levels of economic inequality there will be less concern for people of different backgrounds. The rich and the poor in a country with a highly unequal distribution of wealth such as, for example, Brazil, may live right next to each other, but their lives do not intersect. Their children attend different schools, they use different health care services (and in many cases, the poor cannot afford either of these services). The rich are protected by both the police and private guards, while the poor see these as their natural enemy. In such societies, neither the rich nor the poor have a sense of shared fate with the other, and this makes both groups stick to their own (Uslaner 2002: 189). The comparatively high levels of social capital in the Scandinavian countries may thus be caused by their extensive policies for economic equality and equality of opportunity.

Associativeness and social capital

The individual and the state are not all there is. Between the individual and state structures exists what is usually called the civil society. The term is not always precisely defined, but usually refers to the myriad of voluntary associations and informal networks that exist to a varying degree in different societies. These associations may have a very strong, formal organization (as with labor unions, employers' organizations, large sports associations, industry associations, and student unions, for example). But they may also have a very loose structure (a neighborhood choral group or a village society, for example). Their linkages to and dependency upon the state establishment may also vary considerably. Theories on the significance of the civil society go back to Alexis de Tocqueville's famous book on *Democracy in America* (1840), in which he stated that the ability of Americans to organize was precisely that which made their republican democracy work. The theory gained credence in analyses of the disintegrating Soviet societies in the 1980s, where every form of voluntary association outside the control of the Communist Party was regarded as an illicit conspiracy against the state and the party (Cohen and Arato 1993).

Robert Putnam's study of Italy showed that the source of social capital was the density and weight of the civil society. The asset he and his research team found critical to whether or not democracy could work flowered in the context of *associativeness*. Socialization in the social networks that were the foundation of choral societies, sport clubs, local unions, and other types of associations, for example, gradually taught individuals the art of overcoming the problem of the social trap. The idea that voluntary associations generate social capital has had a widespread and rapid political impact.

However, the notion of the significance of the civil society and voluntary associations to social capital has suffered three serious reverses. The first is conceptual, in that it has proven impossible to find a working distinction between the kind of organizations that produce social trust and those that produce the opposite. Many voluntary organizations and networks are actually built to instill mistrust of other people in general and of members of other organizations in particular. This does not apply only to obvious cases, such as that members of the Hell's Angels are supposed to mistrust members of the Bandidos and that ardent fans of one sports team are not expected to be particularly fond of the passionate supporters of a rival team. Many voluntary associations are of a religious, political, ethnic, and gender-based nature and their existence is partially based on a *logic of separation* – i.e. establishing distance bordering on mistrust from competing associations or networks. This comprises much of the very nature of human organization. All voluntary associations are not like the parent–teacher association (PTA) or bird watching club; their raison d'être may be criminality or other forms of deviation that hardly generate interpersonal trust (cf. Arias 2002). Margaret Levi has aptly used the distinction of social versus "antisocial" capital (Levi 1996). As a colleague from Bosnia said at a conference in 2002, "our problem has been that we have had too much social capital." That is, many of the people of Bosnia have been involved in social networks that created the hate and mistrust that laid the foundation for discrimination, ethnic cleansing, concentration camps, and murder of civilians. The same can probably be said about Northern Ireland and Israel/Palestine, to take two more examples from the depressing pile.

Sheri Berman has stressed that the Nazi takeover of power was considerably eased by the extensive system of voluntary associations in Germany at the time (Berman 1997). The Nazis were able to infiltrate many of those associations but, more importantly, many organizations voluntarily affiliated with the Nazis and began quickly to purge the non-desirable element. The spring of 1933 saw a very rapid coordination (*Gleichschaltung* in German) of voluntary associations from the top down to the grass roots. In his study of the rise of Hitler and the Third Reich, Ian Kershaw writes that hardly a fraction of local associations remained outside the Nazification process that took place in everything from gardening clubs to choral societies. The result, according to one witnesses, was that "there was no social life; you couldn't even have a bowling club that was not 'coordinated'" (cited in Kershaw 2000: 479). Among the very first voluntary associations that chose to tread the Nazi path were the German student organizations, the culprits behind the infamous book burnings of May 10, 1933 (Friedländer 1999: 322).

The definition of social capital presented here implies that it is connected to the opinion or belief that people can generally trust most other people in the society in which they live (or the organization within which they act) – i.e. generalized or social trust. Involvement in an organization that produces the opposite must then be categorized as a minus item on the social capital balance sheet. The problem cannot be solved by typologizing organizations, as their orientation towards the problem is partially dependent on the prevailing political landscape. An obvious example is the political role of religious organizations. In Putnam's study of Italy, it is shown that religious activity does not produce social capital (1993: 107), while in his study of the United States, the opposite is true (2000: 65–79).

In sum, associativeness may contribute to producing, maintaining, or eroding the social capital of a society. To say that a society like that of Northern Ireland or Bosnia around 1992, or Germany *circa* 1933, had abundant but "dark" social capital does nothing but engender conceptual confusion. Individuals who are socialized in associations to generally mistrust other people in their society and behave, through strategies of social isolation and segregation, in ways that make others mistrust them, cannot be said to possess a large supply of social capital. When the balance sheet of social capital is totted up, the sum of their internal trust and internal social contacts must be reduced by the sum of their external mistrust and lack of external social contacts.

The second problem that Putnam's theory on the origin of social capital has encountered is empirical. It has not been possible to prove any correlation on the individual level between involvement in voluntary associations and high social trust. While the theory has proven almost amazingly robust at the aggregated level, a correlation at the individual level is nowhere to be found. That is, if one finds a city, country, or region with a vibrant network of voluntary associations and abundant social interaction among citizens, it is highly likely that one will also find a reasonably working democracy and a growing economy. The problem, which is very common in the social sciences, is that correlations on the aggregated level prove nothing, since such data preclude any conclusions about causal correlations at the individual level. Correlations at the aggregated, or macro, level can be used only as indicators for where on the micro level a further search might be productive. For a causal correlation to be considered extant, one must prove that it holds also at the micro level. This requires two things – a theory on how social mechanisms at the individual level should be understood and explained, and empirical indicators that support such a theory.

Ascertaining whether this is the case often requires data over time or comparative data and the researchers who have been able to work with such data have determined that the correlation does not exist (Claiborn and Martin 2000; Delhey and Newton 2003; Stolle 2000a; Uslaner 2002; Whiteley 1999; Wollebeak and Selle 2002). For example, one recent large scale empirical study concludes that, "perhaps most important and most surprising, none of the four measures of voluntary activity stood up to statistical rests, in spite of the importance attached to them in a large body of writing, from de Tocqueville onwards" (Delhey and Newton 2004: 27). One example comes from a major survey study in Norway that showed that although it is true that members of voluntary associations state that they have higher social trust than people who are not members, there is no difference at all between active and passive members (Wollebæck, Selle, and Lorentzen 2001). In an analysis based on the *Afrobarometer* survey from ethnically divided countries in West Africa (Ghana and Nigeria), Michelle Kuenzi finds a negative correlation between membership in associations and social trust (Kuenzi 2004). The net conclusion from the empirical research is that associativeness and social networks may very well be a good thing for many reasons, but they do not seem to increase interpersonal trust. The correlation between high associativeness and high social trust that does exist is probably due to a process of self-selection by which the people who are most likely to join and be active in associations or networks are those who are already high trusters, often dating back to their childhood, while associativeness itself does not increase people's inclination to trust others (Stolle 2003). Uslaner asserts instead that trustfulness is instilled through the socialization process in the family that children and adolescents undergo – i.e. in plain English whether or not people are inclined to trust others depends on the image of the surrounding society that parents communicate to their children. However, this is a rather impoverished explanation of how social capital is produced in a society, as those socialization processes do not take place in a social or political void. It is only reasonable to assume that the dissimilarities in views of the surrounding society, its institutions, and its people that parents and others communicate to children were caused by something. The question is just what this might be.

The third problem that the civil society/voluntary associations hypothesis has run into is the following. If civil society produces the kind of beliefs necessary for a stable and working democracy, then newly established democracies should have a strong and vibrant voluntary sector. This is, however, not necessarily the case. In a detailed case study of the processes of democratization in Brazil and Spain, Encarnación shows that neither of these countries rates high on civil society indicators. He shows that that civil society has been overrated as the main source of social capital. Instead of civil society, he points to the importance of "the constitution and political institutions" (2003: 8).

Researchers do not have a monopoly on constructing good hypothesis. Their skill lies (hopefully) elsewhere – i.e. in knowing how hypotheses should be constructed to make it possible to answer the question and what methods exist that can provide reasonably correct answers. Hopefully, they also have some knowledge of the current state of research – i.e. what hypotheses have already been put forward and how well they have survived empirical tests. But social capital, especially its qualitative dimensions, touches upon socio-psychological processes close to all of us that are not particularly easy to grasp. In our hunt for the explanation for variations in social capital, we could of course go in the other direction, i.e., instead of asking what kinds of individuals or social networks produce societies with abundant social capital, we could look at what kind of society produces individuals and networks with high social capital. The truth of the situation may be precisely the opposite of what Robert Putnam, and many in his wake, have proposed. The causal connection may not go from the sociological level (individuals–networks) to the political (the state and its institutions), but rather the reverse. It may be that a particular type of state institution produces individuals and organizations with high (or low) social capital. Now that the nearly organic view of the emergence of social capital triggered by Putnam's work is proving incorrect, there is reason to think along different lines. Maybe it is a particular type of political institution that produces social capital, rather than social capital being produced by a particular type of political institution.

"The Pajala connection"

Some movies and novels have the distinctive quality of being both commercially successful and critically acclaimed. One such novel is Mikael Niemi's *Populärmusik från Vittula* (Popular Music from Vittula), published in 2000. The book has not only sold a nearly incomprehensible (by Swedish standards) 800,000 copies, but is now also becoming an international bestseller.[1] There is a long passage in the book that may shed some light on what the socialization processes that Uslaner identifies might actually be like. Because we are interested in how the causal mechanisms may work, such descriptions are doubtlessly valuable, especially when, as in this case, the author has stated that they are (at least partially) autobiographical. The novel may be characterized as a long description of such a socialization process in Pajala, a town in northernmost Sweden where most of the people are bilingual, speaking Swedish and a special Finnish dialect. The passage I found particularly captivating takes place on a Saturday evening when the father and son as usual take a sauna together.

> On this particular night, though, everything was different. I realized afterwards that Dad had planned it all; there was something in the air. Nervousness. We sat down in the changing room where the washing machine stood in the corner. Mum was in a hurry to get away: it was obvious she wanted to leave us on our own . . . Dad finished off his post-sauna beer, then went over to grog: Koskenkorva schnapps and lemonade . . . Dad cleared his throat, but then said nothing for several minutes . . .
>
> "Anyway, now that you're not a little lad anymore . . ." he eventually started, speaking in Finnish . . .
>
> "I expect you've sometimes wondered . . . asked yourself all sorts of questions . . ."
>
> I glanced at him in astonishment, and could see his jaw muscles throbbing.
>
> "Asked yourself . . . about life . . . about people . . . Now that you're grown a bit older, you ought to know . . ."
>
> He paused, took another swig, and avoided looking at me. He's going to go on about the birds and bees, I thought. Condoms.
>
> "What I'm going to say is just between you and me. Confidential . . . Man to man . . . There are two families in this district that have caused us a lot of harm, and you're going to have to hate them forever and a day. In one case, it all goes back to a perjury suit in 1929 and the other it's got to do with some grazing rights that a neighbor cheated your grandad's father out of in 1902, and both these injustices have to be avenged at all costs, whenever you get the chance, and you must keep going until those bastards have confessed and paid, and also gone down on their bare knees to beg forgiveness."
>
> Dad summarized what had happened over the years. There were summons and counter-summons, false witness, bribery and corruption, fisticuffs, threatening

---

[1] It has received two important literary awards, the 2001 August Prize as well what I consider the considerably more prestigious Fritiof Nilsson Piraten Prize for 2002. The English edition from which this quote is taken is titled *Popular Music* and was published by Harper Perennial in 2003 (trans. Laurie Thompson)

letters, damage to property, attempted blackmail, and on one occasion the kid-napping of a promising elkhound that had its ears branded with a knife, like a reindeer. There was no limit to the outrages these madmen had perpetrated on us, and although we'd exacted as much revenge as we could, we were still a long way in debit. The worst thing was that these families were spreading false propaganda about us and were greatly exaggerating the modest counter-attacks we'd managed to pull off. The upshot was that I'd better be on my guard when I went to dance halls and other public gatherings where vengeance could suddenly leap out of the bushes or from dark corners, with the most terrible consequences.

He named the families, and spelt out all their off-shoots and those who'd mar-ried and sometimes changed their surnames as a result, but whose blood was nevertheless the same poisonous sort as before . . . I committed all this to mem-ory, and Dad then tested me on it as it was important that nothing should be forgotten or forgiven through sheer carelessness. He took another swig or two and did a bit of ranting, then got me to grunt and snort and help him to work out a few crafty plots. He suggested I might like to make a career in for myself in local government, because that put you in a position where you could create merry hell and, even better, they couldn't sack you: if you played your cards right you could exploit a bit of nepotism and get the rest of the clan into positions of authority until it was impossible for these perjurers and land thieves to stay around. (Niemi 2000: 262ff.)

This narrative gives us concrete examples of several interesting theoreti-cal building blocks. We are given a highly believable glimpse into how the kind of socialization processes identified by Uslaner may work. We also get a description of "anti-social" capital generated by families or clans that deeply mistrust each other. The role of memories of "the others'" distrustful and deceitful behavior and how it is transferred from one generation to the other is given a vivid illustration. Most importantly, we are given an illuminating description of how public institutions, by setting aside fundamental lib-eral principles such as equal treatment and impartiality, can help erode the already fragile trust in a society. In their official capacity, city officials in the society that Niemi portrays in his novel can clearly use their power to discriminate against individuals to the point where they would be forced to leave the community.

The state and social capital

This leads us to ask whether social capital is produced by the political sphere, more specifically public institutions. While Putnam's theory offers a soci-ological explanation to how social capital is produced and/or destroyed, it should be added that although his chief interest has been socio-cultural factors such as associativeness and social networks, he has also stressed the possibility that there may be other explanations. He writes that: "the myriad ways in which the state encourages or discourages the formation of social capital have been underresearched" (Putnam 2002: 17). There are also passages in his book about Italy that points at the importance of political and institutional variables (1993: 159, 165ff.). However, the main theme in research about social capital and social trust has been that "states destroy the social cohesion of traditional communities, undermine cooperation, and destroy trust among individuals" (Levi 1998b: 81f., cf. Herrero 2004: 72).

However, states can be of diverse natures and they encompass many different institutions. Some things stand out instantly even upon hasty inspection of the data – high social trust is associated with *stable democracy* (Inglehart 1999), little *corruption* (della Porta 2000) and a *low degree of economic inequality* (Uslaner 2002). Societies that want high social capital need only create those conditions. Oil-rich Nigeria could simply decide to establish the same political institutions found in equally oil-rich Norway, to give one example. We will return to the subject of opportunities for institutional change later, but there is reason to try and discover how the causal mechanisms between public institutions and social trust work. We could reverse the argument and say that in societies with undemocratic and corrupt institutions, the oppressed peoples choose to enclose themselves in solidaristic networks in which they develop trust in their fellow humans, but any such correlation cannot be found, either in the comparison of survey data from different countries or in analyses of, for example, societies in the former Soviet Union (Sztompka 1998).

Many survey studies of public trust in political institutions such as government administration, political parties, and parliament are being made in various countries today. The main finding of this research has been that there is no strong correlation between political trust, defined as trust in democratic institutions, and social trust. We find a clear example in Sweden, where public trust in the political institutions listed above has declined rather dramatically since the mid-1980s, while social trust remains at a high and stable level (Rothstein 2002). Apparently, people's trust in parliament, political parties, and government can decline without affecting their trust in other people. This has led many researchers to conclude that there is no causal connection showing that trust in democratic institutions produces social trust and social capital (Newton 1999a).

However, from a causal mechanism perspective, it is difficult to see why such a connection should exist in the first place. Politics in representative democracy is by nature partisan and interest-driven. Political parties and political majorities believe that promoting their own programs, which often entails supporting the interests of particular groups, is one of their main tasks. Representational politics is by nature partisan, and if you are not supporting the party in power, there is no reason why "trust in government" should have an impact on your trust in other people. If I, as an individual, consider myself a member of the political majority that is currently in control of my city or my country, I have reason to feel confidence in the government administration and parliament (or the city council). But if I belong to the political minority, the opposite should occur – i.e. I have reason to mistrust the administration, the parliament, or the city council (cf. Norén 2002). It is difficult to find any conceivable logic as to why these conditions should affect my trust in other people in the least. The causal mechanisms are, to put it delicately, not particularly well specified in this line of research on the meaning of social capital.

However, the institutions of the democratic state are not limited to the representative side of politics. They are joined by the comprehensive and numerous political institutions whose mandate is to implement policy – i.e. the administrative side of the democratic establishment (Rose-Ackerman, 2001 329]. The impact of these institutions on how democracy works and its legitimacy is often, as Lundquist (1996, 2000) has asserted in numerous works, gravely underestimated. In modern welfare states, administrative institutions encompass everything from law enforcement to courts to unemployment offices, public health care, social services offices, and public schools. These institutions are vital to the legitimacy of the political system for two reasons. Their actions *vis-à-vis* citizens can often be of an exceedingly interventionist nature and crucial to their welfare. It may be distressing if members of parliament from one's own constituency do not adequately represent one's opinions (or one's gender, ethnicity, social class, sexual orientation, etc.), but nothing that is immediately and palpably deleterious or dangerous to one's welfare is likely to occur. If on the other hand judges, doctors, teachers, policemen, etc. act unethically and/or incompetently, things may occur that are immediately and seriously disagreeable to the individual. His children may be mercilessly bullied or discriminated; if he is ill he may suffer unnecessarily or even die; and he may be convicted of a crime despite his innocence, etc.

In most societies, the public also has much more frequent contact with the administrative institutions of democracy than with the representative institutions. This is especially true in comprehensive welfare states where both the extent of public policy and its impact have increased. In the Nordic type of welfare state, people leave their children in public daycare centers and hope to get them back relatively unharmed, they entrust large portions of their income to a social insurance system and hope to get the benefits they have been promised when they retire, become ill, or unemployed. The policy implementation side of democracy is thus in many ways more central to the welfare of citizens than the representative side. As Staffan Kumlin (2004) has shown, citizens' direct experiences of how they have been treated by different public service institutions have a considerable impact on their political views and ideological orientations. Compared to the individual's economic situation, the impact of experiences from social service institutions is of greater importance for the formation of political opinions.

The task of administrative institutions is actually, in concrete and specific terms, to supply citizens with their democratic and social rights. Accordingly, they are more closely connected to the aspect of democratic theory that has to do with ensuring liberty and civil rights than to democracy as an aggregation of preferences. One thing that makes these institutions trustworthy is precisely the opposite of partisanship, namely impartiality (Levi 1998b: 91; Offe 1999: 74; Rothstein and Stolle 2003).[2] Impartiality implies fairness in procedures and no corruption, clientilism, nepotism or discrimination.

What we have here is a contradiction within the institutions of the democratic state that I believe is both interesting and undertheorized (cf. Zakaria 2003). While the main idea of the representative aspect of democracy is partisanship – i.e. the objective is to ensure the implementation of the political majority's programs the implementation itself must be impartial. That is, there is nothing to stop the political majority from choosing to favor certain groups (families with children, farmers, senior citizens, union members, small business owners) when formulating a policy, but when the policy is to be implemented, impartiality as one component of the rule of law implies that individual citizens must be treated according to the principles of equality before the law. A political majority may pass reform legislation in order to, for example, benefit families with children as a group, but according to the constitution, no individual family may be accorded special treatment when the reform is implemented.

Upon initial review of the SOM Institute's data on trends in political trust in Sweden, we find that there could be a correlation between confidence in policy administration and social trust. The reason is that the sharp decline in trust in representative political institutions since the mid-1980s lacks any equivalent with respect to administrative institutions. The main tendency has been that trust in administrative institutions is high or very high and rather stable, *coinciding with high and stable social trust.* Table 5.1 shows data from the SOM Institute's 2000 survey that measured trust in social institutions.

---

[2] In the Swedish Constitution, which dates from 1974, this is stated in the following way: "Courts, public authorities and others performing functions within the public administration shall observe in their work the equality of all persons before the law and shall maintain objectivity and impartiality" (chapter 1, article 9).

Table 5.1. *Trust in social institutions in Sweden, 2000 (percent)*

Institution	Very great	Fairly great	Neither great nor little	Rather little	Very little	Total percent	Balance measurement
Public universities	8	46	39	5	2	100	+ 47
Public health care	14	46	25	12	3	100	+ 45
Police	8	45	30	13	4	100	+ 39
Courts	9	38	37	12	4	100	+ 31
Primary school system	5	35	38	14	5	100	+ 26
Parliament	4	27	44	18	7	100	+7
The cabinet	4	27	41	21	7	100	+3
City council	2	17	47	25	9	100	−15
Unions	2	18	41	27	17	100	−19
Political parties	1	14	45	28	12	100	−25
European Parliament	1	10	38	25	25	100	−39

Source: National SOM survey (2003). The table shows results from the two national SOM surveys performed in 2000 (number of responses = 3,546). The balance measure ranges from 100 (if all respondents answer "very great") to −100 (if all respondents answer "very little").

As table 5.1 shows, there is a large "trust gap" between the five implementing institutions in the upper half of the table and the six representative institutions ranked below them. While, for example, 60 percent state that they have "very great" or "fairly great" trust in the health care system, the corresponding figure for the political parties is only 20 percent. Only 7 percent say that they mistrust universities and colleges, while a full 40 percent say that they mistrust political parties. Even trust in the police and the courts is much higher than trust in political parties and unions. Trust in the implementing organizations remains high or relatively high, even when respondents are asked about the occupational categories (doctors, health care personnel, teachers, policemen *et al.*) that populate them, and the difference compared to politicians and political consultants is very high here as well (Holmberg and Weibull 2004). The question thus becomes: Is there any correlation between trusting social institutions and trusting other people? The

Table 5.2. *Correlations between social trust and trust in social institutions, 1996–1999*

Institution	1999	1998	1997	1996	Mean value 1996–1999
Courts	0.20	0.19	0.22	0.18	0.20
Parliament	0.23	0.22	0.19	0.15	0.20
Police	0.21	0.19	0.18	0.18	0.19
Health care system	0.17	0.20	0.21	0.16	0.18
Government (cabinet/ministries)	0.21	0.18	0.19	0.12	0.17
Municipal executive board	0.19	0.18	0.20	0.13	0.15
Primary school system	0.14	0.15	0.11	0.10	0.12
Daily newspapers	0.13	0.14	0.12	0.07	0.11
Swedish church	0.11	0.11	0.13	0.10	0.11
Royal house	0.13	0.11	0.08	0.10	0.10
Big business	0.10	0.12	0.11	0.08	0.10
Radio/TV	0.10	0.11	0.08	0.10	0.10
Unions	0.10	0.09	0.12	0.08	0.10
Banks	0.11	0.07	0.06	0.05	0.09
Armed forces	0.11	0.11	0.08	0.08	0.07

Source: National SOM surveys (1996, 1997, 1998, 1999). N varies between 1,707 for 1996 and 2,586 for 1999. For further information on the design of the surveys, statistical decline, etc., see the reports for each year from the SOM Institute.

question on social trust has been asked in the SOM Institute's annual surveys since 1996, along with questions about the extent to which people have trust in social institutions. Table 5.2 shows the correlations (Pearson's r) between these measurements.

The measurement used (Pearson's r) can technically range from $+1$ to -1. As I interpret the results, the correlations between social trust and trust in institutions are all weak. However, all sixty correlations are in the expected direction – i.e. they are weakly positive, as the theory of social capital predicts. The more trust people have in political and administrative institutions, the more they are inclined to feel social trust in their fellow human beings, or the reverse: the more people believe that other people can generally be trusted, the more they trust in social institutions. The third conclusion is that the results from the measurements taken in different years are surprisingly stable. The fourth and perhaps most interesting result from our perspective is that the relationship between social trust and trust in the courts and police – i.e. what is usually called the rule of law – is one of the least weak correlations.

I must admit this surprised me at first. Why should people with high trust in other people feel any particular confidence in the police and the courts? And how should we understand the causal mechanisms between these two beliefs? According to Putnam, there is no reason to expect that the legal system has a positive effect on social capital (Putnam 2000: 136). Societies that rely heavily on the use of force do not have a large stock of social capital.

However, contrary to Putnam, I think that it is possible to argue why societies where trust in the legal institutions is high would also have higher levels of social capital. This argument has three steps. First, legal institutions have a special task compared to other government institutions, namely to track down and punish people who have committed acts that make them undeserving of our trust. Secondly, if most people believe that these institutions perform that task effectively and fairly, they also have reason to think that most other people are of the same belief.[3] Accordingly, it is reasonable to conclude that most people refrain from treacherous behavior because they believe that the legal machinery will find and punish them. Logically, as a result it is reasonable to think that most people can be trusted, which is likely to increase the amount of reciprocal relations. This can also be phrased in game theoretic terminology: a state that is efficient in finding and punishing free riders will create not only trust in government, but trust in other citizens as well, simply because there will be fewer citizens who choose to take a free ride (Levi 1998b: 90f.).

Further analysis of data from the SOM Institute and the World Values Study shows that this might be the case. Table 5.3 shows an analysis of survey data from the World Values Study conducted in Sweden and sixty other countries.

What emerges from this analysis is that, as far as Sweden is concerned, trust in the legal system and the belief that bribe taking and corruption are uncommon have significant impact on interpersonal trust, even when we control for respondents' level of educational. However, factors such as activity in voluntary associations, "happiness," interest in politics, and subjectively perceived health are not significant – i.e. control for the rule of law variables eliminates the effect of those factors. The results are more mixed for the total survey of sixty-one countries, but the variable that has the greatest effect on trust in other people is the belief about whether bribe taking and corruption are widespread.

The results found using data from the World Values Survey can be validated to a surprisingly great extent by the SOM Institute's survey of people

---

[3] Game theoreticians commonly use the expression "opportunistic behavior," which I think is a far too benign term for describing the phenomenon.

Table 5.3. *Trust in others according to World Values Survey, 1995–1997 (world and Sweden)*

Dependent variable:
Trust in others:

[spanname = "2to3"]

Independent variables	World Value data		Swedish data	
	Bivariate regression b	Multivariate regression b (sign)	Bivariate regression b	Multivariate regression b (sign)
Education (9-point scale)	0.222	0.034 (0.000)	0.434	0.244 (0.001)
Interest in politics (4-point)	0.122	0.100 (0.000)	0.187	0.088 (0.127)
Activity in associations (3-point)	0.075	0.059 (0.000)	0.120	0.037 (0.491)
How widespread do you think bribe taking and corruption is in this country? (4-point)	0.217	0.176 (0.000)	0.369	0.251 (0.000)
Trust in the legal system (4-point)	0.100	0.067 (0.000)	0.452	0.313 (0.000)
Happiness? (10-point)	0.000	0.002 (0.267)	−0.007	−0.013 (0.638)
General state of health? (5-point)	0.144	0.106 (0.000)	0.262	0.105 (0.165)
N		56 204		906
Constant		−0.013 (0.071)		0.046 (0.589)
F		316		13.0
R^2		0.038		0.085

Notes: The "World" category includes the sixty-one countries or regions in which World Values Survey interviews were held. The Swedish part of the study was performed by TEMO in cooperation with Thorleif Pettersson of Uppsala University. All variables in the models are coded between 0 and 1 so that the *b* values in the table can be read as percentages. I would like to express my gratitude to Professor Thorleif Petterson, who was kind enough to put these data at my disposal.

Table 5.4. *Multivariate analysis of interpersonal trust*

Dependent variable: Independent variables:	[spanname = "2to3"] Generalized trust in others, 0–10 scale	
	B	*(sign)*
Education	0.038	(0.006)
Interest in politics	–	–
Income bracket	–	–
Involvement in associations	0.028	(0.000)
TV index	0.123	(0.000)
Trust in the police	0.060	(0.020)
Trust in legal professions	0.110	(0.000)
Trust in the rule of law	0.193	(0.000)
N	**1,692**	
Constant	**0.261**	**(0.000)**
F	**32.8**	
$R^2 =$	**0.131**	

Source: Western SOM (2000). For information about data collection and study method, see Nilsson (2002).

living in western Sweden, in which respondents were asked specific questions about their trust in the institutions of the rule of law (table 5.4).

Here also, the results show that variables related to the rule of law have greater explanatory power than education and involvement in associations with respect to how much people state that they trust others, while interest in politics and income bracket are not significant. On the other hand, the results tend to show that how often people watch television has a relatively strong but negative impact on social trust.

As shown above, the idea that citizens are able to differentiate between the representational and the implementation side of the democratic system is confirmed. This implies that one should not conflate these into one "trust in government" variable because people do not tar all public officials with the same brush. This means that in analyzing the relationship between social trust and how the democracy works, we must disaggregate the concept of political trust: there is a considerable difference between how citizens view their elected representatives versus public officials appointed according to some kind of impartial assessment of their merits. Trust in the representative side is low, but trust in the implementation side is high. This is in itself a not entirely insignificant problem for democratic theory: the public officials whom the people have elected and can vote out of office enjoy considerably

Table 5.5. *Factor analysis of dimensions in institutional trust*

	Component 1	2	3
	Trust in representative institutions	Trust in implementing institutions	Trust in control institutions
Government (cabinet and ministries)	**0.876**	0.161	50.411E-02
Parliament	**0.874**	0.204	0.100
Municipal executive boards	**0.672**	0.254	0.191
Police	0.198	**0.733**	50.239E-02
Health care system	80.773E-02	**0.743**	30.442E-02
Armed forces	0.159	**0.625**	70.120E-02
Primary school system	0.130	**0.527**	0.287
Courts	0.353	**0.531**	0.156
Daily newspapers	0.145	90.247E-02	**0.815**
Radio/TV	90.033E-02	0.153	**0.833**

Note: Principal component analysis (PCA). Rotation method: Varimax with Kaiser's normalization.
Source: Rothstein and Stolle 2002; data from National SOM surveys (1996–2000).

less trust than the officials who cannot be voted into or out of office. We will return to this problem later.

A more advanced analysis of this dimension can be done by exploiting the opportunity to combine SOM surveys from several years to arrive at a very high number of respondents (approx. 12,000). Table 5.5 shows a factor analysis of data from the five years 1996–2000, aimed at discovering whether there is a correlation in such a way that positive versus negative opinions on trust in institutions are connected in separate opinion dimensions in the respondents. That is, whether those who have high trust in, for example, the police also have high trust in the courts, but not in the government and parliament, and vice versa. The division is between *implementing* institutions, *representative* institutions, and *control* ("watchdog") institutions.

The results of the factor analysis show clearly that we are dealing with different cognitive dimensions of political trust among Swedish citizens. Those who trust some *implementing* political institutions probably trust the others as well. If people trust, for example, the courts and the armed forces, they probably also trust the police and the health care system. However, the likelihood is not nearly as great that they for that reason trust the media or parliament and government administration.

Table 5.6. *Correlations between social trust and trust in social institutions*

		Social trust
Representative institutions	Pearson's r	0.170
	N	12,629
Implementing institutions	Pearson's r	**0.201**
	N	12,629
Watchdog institutions (media)	Pearson's r	0.078
	N	12,629

Note: All correlations significant at the 0.01 level.
Source: Rothstein & Stolle 2002; data from National SOM surveys (1996–2000).

One further question is: what kind of impact does this large data material have with respect to the correlation between trust in these different types of political institutions and trust in other people? The results of these correlations are shown in table 5.6.

The correlations are based this time on statements from more than 12,000 respondents, and show that there is a stronger connection between social trust and trust in implementing institutions than between social trust and trust in representative or control institutions.

Answers to the question about social trust in SOM Institute studies have remained stable over the years (see chapter 4), making it possible to combine the data from multiple years in order to reach a considerably larger number of respondents. In so doing, we reach an *n* of more than 12,000 respondents for the years 1996–2001, which allows us to control for a substantially larger number of variables. In the theoretical discussion, thirty-two independent variables were thought able to influence individual social trust. After performing a multiple regression analysis controlled for all thirty-two, only trust in the courts and the level of education attained by individuals remained statistically significant.[4]

To summarize this far, a fairly unambiguous result emerges from these various survey studies – i.e. that there is a positive correlation between how people perceive the functions of administration, particularly legal institutions, and the extent to which they believe other people can generally be trusted. The correlation we have found in the Swedish data is also found

---

[4] For reasons of space, the tables are not shown here but are available from the author (Bo.Rothstein@pol.gu.se).

in other countries: a comprehensive work including survey and historical data from between sixty and 140 countries shows that the level of social trust in different countries covaries positively with the efficiency of the legal institutions in those countries, whether measures to fight corruption had been taken, and with the quality of public administration (La Porta *et al.* 1997: 336). The question is how we might be able to determine how the connection between the two beliefs is constructed and conceivably congruent. Once again, I want to emphasize that this search for causal mechanics is not a matter of finding another intermediate variable that might increase the explained variance in the regression analyses. Instead, this must be resolved theoretically. We know the correlation exists, but we must specify a credible theory for why it may be that trust in other people is dependent on trust in state bureaucracies, particularly legal institutions. We must once again employ the more insightful picture of human behavior that culture can provide. In this case, we shall take ourselves to the promised land of the cinema, Hollywood.

Francis Ford Coppola's *The Godfather* and the question of trust

There is a kind of cultural arrogance among many Scandinavians that can be rather irritating in discussions concerning the problems of corruption and social trust. The basic premise in such discussions is often that the lack of trust in others and in public political institutions, and the occurrence of corruption, should be understood as resulting from a cultural legacy, or something that is "in the nature" of certain peoples or nations but foreign to Swedes or Scandinavians. I question this line of reasoning for many reasons, including that this kind of primordial or culturally essentialist reasoning often lacks empirical capacity. With respect to the Swedish state administration, we can, for example, go back to political scientist Gunnar Heckscher's classic work from 1952 about the Swedish public administration, where he writes that "at the dawn of the 19th century, Swedish state administration was actually rather in decay" (Hecksher 1952: 18). Noteworthy among Heckscher's examples of this decay was the practice of holding and thus severely mismanaging multiple offices at the same time and the existence of widespread corruption. Purchase of official posts and circumvention of rules to benefit private interests were common in Swedish state administration at the time, when public offices were regarded as a kind of personal reward that office holders could use to feather their own nests to the best of their ability (Rothstein 1998b).

To illustrate the point, we can look at the opening scene of Francis Ford Coppola's cinematic masterpiece, *The Godfather*. In a recent poll, the National Society of Film Critics in the United States ranked it the most important film of the twentieth century, ahead of masterpieces such as *Citizen Kane, Gone With the Wind, Schindler's List, Casablanca, The Promised Land*, and *A Clockwork Orange*.

The Godfather can be put in a class of its own for many reasons, not least among them the purely artistic qualities of Coppola's creation.[5] However, this film may also have important things to tell us about what it means to be a human being, about core issues such as family loyalties, immigration and social exclusion, multiculturalism, the patriarchy, society, and the eternal questions about the nature of good and evil. The two main characters in the film appear at once to be caring fathers and cold-blooded murderers, absolutely loyal friends, and men capable of the most ruthless treachery. "I also made them out to be good guys . . . except that they committed murder once in a while," said scriptwriter Mario Puzo in a filmed interview shown before the movie in the new widescreen video edition. This film (or the three films of the *Godfather* trilogy, to be correct) can probably be analyzed in countless ways, but from my perspective, *The Godfather* is first and foremost a story about trust.

Trust, writes the Polish sociologist Piotr Sztompka, may be defined as a "bet on the future contingent actions of others" (Sztompka 1998: 20). When we decide to trust an individual or an institution, we are not completely certain what is going to happen – i.e. if the person or institution is going to live up to our trust and in fact prove trustworthy. That is why we differentiate between "blind faith" and trust. Even if we do not sit down and perform a probability analysis of the risks that our trust will be abused every time we decide to trust someone, there is usually an element, however small, of uncertainty. If we were entirely sure that someone was trustworthy, we would have no need for a word such as "trust".

The very first scene in the first film of Coppola's trilogy can illustrate this problem. The first sentence spoken is: "I believe in America," by the pitiful undertaker Amerigo Bonasera, a man who emigrated from Sicily and has found fortune and happiness in America, the land of opportunity. But now, he has been hit by a great misfortune, as his daughter is in the hospital recovering from a grievous assault. A couple of "all-American" boys tried to rape her and when she, to the not inconsiderable pride of her father, defended her "honor," they beat her to a pulp "like an animal," he relates during his audience in the Godfather's office. Bonasera wanted to be a real American and had allowed his daughter to socialize with the young men without a chaperon from the family. Between the lines, we understand that

---

[5] I also agree with Mårten Blomkvist, film critic for *Dagens Nyheter*, that Tom Hagen's character is grossly underestimated. See *Dagens Nyheter*, October 23, 1997: B1.

the two young men are not from the Italian immigrant community: they are White Anglo-Saxon Protestant Americans – "WASPs."

This kind of situation can be managed in various ways, but since our man Bonasera *believed in America*, he went to the police "like a good American" to get justice and not to the local Don, as he would have in the old country. There are many analyses as to why it is not a good idea to rely on the Sicilian police in cases such as this. I believe one of the best to be found in literature is Frank Viviano's *Blood Washes Blood* (Viviano 2001). Anyway, what Bonasera believed in America was that the authorities could help him, ensure justice, and redress the wrong done to his family and his daughter.[6]

He tells the Godfather – Don Corleone – that he went to the police, who arrested the youths and investigated what had happened in accordance with the law. So far, everything seems to have gone according to the poor man's expectations. But once the perpetrators were put on trial, things went astray. It turned out that they were given only suspended sentences due, we understand from the subtext, to their backgrounds and connections. They sneer at the unfortunate Bonasera when they are immediately released and can leave the court with no further consequences. So now the despairing and deeply offended Bonasera is sitting with Don Corleone and asking him to give him justice, because his trust in the American legal system has been breached.

But the Godfather is irritated with his old friend. "Why did you go to the police? Why didn't you come to me first?" he asks. The matter would have been dealt with immediately, he assures him. But he is also displeased because Bonasera has avoided him for many years and rejected his "friendship." Don Corleone says to Bonasera: "We've known each other many years, but this is the first time you came to me for counsel, for help. I can't remember the last time that you invited me to your house for a cup of coffee, even though my wife is godmother to your only child. But let's be frank here: you never wanted my friendship. And uh, you were afraid to be in my debt." "I didn't want to get into trouble," says Bonasera delicately. "I understand," says Don Corleone. "You found paradise in America, had a good trade, made a good living. The police protected you; and there were courts of law" and he makes it clear that he wonders how in the world his old friend could have been so incurably gullible to have trusted in the impartiality and honesty of those institutions. The idea that a Catholic immigrant family from Sicily would get a fair trial in a court dominated by WASP Americans

---

[6] Mario Puzo's novel, on which the film is based, begins with the words: "Amerigo Bonasera sat in New York Criminal Court Number 3 and waited for justice; vengeance on the men who had so cruelly hurt his daughter, who had tried to dishonor her."

whose roots probably went all the way back to the *Mayflower* seems absurd to him, especially because he has a number of judges and politicians on his "payroll" to help with the sundry matters upon which assistance might be needed in the kind of business run by the Corleone family.

Don Corleone gets even more irritated when Bonasera offers him money to have the two youths murdered. He feels insulted to be seen only as a simple criminal who murders for money. And he tells Bonasera "That is not justice; your daughter is still alive." It emerges that what the Godfather wants in return for administering "justice" is not money, but Bonasera's trust and loyalty. "Had you come to me in friendship," he says, "then this scum that ruined your daughter would be suffering this very day. And that by chance if an honest man such as yourself should make enemies, then they would become *my* enemies. And then they would fear you." It is only when Bonasera bows to him, calls him Godfather, and submissively asks to be allowed to be his "friend," that Corleone "takes on the case" by ordering one of his *capos* to see to it that both of the youths are crippled as punishment. Corleone then speaks the crucial words of the scene, telling Bonasera that he should regard this as an act of friendship and that some day he may call upon him to do a service for him (and that day comes, but that is another story).

We can conclude a number of things from this remarkable scene. One is that Bonasera and his family stop being generalized trusters and instead become particularized trusters, to use Eric Uslaner's terms. They will no longer believe that they can "trust people in general," but rather that they can trust only their own small and socially homogeneous ethnic group. They will no longer look at the future with optimism and believe that they can shape their own lives. They will begin mistrusting most political and legal institutions and believe that those institutions are structured to stack the deck against them.

The logic in this pivotal scene in *The Godfather* is that the scarcity of social capital that plagues Sicily and many other parts of the world comes about when people do not believe that they can trust the political institutions, and especially not those that have to do with the legal system. As Diego Gambetta, one of the most highly regarded specialists on this problem, writes, it is hardly irrational to acquire protection from the mafia in a situation like this (Gambetta 1988: 173). The unfortunate Bonasera actually does not have much of a choice when the institutions he trusted have so blatantly betrayed him. One kind of trust is replaced with another, but this should not be seen as some kind of moral defect among the individuals who live in these societies, nor as a defect in their culture. If people cannot trust that public officials will act according to norms such as impartiality, objectivity, incorruptibility, and non-discrimination, they cannot trust "people in general" either.

The critical importance of credible public institutions was illustrated by an article on measures to fight the criminal culture of the Mafia published by the Italian special prosecutor Paolo Borsellino in 1989, a couple of years before July 19th, 1989, when he was blown to bits by the Sicilian mafia shortly after the murder of another renowned mafia prosecutor in Palermo (Giovanni Falcone). Borsellino wrote:

> The removal of the causes that constitute the strength of Cosa Nostra can only be accomplished by the restoration of faith in public administration. No influx of financial resources, however massive, will produce beneficial effects if the State and the institutions in general are not able and do not appear to be impartial holders and distributors of the trust necessary for the free and orderly progression of civil life. Otherwise the recourse to alternative organizations that ensure materialistic advantages will continue and the consensus around them, whether expressed or passive, will continue. (Quoted from Jamieson 2000: 127)

An attempt to clarify the causal mechanism

We are approaching a conclusion in our hunt for the causal mechanism: social capital can be both produced and destroyed when the state organizes the public institutions intended to implement public policy. It should be repeated that by "causal mechanisms", I mean the property that is actually in the change of the x variable that causes the change in the y variable. This is a matter of identifying the kind of personal experiences and/or general information that can change how much people trust other people according to the analysis presented in chapter 2. I propose a three-part causal mechanism based on people making three different inferences:

1. *The inference from public officials.* If public officials in a society are known for being partial or corrupt, citizens will believe that even people whom the law requires to act in the service of the public cannot be trusted. They will therefore conclude that *most other people cannot be trusted either.*

2. *The inference from people in general.* Citizens will be able to see that most people in a society with partial or corrupt officials must take part in corruption, bribery, and various forms of nepotism in order to obtain what they feel their rightful due. They will therefore conclude that *most other people cannot be trusted.*

3. *The inference from oneself.* In order to act in such a society, citizens must, even though they may consider it morally wrong, also begin to take part in bribery, corruption, and nepotism. They will therefore conclude that since they cannot themselves be trusted, *other people cannot generally be trusted either.*

The causal mechanisms specified here imply that individuals, in the method-ical language of the social sciences, make an inference from the information they have about how their worlds work. This information need not be cor-rect, of course, but individuals have no other choice than to act on the information to which they in fact have access. The first clarification implies that individuals think something like this: If it proves that I cannot trust the local police, judges, teachers, and doctors, then whom in this society can I trust? The ethics of public officials become central here, not only with respect to how they do their jobs, but also to the signals they send to citizens about what kind of "game" is being played in the society.

The two following clarifications are logical outcomes of the first. People draw personal conclusions from the actions they observe in others – and they also draw conclusions in the other direction: "To know oneself is to know others." The process identified here puts the spotlight on what socio-psychological research calls *procedural justice*. This research has shown that people do not care only about the final result of personal interaction with public institutions (I was granted a benefit, I was convicted in court, am I happy with the daycare center). They are often at least equally interested in whether the procedure that eventually led to the final result may be con-sidered fair (Lind and Tyler 1997). There are many aspects of procedural justice: Whether one has been treated with respect and dignity, whether one has been able to express one's opinion to the responsible officials throughout the process, and a great deal else (Tyler 1998). Another aspect of procedural justice commonly noted has to do with whether people have been treated in the same way as everybody else in relation to existing regulations and stan-dard practice. A positive correlation has been shown between how people perceive procedural justice and the absence of things such as discrimina-tion, partiality, nepotism, corruption, bribery, and patronage (Rothstein and Stolle 2003, cf. Uslaner 2004).

How do people react when they feel that they have not been treated equally in personal contacts with the programs and agencies of the welfare state? Staffan Kumlin (2004) has shown that there is a correlation between beliefs about procedural justice in the context of interaction with the institutions of the welfare state and generalized political trust, operationalized through survey questions concerning "trust in politicians" and "content with democ-racy" (Kumlin 2004).

Needs-testing, universalism, and social capital

As corruption is not a prominent feature of Swedish society, it is no simple matter to determine how an empirical test of the linkage between public administrative institutions and social capital can be examined. This would be true even if we had empirical material from countries where corruption is rampant, simply because the validity of the answers obtained in survey studies is probably too low to be useful. By the very nature of the subject, it is impossible to get people to honestly answer questions about whether they usually take or give bribes. However, experiences of bald-faced corruption are not the only reason that citizens may begin mistrusting public agencies. More generally, we can ask how interaction between citizens and public institutions can be designed in order to as far as possible uphold the principle of equal treatment and prevent suspicion of discrimination and cheating. As one alternative, I will begin with the distinction between *selective* and *universal* forms of public service (Rothstein 1998a). Selective public service is allocated to individuals only following individual needs-testing. The citizen must meet a number of more or less specific conditions to gain access to a program. These conditions may be of a financial nature, as with social assistance (cash benefits) and housing subsidies, but may also be related to the individual's health or capacity to care for herself (disability pensions, various forms of elder care, or different types of labor market policy measures).

Needs-testing puts heavy demands on both the public worker and the citizen who is applying for financial assistance or other service. The bureaucrat must actively interpret general regulations and apply them to the individual who is seeking access to a public service. The difficulty lies in the regulations, which are rarely so precise that they provide clear-cut guidance towards the right decision in an individual case. To manage this difficulty, "street-level bureaucrats" must develop personal interpretive structures, as Michael Lipsky shows in his book *Street-Level Bureaucracy* (1980). This interpretive structure is often of an informal and less explicated nature. As a result, the bureaucrats carrying out the needs-testing process can easily be suspected of applying "prejudice, stereotype, and ignorance as a basis for determination" (Lipsky 1980: 69). In this situation, the citizen is given the incentive and the opportunity to withhold relevant information from the bureaucrat and to try by various means to persuade her that she should be given access to the program in question. Soss (2000: 46) writes of needs-tested benefits in the United States through Aid to Families with Dependent Children (AFDC):

> The act of welfare claiming, especially in a public assistance program, can be mortifying. The degraded identity it conveys can effectively strip individuals of full and equal community membership.

For these reasons, needs-testing and bureaucratic discretionary power are often more difficult to combine with the principle of equal treatment than is the case in public service programs with universal access. Because selective welfare institutions must examine each case individually, they are more vulnerable to suspicions of cheating, arbitrariness, and discrimination than are universal public programs. Research on public support and legitimacy of various welfare programs has clearly shown that selective programs fare less well in those respects than universal programs (Svallfors 1996). My argument is based on the premise that selective, needs-tested public programs stimulate suspicions of cheating and arbitrary treatment more readily than do universal programs, and that information about equal treatment and cheating within public agencies affect how citizens estimate the trustworthiness of public workers and other people in general. These assumptions give rise to two hypotheses on needs-testing, universalism, and social capital. First, if the assumptions are true, we may suspect that people with many personal experiences of selective, needs-testing welfare institutions will demonstrate lower interpersonal trust than others. And, conversely, people with many personal experiences of universal, non-needs-testing institutions will evince higher interpersonal trust than others. As shown in figure 5.1, such an assumption can be confirmed by survey data.

We see here that people who are the target of selective measures such as determining eligibility for social assistance and disability pensions have significantly lower trust in other people than the rest of the population. We also see that having been granted sick pay, which is a general benefit, does not affect trust in other people to any significant extent.

The same result emerges from a research that Staffan Kumlin and I carried out which was based on the survey performed by the SOM Institute in the West Götaland region of Sweden (Kumlin and Rothstein 2002, 2005). In that study, respondents were asked to state whether they had dealt with any of the following selective welfare institutions: housing subsidy, subsidized transportation, disability pension, assistance to people with disabilities, elder care, and the employment office/labor market policy measures. A variable was created to record with how many of those institutions each respondent had recently interacted. The difference between those who had had no contact with selective institutions and those who had interacted with two or more such institutions was one step on the scale of 0–10 used to measure interpersonal trust. Initially, this was not particularly surprising, as people who have frequent dealings with selective welfare institutions often also have other characteristics that according to research apply to "low trusters," such as low income and low education. In order to find out whether contact with needs-testing institutions had an independent effect, this was tested in a multiple regression analysis in which the effect of many of the other variables could be controlled. The interesting point as far as we are concerned was that the negative effect on social trust caused by interactions with needs-testing institutions remained (was statistically significant) when the test was controlled for the following variables: age, level of education,

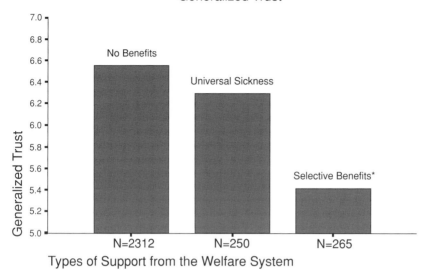

Figure 5.1. Universal and selective benefits and generalized trust, 2000
Source: National SOM survey, 2000, from Rothstein and Stolle 2003.
Note: "Selective benefits" refers to people who have been granted social assistance (cash benefits) and disability pensions.

class affiliation, income, extent of activity in the civil society, interest in politics, general happiness, political ideology (left–right), and job market status (employed or unemployed). Dietlind Stolle and I were able to confirm the principal aspects of this result in a joint analysis of data material from the 2000 National SOM survey (Rothstein and Stolle 2003).

The questions asked in the western Sweden survey also made it possible to test whether citizens' beliefs about how they had been treated by various welfare institutions affected how much they trusted other people. Again, the data showed that a belief that one had been treated well by most of those administrations had significant positive effects on trust in other people (Kumlin and Rothstein 2002, 2005).

Our results are replicated in a couple of other studies. For example, drawing on World Value Study data from twenty-five countries, Letki (2003) finds that the extent to which citizens are trustworthy and law-abiding is not affected by the extent to which people live in a context marked by a vibrant civil society. Rather, what seems to matter is the extent to which central elements of democratic and bureaucratic institutions are perceived to perform well, as well as on the extent to which institutions perform well as measured by "objective" indicators. Letki (2003: 21) thus concludes that "the trustworthiness of efficient institutions influences individuals' attitudes and behaviour". In a study based on data from sixty countries, Delhey and Newton (2004) conclude that "government, especially corruption free and democratic government, seems to set a structure in which individuals are able to act in a trustworthy manner and not suffer, and in which they reasonably expect that most others will generally do the same (2004: 28). They also report that none of the four different measures they use for assessing activity in voluntary associations had a significant effect on social trust.

On the implications of origin, and other conclusions

There is thus significant empirical support for the importance of institutions in creating social trust in general, and in particular the notion that personal experiences of selective, needs-testing welfare institutions undermine interpersonal trust, while experiences of universal institutions tend to increase it. Views on the constitutionally protected right to equal treatment by public agencies seem to be an important link in this causal chain. If the theoretical interpretation of the correlations is accurate, we may have stumbled onto one of the explanations as to why Sweden is a country with a high degree of interpersonal trust: relatively few Swedes have experienced selectively distributed public welfare and service, while many encounter universal programs.

Robert Putnam gives a completely different explanation in his comprehensive study of the decline of social capital in the United States. His analysis shows clearly that there are large differences in social capital among various US regions, especially between southern states such as Louisiana and Alabama and states in the upper Midwest such as Minnesota and Illinois. As in the book on Italy, Putnam's explanation of these differences is historical and cultural. He writes: "One surprisingly strong predictor of the degree of social capital in any state in the 1990s is, for example, the fraction of the population that is of Scandinavian stock" (Putnam 2000: 309).

Of course, this is good news for individuals who happen to be of Scandinavian "stock." But for everyone who does not have such origins, including the author of this book, Putnam's conclusion makes for less encouraging reading. We cannot do much about our "stock" if it should happen to be Latin American, African, Turkish, or Eastern European – i.e. originating in cultures with a paucity of social trust. This clearly illustrates the structural determinism proposed in chapter 2 as a particular problem for these kinds of cultural explanations. It also proves that explanations of this kind, contrary to what is frequently assumed, do not necessarily have an emancipating, radical, or progressive political import. To take it as an axiom that human norms and beliefs are socially constructed pretty much leaves people high and dry when it comes to their opportunities to change their situation. This historical determinism was also a prominent feature of Putnam's book on Italy. In one passage, he writes that "the astonishing tensile strength of civic traditions testifies to the power of the past" (Putnam 1993: 162). He also recounts a conversation with a regional president in one of the regions with low social trust, who when treated to this historical determinism, exclaims: "This is a counsel of despair! You're telling me that nothing I can do will improve our prespects for success. The fate of the reform was sealed centuries ago" (1995: 183).

The discussion of the significance of "history" and "origins" naturally becomes even more problematic in light of the results of various survey studies in the United States showing that black Americans (i.e. people who are mainly of African origin) have considerably lower social trust than people of European origin. This applies even to the trust African Americans feel in each other and the result holds up even when studies are controlled for factors such as income and education (Patterson 1999).

A sociological explanation of this circumstance in the spirit of Putnam builds on the notion that there is something wrong with the inherited tradition (i.e. the stock) for how social networks are built that leads to problems in the production of social capital. As shown above, support for such a thesis at the individual level is scarcely to be found. A thesis in line with the theory on the significance of administrative institutions like that presented here would provide a very different explanation of the low social capital found among the African American population in the United States – i.e. that African Americans have been, or believe themselves to have been, victims of systematic discrimination, special treatment, and other offenses by public agencies in the United States on such a grand scale that the three causal mechanisms I have specified above were triggered and came to enclose their worldviews and beliefs about the institutions of the society and its citizens. There is nothing wrong with their "stock" when it comes to the creation of social trust. The problem of low interpersonal trust comes from discriminated groups having been forced to live under public political institutions that have been, or which they have believed to have been, deeply dysfunctional for them. The *collective memory* of things such as gross police brutality, public lynchings,[7]

---

[7] Anyone who saw the exhibition on public lynchings of black people in the United States at the New York City Museum in the spring of 2001 will have no difficulty imagining how these "cognitive maps" and processes can come into being.

and systematic discrimination has a tremendous effect on the belief systems of which the individuals in a group such as this become the bearers (Harris 1999). This conclusion also finds support in research that shows that African Americans, to a much greater extent than other Americans, are fascinated by conspiracy theories, most of which are based on the presumption of grossly devious behavior on the part of the authorities. A higher percentage of African American citizens than other Americans believe that AIDS was deliberately spread by the government, that the government spreads drugs to minority groups, and that the FBI murdered Martin Luther King, to give a few examples (Goertzel 1994).

The institutional theory on how social capital is created that I present here is consistent both with Uslaner's results emphasizing childhood socialization processes and Yamagishi's theories on how social intelligence is acquired. In Uslaner's case, beliefs about social institutions and the trustworthiness of people in general are created to a great extent through the means by which parents transfer information about how society works to their children, whether in Pajala or Memphis. As for Yamagishi's theory, it is easy to understand that a society characterized by segregation and racism bars many young individuals from the kind of extroverted interactions that teach them to interpret signals concerning trust or its opposite – i.e. the society prevents them from developing what Yamagishi defines as "social intelligence." A society or an organization in which interactions among individuals are to a great extent based on racial, ethnic, gender, or religious prejudice probably does not encourage people to engage in social interactions outside their own group. However, institutions oriented towards working by rules that prohibit any consideration of those characteristics or affiliations may, if the theory I present here is correct, break such a pattern.

I have added an element of "non-determinism" to my institutional theory on social capital. Uslaner's and Yamigishi's theories include very little that points towards change. Much of the political process in a democracy has to do with how we should design the political institutions identified here as significant. Institutional design thus becomes a central element (cf. Goodin 1995, 1997). In the areas of social and gender equality, immigration, and welfare policy, institutional design has been decided in various ways, in Sweden and elsewhere. As I have shown in earlier writings, the outcome of such political processes has, in many important cases, been anything but a foregone conclusion based on structural factors (Rothstein 1998a). We shall see more on this in chapter 6.

6

The problem of institutional credibility

We can conclude from chapter 5 that variations in the supply of social capital in a society are rooted mainly in the design of political and administrative institutions. The causal factor seems to be the degree of *universalism* in those institutions, understood as impartiality, objectivity, and equal treatment. We also presented a theory that specifies how the causal mechanism (or mechanisms) is constructed as a link between state institutions and individual worldviews and which produce – or destroy – social capital. The connection between how political institutions are constructed and the belief systems of the people is central here, as it implies that the design of political institutions should not be regarded solely as an effect of a society's historical and cultural legacy. On the contrary, it is possible to show, in Swedish political history, for example, that highly deliberate choices have been made by key politicians in the construction of political institutions with the express purpose of influencing the belief systems of the people. This applies, for instance, to the design of the pension system in 1912, to the choice between general and selective social insurance programs during the 1940s; and to the design of unemployment insurance in the 1930s (Olsson 1993; Rothstein 1992c, 1998a; Svensson 1994).

As shown by Hilton Root's studies of societies such as Hong Kong and Singapore (Root 1996), for example, institutional design is not culturally determined. Those societies have experienced remarkable economic growth, and Root shows that the prerequisite for that growth was the establishment of the type of universal administrative institutions I have identified here. First and foremost, he points to the comprehensive and powerful measures to eliminate corruption carried out in those societies in the 1970s. In a comparative perspective, those countries are distinguished by a relatively low extent of corruption. In the latest measurement published by Transparency International (TI), Singapore was rated to have an index of 9.3 on a scale of 0–10, sharing fifth place with Sweden, while Hong Kong was in fourteenth place (index 8.2). The measurement shows that nearby countries, which can be reasonably placed in the same cultural sphere, can be considerably more corrupt. China is in fifty-ninth place with an index of 3.5. Indonesia, Singapore's neighbor to the south, ended up far down on the list in ninety-sixth place with an index of 1.9, and its northern neighbor Malaysia was ranked thirty-third (index 4.9).[1] We can conclude from these differences between nearby countries that the extent of corruption is *not* culturally determined (cf. Hodess, Banfield, and Wolfe 2001). Root shows persuasively that the low extent of corruption, and consequent successful economic growth, were achieved through highly specific institutional arrangements introduced and implemented by political leaders in those countries.[2]

How are credible institutions created?

Based on the preceding discussion, one might conclude that the matter of creating social capital should really be very simple. Countries, societies, or organizations suffering from a low supply of social capital and attendant problems need only duplicate the universal institutions that exist in countries with a high supply of social capital (and therewith gain a working democracy, strong economic growth, and rich, happy people). Aid from the rich industrialized world to developing countries could be redirected from consisting of physical resources and education to export of reliable institutions. This has happened to a certain extent. For instance, Swedish aid to developing countries has become progressively more oriented towards democracy aid (Brodin 2000).[3] Current publications from the World Bank, the United Nations Economic and Social Development organization, and other similar international institutions emphasize the importance of *good governance*, which is probably their way of achieving a politically correct circumlocution for "eliminating corruption" (Easterly 2001: 242). The problem is that the formal design of institutions is far from the only thing, and perhaps not even

---

[1] www.transparency.org – Corruption Perception Index (CPI) (2002).

[2] Root also shows that these countries, contrary to what is predicted by economists of the Chicago School, can by no means be characterized as laissez-faire economies where the state has withdrawn from the fray. On the contrary, these states are certainly limited but they are very strong and, beyond upholding the rule of law, are engaged in a wide array of educational and sociopolitical activities.

[3] As Robert Barro (2001) has shown, there is unfortunately a great deal of empirical evidence indicating that legal administrative institutions are the primary engines of economic growth, rather than democracy. Examples include Hong Kong and Singapore.

the most important aspect, that will determine how it will be perceived. It may suffice to mention that, on paper, the 1936 constitution of the Soviet Union is thought to be one of the most democratic documents the world has ever seen. Naturally, it does not help much if the leaders of a corrupt state or administration decide one fine day that corruption shall cease as of January 1 the following year. People will decide whether they should trust institutions based on concrete experiences and other information they deem credible, and not based on political declarations or resolutions. Proclamations, be they never so wonderful, issued by politicians they have come to distrust, do not change popular belief systems about the nature of the political world. Trust, whether in individuals or institutions, is difficult to earn but easy to shatter.

In economic theory, this dilemma is usually called the "problem of credible commitments" (Falaschetti and Miller 2001; Milgrom, North, and Weingast 1990). Obviously, it does not suffice for the leading, responsible politicians in a country to write documents in which they promise to follow certain rules of the game if the citizenry has no confidence that the promises will be kept. It is on this particular point that the weakness shows up in Russell Hardin's argument that trust in government agencies cannot exist (see chapter 4). His argument is that we can talk about trust only in situations where we have knowledge about the individuals we choose to trust, by which we know it is in their own interest to act in our interest. That is, that the "trusted" is acting according to such an incentive structure known to the "truster" that the latter can predict that the former is not going to act deceptively. According to Hardin, it is impossible to have such information about civil servants because the control system intended to supervise their actions is too complex to allow us, as individuals, to acquire sufficient knowledge about whether the system is constructed in such a way that it lies in the interests of civil servants to act in our interests (Hardin 1998). Hardin puts it this way: To say that I trust you implies that I "have reason to expect you to act, for your own reasons, *as my agent* with respect to the relevant matter. Your interests encapsulates my interests" (Hardin 1999: 26, italics in the original).

However, when we choose to trust, or not trust, a government agency and its officials, it is not a given that we believe they will act as our agents or representatives. On the contrary, we could say that a public official who acts as my agent (or representative) is someone I have bribed or who for some other reason has set aside the principle of avoiding conflict of interest. What we expect from, or what we choose to trust about the official or agency, is instead that they live up to the ethical norms such as objectivity, impartiality, and equality before the law. This type of trust in state institutions is thus essentially different from the trust we may feel in family and friends.

This argument enjoys strong empirical support in research conducted by psychologist Tom Tyler on why people accept the principle of compliance with the law. He tested five factors in his study and found that the strongest was whether citizens believed that the procedures applied by officials in the implementation of laws were fair. *Procedural fairness* was a more important factor than the risk of being caught and punished or the general moral norm that people should obey democratically passed laws, and more important than whether or not the individual believed the outcome of the case to be in his favor (Tyler 1992). Tyler's argument is that the basis of public support of laws and authorities lies in how citizens judge the way in which authorities exercise their power (Tyler 1998). In her work on why young men voluntarily came forward and risked their lives to defend their countries, Margaret Levi arrived at a similar result with respect to the significance of the perception of procedural fairness (Levi 1998a). In earlier contexts, I have argued that the advantages of universal social political programs in relation to meeting demands for procedural fairness explain much of the support for that policy in the Scandinavian countries (Rothstein 1998a). Ylva Norén (2002) has shown that the beliefs of Swedish citizens about the nature of authorities mandated to administer justice has greater influence on their trust in political parties, city councils, parliament, and the prime minister and cabinet ministers than their involvement in voluntary associations, for example (Norén 2002).

On the whole, empirical research shows, in contrast to Hardin's opinion, that discussion of trust in state institutions is more than legitimate. What probably confused Hardin is that this trust is not a matter of whether state institutions act in our personal best interests, but rather whether they are deemed to respect the ethical principles outlined above. There is a tremendous difference between trusting that someone will act objectively and impartially and trusting that she will act in our own interests. We can designate the former as *universal* institutions and the latter as *particular*. Particular institutions are such that are established to benefit a particular individual, party, or group in the social dilemma at hand. Apartheid laws in the former South Africa are perhaps an excruciatingly clear example; another may be labor laws that especially favor either unions or employers, or various groups of employees (Hattam 1993).

Are efficient institutions really efficient?

Game theory literature refers to this type of institution as "efficient" because it helps solve problems of the nature of the social trap (Tsebelis 1990: 106ff.). However, the terminology is a tad unfortunate because it can conceal the truth that imbalances of power and other kinds of disequilibria may remain, even under such institutions. That which is efficient for one party may be inefficient for another (Galaz 2004). Significant disequilibria between the actors may remain even after successful resolution of a social dilemma; all that is required is that the subordinated actors also realize that a "non-solution" may make their situations even worse. It is easy to imagine an ethnic group whose only choice is either to accept some form of discrimination or start a full-blown civil war to establish a separate state. Starting such a conflict may entail significantly greater risk to the group than continuing to fight the discrimination against it within the framework of universal institutions and by peaceful means. Thus, instead of "efficient," I will be using the term *universal* institutions.

Digression: social services and universalism

A conflict could arise between these universal principles and the capacity to deliver the kind of social services required of public sector employees in the welfare state who must perform curative and caring work. Following feminist theorist Joan Tronto, Helena Stensöta (2004) has argued that we expect, for example, pre-school teachers, medical professionals, and social workers to demonstrate empathy and compassion and not be governed by some general and abstract logic of fairness. The logic of care and concern within social services leads to a more context-dependent ethic and may come into conflict with the ethic more oriented towards principles founded on the abstract, universal logic of fairness. I am prepared to agree with Stensöta, but still maintain that this conflict may rest in a dimension other than that which I have tried to specify here. Certainly, most of us want our preschool children to be approached with empathy and concern, rather than some dry-as-dust objectivity and impartiality based on principle. But Stensöta does not claim that the principles of care and concern should be put on an equal par with particularism. Obviously, many people would be angry if preschool staff deliberately directed their care and concern only towards certain children and thus in practice discriminated against other children. If such treatment occurred based on gender or ethnicity, for example, many would perceive it to be immediately disturbing and offensive. There may also be a conflict between care and concern and equality before the law, if it means equal treatment in a more restricted form, as in that everyone should be given exactly the same measures of everything (e.g. exactly the same amount of comfort whether the child in question is sad or not). However, as I showed in an earlier work, this interpretation of the concept of "equality before the law" is too narrow (Rothstein 1998a: chapter 2). It is not a matter of precisely equal treatment, but rather that everyone is assured that his or her needs will be tested on equal terms with everyone else's. On objective and professional grounds, public sector employees may assess needs for, in this case, social services as being so different that social programs or interventions must be varied. This is no stranger than that someone who needs a kidney transplant needs more healthcare resources than someone with a sore throat. There is no breach of universal norms until public servants discriminate in their assessments of the need for social services for reasons that have nothing to do with the applicant's needs – i.e. until they take circumstances into consideration that are unrelated to the "case."

But is it actually possible to create universal institutions?

If we accept that universal institutions are vital to the production of social capital, then how can such institutions be achieved? Accepted economic theory tells us that it is a walk in the park: those in high places in the system must create an incentive system by which the risk and costs entailed in the discovery of corruption and other irregularities are greater than the potential gains to be made from participating in such activities (Weibull 1995). That is, the society institutionalizes a system in which the fear of getting caught triumphs over the greed of individuals and civil servants. When fear is higher than greed, things go well. The problem with this solution is in part theoretical: it raises the problem only to an underlying level. Why should self-interested utility maximizing senior civil servants, who have the most to gain through bribery and corruption, be in the least interested in implementing such a system? And why should their political bosses, who stand to profit even more by a corrupt system, be the slightest bit interested in such a change? This has been formulated as the question of "who will execute" the reforms needed to change a corrupt structure if top management is made up of self-interested utility maximizers (Shleifer and Vishny 1998: 5). As Hans Blomkvist has asserted, much of the advice emanating from organizations such as the United Nations Development Program (UNDP), the International Monetary Fund (IMF), and the World Bank on the importance of action against corruption and the establishment of working administrative bodies under the rule of law (i.e. good governance) is based precisely on the presumption of access to the kind of administrative praxis that these countries lack; that is, they presume that the desired end already exists (Blomkvist 2001). One can define this problem as a social dilemma of the second order, meaning that the achievement of social norms of trust and confidence, without which universal institutions cannot be created, is in itself a social dilemma (Ostrom 1998).

Douglass C. North has expressed this as the fact that such universal institutions and administrative behavior are precluded within a strict utility maximizing model. If political leaders successfully shape a state that is administratively strong enough to protect the rights of individuals from corruption and the abuse of power, they will also have access to an administrative machine that can violate those rights (North 1990: 59). If those in control of the state are the type of actors assumed by the utility maximizing model, they will also exploit that power to enrich themselves at the expense of the people's rights (Weingast 1993: 287). In so doing, they inevitably create distrust of the state as an institution, which is a barrier to civil willingness to invest or take other economic risks. Creating the type of universal institutions I refer to here is neither easy nor uncomplicated. As de Soto has shown, it took centuries for the universal institutions upon which modern Western market economies are predicated to emerge in the industrialized countries (de Soto 2001). The jurisprudential regulations are complicated; the institutions required are many, costly, and comprehensive. It is not solely a matter of police and public courts, but also of institutions such as registrar offices that establish ownership rights to real property, a working land survey office, receivers, official agencies for the collection of debts, taxation and inspection authorities, etc. The holding of "free and fair elections," to take another example, is a highly complex matter from the administrative perspective (Choe 1997). Democratic elections are dependent on the existence of an array of agencies and authorities that must all be perceived as impartial by the competing parties. Just how problematic this can be was clearly demonstrated by the presidential election in the United States in 2000.

The second problem is of a more empirical nature. It has proven very difficult for high-ranking bureaucrats to actually introduce and manage a control and supervision system sufficiently effective to deal with bureaucrats oriented towards attempted fraud. Research in the field of organizational theory shows that attempts to govern and control organizations by means of economic incentives alone usually do not work, because supervisory officials cannot acquire sufficient information to design effective incentives. That information is the province of lower-ranking bureaucrats, and if they know that their superiors want to get at such information in order to increase control and supervision, they will attempt to hide or distort the information in all manner of ways. What is even more troubling is that the use of economic incentives will only aggravate this problem of asymmetric information (Miller 1992). In one of the most comprehensive studies of civil servants in the United States, researchers concluded that control from above and supervision by superiors played an obscure role in the actions of civil servants, while the personal normative beliefs held by lower-ranking officials on the meaning of their work were critical to their performance (Brehm and Gates 1997). The bureaucratic ethic thus becomes a determining factor in whether universal institutions can be established (Lundquist 2000).

Attempting to achieve non-corrupt administration through administrative control and economic incentives thus conflicts with efforts to exert influence by means of ethical and moral codes.

The four no solutions: market – hierarchy – norms – institutions

Theoretical research on cooperation – i.e. potential solutions to the problem of the social trap – has been conducted primarily within the rationalist paradigm. Marc Lichbach (1995) has written one of the more important works in the field. In his comprehensive review, he showed that researchers have labored mainly with four potential solutions. That which inspires people to maintain respect for contracts and behave in a trustworthy manner may be the *market*, the *hierarchy*, *social norms*, or *institutions*. After a thorough analysis, his conclusion is quite pessimistic: "The major difficulty with every solution to the Cooperator's Dilemma is that each presupposes the existence of at least one other solution. All solutions to the Cooperator's Dilemma, in other words, are fundamentally incomplete. This is, or course, quite troubling" (cf. Falaschetti and Miller 2001; Lichbach 1995: ix). This means that utility maximizing actors acting solely according to market principles cannot solve the problem of the social trap, because the nature of public goods makes is impossible to divide the good into individual property. Nor can the social trap problem be solved by means of hierarchical supervision and control alone, or only through the establishment of universal institutions, because the creation of such institutions is a just another collective action problem. Finally, systems based only on social norms do not work either because they come into conflict with the basic principle upon which the rationalistic model is built. Each such intra-theoretical solution presumes that one of the solutions is already in place. To cite one example, a market that lacks institutions or social norms will, given self-interested agents, sooner or later break down through corruption. The conclusion, according to Falaschetti and Miller is that "there is no solution!" (2001: 405).

An article by Douglass North, William Summerfield, and Barry Weingast (2000) contains a textbook example of the problem. On the one hand, we are told that "establishing credible commitments requires the creation of political institutions that alter the incentives of political officials." However, early on in the paper, the authors assert that the analysis has to start with the "beliefs" held by citizens in the society, "because it is the beliefs which translate into the institutions that shape performance." (North, Summerfield, and Weingast 2000: 27, 22). This is circular reasoning of precisely the kind noted by Lichbach – it may be true that beliefs create working institutions even as working institutions create beliefs. But given the presumption in rationalistic theory, opportunistic behavior will sooner or later drive agents into the social trap.

As Lichbach shows, rationalist researchers often try to save the analysis by falling back on functionalist arguments. Universal institutions arise through some kind of automatic mechanism because the market is thought to need them. But, as Jon Elster has shown, functionalist explanations lack validity in the social sciences. The existence of a need for a solution to the social trap cannot explain why such solutions have come into being (Elster 1989b). Functionalist explanations are usually post hoc – i.e. the scholar rationalizes an answer into being without specifying the causal mechanisms that explain why agents have succeeded in creating universal institutions. The primary argument against this type of explanations is that history is obviously not efficient. It is not true that all societies or organizations faced with a social dilemma manage to find solutions that keep them out of destructive social traps. Sadly, there is a great deal that indicates the opposite – that history is most often not efficient and that no solutions to the social dilemma are found (Lichbach 1997: 212ff.).

The solutions presented here have dealt with opportunities for coopera-tion between two actors that have repeated interactions with one another. The problem of corruption and similar in that it involves a great many actors who sometimes have repeated interactions and sometimes do not. Unfortu-nately, the notion that we cooperate because we know that the cooperation will be repeated does not work in these contexts. Since it is, again, impossible rationally to decide to forget, the memory of untrustworthy behavior does not easily go away.

The problem of naïve rationalism

Researchers within the economic rationalist paradigm have made a number of attempts to find a solution to the problem of how universal institutions can be created. I will illustrate and criticize three such attempts here. The first solution to the problem of the origins of credible institutions was proposed by Paul Milgrom, Douglass C. North, and Barry Weingast in an oft-quoted paper (Milgrom, North, and Weingast 1990). Their example is how mer-chants in a certain region of Europe in the fourteenth century could develop legal praxis that oiled the wheels of trade despite the lack of credible state institutions. The problem they were facing was naturally that of managing situations in which contractual disputes arose between two merchants – i.e. how they should handle the deceptive behavior of certain merchants in the form of various kinds of breach of contract. The situation may be likened to a classic social trap – all merchants have a vested interest in everyone behav-ing honestly, but there is no point in being the only honest actor if everyone else is engaged in trickery and deceit of one kind or another. But if "everyone does it," the financial gains to be had from trade decline substantially, in part because fewer transactions are completed and in part because the actors are forced to devote considerable resources to protecting themselves from the deceptive actions of others. The costs incurred by merchant A to enter into a financial contract with merchant B, who intends to swindle A, are substantial. Even if the wronged A spreads information that the dishonest merchant B is not to be trusted, B could of course counter that information with contrary disclosures. Absent credible information institutions, other merchants have little or no means of determining who was in the right.

Milgrom *et al.* claim that in order to avoid that social trap the merchants' guilds of fourteenth-century France appointed "law merchants." The law merchants were empowered to act as judges in disputes between merchants and to publicize information about merchants who refused to voluntarily accept the verdicts of their deliberations (e.g. by paying compensation to the wronged party). This made deceptive behavior and refusal to comply with the verdicts of the law merchants an expensive business, since merchants who did so gained a reputation for lacking credibility and for being unreliable trading partners. This led to a strong decline in deceptive behavior, because it was in the merchants' own interest to avoid getting such a reputation. Therewith, according to Milgrom *et al.*, an institution for solving the problem of the social trap had blossomed from the market's own inherent logic. The actors had a self-interest in both establishing the institution and in obeying the verdicts of the law merchants, which made the institution self-reinforcing. According to this analysis, a type of society under the rule of law had sprung up by itself; the problem of the social trap had been resolved by the self-interested utility maximizing actors of their own volition and with no outside involvement by something like a state or some form of social norms.

This is a charming analysis to be sure, but also supremely idealistic, if not to say naïve. Merchants and trading companies are not homogeneous quantities. Market logic dictates that some will eventually become much more financially strong than others. If they are only economic rationalists, the large trading houses will use their financial strength to bribe or corrupt the law merchants in one way or another to gain economic advantages. They will also try to get their confidants in corruption installed in those positions in order to render verdicts in their own trading house's favor. And if they are economic rationalists, the integrity of the law merchants will be for sale as long as the price is right and the transaction can be kept secret. Secret interactions are the hallmark of corruption. Such a scenario is a rather apt description of events in Russia after the privatizations of the 1990s (Hedlund 1999). The economic oligarchies seem to have become so strong that they have managed to block attempts to build universal legal institutions out of existence (Glaeser, Scheinkman, and Shleifer 2002).

One can object that the offer and acceptance of bribes entails significant risk for both the giver and taker in such a system. However, taking risks is partly what the logic of the market is about – if no risk is taken, there is no market – and there are always individuals who are willing to take substantial risks as long as their chances for making a profit are reasonably proportional to the risk. My point is that in the absence of some kind of social norms among the law merchants that made them immune to bribes and patronage, an institution of the kind Milgrom *et al.* identified is *not* self-reinforcing. If it is made up only of self-interested utility maximizers, the system will be gradually invaded by dishonest agents, become instable, and break down. If merchants began to suspect that certain trading houses had bought certain law merchants, the problems that the system was meant to resolve would rise again. In game theoretical terms, the equilibrium identified by Milgrom *et al.* is not stable in the long term. And when all is said and done, that is what the real world shows us; as North himself in a later paper emphasized: efficient institutions are the exception rather than the rule (North 1998: 494). Sooner or later, self-interested utility maximizers will give into the temptation to act as free riders on the honest actions of others (Dagger 1997: 107). This occurs as soon as it becomes more profitable to engage in deceptive behavior rather than trustworthy behavior, which in such a situation "everyone" knows that "everyone else" is prepared to do. This destroys whatever credibility and trustworthiness that may exist. In the same paper, North admits that "creating cooperative frameworks of economic and political impersonal exchange is at the heart of solving problems of societal, political, and economic performance. While formal rules can help in creating such frameworks, it is the informal constraints embodied in norms of behavior, conventions, and internally imposed codes of conduct that are critical" (North 1998: 506).

Simple observation of the judiciary also tells us that there is something fundamentally twisted about the attempt to erase the significance of social norms to making the institution work. If it were true that its genesis and function could be explained solely by rationalist reasons, all of the insignia with which the judiciary is associated should not have come into being or have been found necessary to uphold. Among such badges of honor can be mentioned special judicial oaths that underline the ethical dimensions of the profession, the existence of judicial robes, special titles, manners of addressing judges during legal proceedings, special terms of employment, etc. (SOU 2000). If it were always in the interest of judges to behave honestly and follow universal principles of objectivity, impartiality, and equality under the law, there would have been no need to invent these phenomena, which are all oriented towards the ethical dimensions of the profession, or they would have eventually become obsolete. The same can be said about the codes of ethics established in many countries for other public officials (Lundquist 1996).

Trying to solve the problem within the rationalist paradigm, Barry Weingast returned to the issue in an article that deals with nothing less than the origins of democracy and the rule of law. His empirical illustration is the conflict between Franklin D. Roosevelt and the Supreme Court of the United States in the 1930s. The Court which then as now was invested with great political power, got in the way of Roosevelt's New Deal policy by ruling in several cases that his reforms were unconstitutional. Roosevelt discovered an escape hatch in the constitution: there was no provision stipulating how many judges should sit on the Supreme Court bench. He believed that he could break down the Court's resistance by appointing additional judges who were more kindly disposed towards his reform policy. In his analysis of why the strategy failed – i.e. why respect for the rule of law was maintained in this critical time in the political history of the United States – Weingast falls back on a fundamentally idealistic and non-rational explanation. According to Weingast, Roosevelt's plan failed "because it constituted a direct assault on the constitutional principle of the separation of powers, large number of citizens, including many of the intended beneficiaries, viewed the plan as illegitimate" (Weingast 1997: 254). This may be certainly an accurate rendering of history, but once again, it means that the rationalist Weingast finds explanations that conflict with the fundamental axiom upon which his theoretical model is built. If those who would have benefited from the "packing" of the Supreme Court turned against it because they viewed the process as illegitimate, we are left with a idealistic normative, not a rationalistic, explanation for the preservation of the rule of law in the United States.

A third example of the peculiarities of this problem within the rationalist school may be taken from two other well-known researchers in the field, Gary Miller and Thomas Hammond (1994). Their analysis deals with how cities in the United States have managed to extract themselves from systems fraught with corruption between elected politicians and financial entrepreneurs, the so-called "political machines" that plagued many cities. The solution, according to their analysis, was the hiring of a new corps of civil servants known as "city managers." They were known for being non-self-interested public servants and for their generally high morals (Nalbandian 1991). Miller and Hammond conclude that it was possible to make it out of the morass of systematic corruption in American cities by hiring such individuals. According to them, the reason it worked was that these city managers "have been selected and/or trained not to be economic actors."

These two rationalist researchers have a simple word of advice to countries and societies plagued by corruption, namely to "find out how such disinterested altruistic actors are created, and then reproduce them throughout the political system" (Miller and Hammond 1994: 23f.). There are just two problems with their analysis. First, according to the assumptions upon which their economic rationalist theory is founded, that type of actor should not exist. Secondly, as advice to my friend in the Russian tax administration, the analysis is even more naïve and idealistic than that of Milgrom *et al.*

It is slightly odd that when scholars working within rationalist school are faced with the utterly central problem of how universal institutions can be created, they end up delivering such idealistic arguments. It is even more peculiar that they fail to reflect more deeply about what that means to the premises of the theory. This probably has to do with the insight that there is no solution to be found within the framework of their own theory to the problem of creating the kind of universal institutions that help eliminate social traps. One might say that the theory of economic rationalism has helped draw our attention to a critical problem that unfortunately cannot be solved within its own theoretical boundaries. Miller and Hammond's conclusion is that politics is more important than economics, but that does not solve the problem, as politics can be both constructive and destructive in the creation of universal institutions. Faced with reality, they fall back on the pre-existence, for reasons unknown, of some form of generalized knowledge or some kind of social norms or other informal institutions that make cooperation possible. But, as Michael Hechter has expressed the problem, the existence of such informal institutions represents precisely the problem that rationalist theoreticians are supposed to explain *in the first place* (Hechter 1992). Why should self-interested utility maximizers refrain from acting as free riders on the cooperation that has arisen based on social norms? To follow the lead of Weingast, North, Miller *et al.* and allow that which is to be explained to become part of the explanation is neither theoretically nor methodologically acceptable.

There is also something of a paradox here. Researchers of the rationalist school are wont to present themselves as hard-boiled realists whose fundamental premise is that people are driven by self-interest and material circumstances, especially monetary rewards (Lichbach 1995: 344). They often dismiss things such as norms and ethics as points of departure that are far too idealistic to be used in analyzing human behavior (Eriksson 2005). But, as we have seen above, when faced with the problem of the social trap and the matter of universal institutions, they retreat into the corner of naïve idealism.

There is reason to reflect upon the magnitude of this problem. The rationalist theory is built upon the foundation that universal (or effective) institutions are needed to prevent societies from falling into social traps (cf. Rodrik 1999). Yet, as shown above, the theory offers no solution to how such institutions can be established or, if established by some ad hoc event, reproduced. Jonathan Bendor and Piotr Swistak, who work within this approach have recently come to a similar conclusion:

> The very existence of globally stable equilibria is consistent with the economist's vision of a homo economicus who maximizes payoffs in equilibrium. But the stability of this behavior comes at a surprising price to the economic paradigm of man: it requires homo economicus to be an intrinsically social creature – one that rewards and punishes others not for what they do to him, but for what they do to others in the group. (2000: 13)

In other words, without agents who act out of a script other than "*homo economicus*," meaning that they without any personal gain punish treacherous behavior, the social trap will close. The conclusion is that the rationalist school offers no valid explanations for why universal institutions can arise because, as we have seen, they refer to agents and behaviors that are not supposed to exist within their models. Given the importance of the rationalist approach within the social sciences, not only in economics but also in political science, this result is quite troubling. It should be added that this is not a theoretical problem. Economists working within the rationalist school have been successful when arguing for establishing institutions such as independent central banks in which economic experts would steer monetary policy insulated from opportunistic politicians and interests groups. But this comes with two problems. First, it is built on the theory that these experts are in fact idealistic servants of the public interest and do not have an agenda that serves their own interests or can be tempted by material rewards to serve special interests (Svensson 1996). As stated by Falaschetti and Miller, "left unchecked, these agents possess an incentive that is inconsistent with the objective for which they are designed – namely to opportunistically redistribute any efficiency gains that they help create" (2001: 398). Secondly, some analysis shows that the reason these institutions work is precisely because they are not insulated from politics and interests groups (Lohmann 2003).

If we look at empirical research on how people in some parts of the world have successfully broken the logic of corruption, much of it has to do with how it has been possible to change ethical and social norms in a variety of ways within the administrative apparatus and the surrounding society (Basu 1998; Hope and Chikulo 1999; OECD 1999; della Porta and Mény 1997; Rose-Ackerman 1999; Stapenhurst and Kpundeh 1999; Thorp 1996). Despite persistent attempts, I have not been able to identify a single empirical study within the framework of the rationalist school that has shown how it has been possible to make the transition from corrupt to universal institutions. As I showed above, the rationalist researchers that have tried to do so have failed (cf. Lichbach 1997: chapter 7). Following the axiom of rationalist theory, no actors will help create institutions that they do not know in advance will benefit themselves, and such institutions are by definition not universal. As Leif Lewin has asserted, there is a conflict between the "public interest" and the capacity of rationalist actors to create institutions that lead to the realization of that public interest (Lewin 1991: 142).

The weakness of universal institutions

However, it is not only that the genesis of universal institutions is hard to explain. According to Russell Hardin's analysis, even once universal institutions have been well and truly established they are weak because, according to rationalist theory, no one has a self-interest in defending them. Instead, most actors want institutions that favor their particular group – i.e. redistributive institutions (Tsebelis 1990). Empirical and theoretical research on the influence of special interest groups on the political system has made us familiar with the phenomenon. For once, the research position is rather unequivocal – in theory, all firms and industries are in favor of full and open competition, while in practice, they generally act to promote state establishment of various forms of subsidies and rules that limit competition in their particular field. The power of special interests over politics is one of the eternal problems of democracy studies, but it has also caught the interest of many economists (for a current overview, see Naurin 2001). We should remember that this does not apply only to firms – the main reason that English workers formed the first International was that they wanted to prevent English employers from importing French workers who were willing to work for lower wages than those the English had successfully negotiated in collective bargaining (Wheen 2000). The problem exists even within the administration – my first teacher in my postgraduate political science studies, Professor Nils Stjernquist of Lund University, was fond of relating his experiences in the 1940s with the government committee on the famous Swedish principle of public access to official documents. All the civil service departments and government agencies the committee visited (and they were many) presented variations on the following theme: They believed on the one hand that the principle of public access to official documents was a fundamental component of Swedish democracy and considered it absolutely essential. But on the other hand, it was perhaps not such a good thing for their particular agency since they had to deal with such especially sensitive information, and so they wanted special exceptions to apply to them.

Russell Hardin (1995) has contributed an important observation here – i.e. that universal institutions are not only difficult to establish, they are also weak and therewith at risk for dissolution. His argument is seductive in its simplicity. Precisely because they are universal, there is no political or economic group that has reason to defend them. Instead, self-interest leads to a logic wherein the universality of universal institutions will be doubted. Most of Hardin's examples are taken from societies with many competing ethnic and religious groups, but they can be easily generalized. Hardin points out that there is a self-interest among what he calls "political entrepreneurs" in challenging universal institutions using arguments that their own group is being discriminated against or otherwise treated unfairly by existing universal institutions. The school system is a typical example, but many other institutions (law enforcement, courts, administrative agencies) are subject to this criticism. Such political entrepreneurs, according to Hardin, get around the problem of collective action by claiming that, for their own group, the situation is a matter of "one for all/all for one" logic. If each one supports the others in the establishment of an institution that favors their own group, all within the group are also potential winners. Those who resist mobilization can be dismissed either as victims of false consciousness or as traitors to the "cause," because they are loyal to the ruling order for all kinds of fishy reasons. In situations of extreme conflict, there is seldom room for neutral viewpoints – "one for all and all for one" is the word of the day. The risks to those who try to remain outside such a conflict are often substantial.

Mobilization of the group is of course easier if there is from the outset a lack of trust in how political institutions act when it comes to upholding the principles of universalism. The capacity of the political entrepreneurs to mobilize the group depends on how convincingly they assert that their own ethnic, social, or religious group is being systematically discriminated against. Hardin says that their demands usually are of two kinds. They either demand special rules to be created that will benefit the members of the group or else they demand institutions over which their own group (ethnic, social, etc.) will have control. In the latter case, other groups will naturally not accept those institutions. There is also some doubt as to whether they will be loyal to the universal institutions that already exist, as they may feel in the context of the struggle that they need to recast them as particular institutions that benefit their own group.

We need not resort to the many hotbeds of ethnic conflict to find examples of this logic – they can be found much closer than Bosnia, Rwanda, India, Northern Ireland, the Baltic countries, etc. One example can be taken from research on neo-corporatist political structures in which special interest groups have been given influence over policy administration. Without exception, this has been a matter of creating trust not only in the general objectives of the policy, but also in how the policy will be implemented. Labor, industrial, and agricultural policies, to name only a few, are of such a nature that many decisions related to distribution must be made in the administrative arena. Who should be given which grants, subsidies, directives, or concessions cannot as a rule be determined directly from a central set of regulations but must instead be decided at the administrative end because the administrators possess the requisite information. Because the decisions can have serious impact on individuals, there are usually high requirements concerning trust in the actions of officials. Aimed at engendering trust in bureaucratic decisions, policy makers have often allowed representatives of the group towards which the policy is directed to have an influence over policy administration. This has taken place either through some kind of local board or through hiring people of the "right" background to work in administrative positions (Rothstein 1992a, 1996b; Streeck and Schmitter 1985). In Sweden, this has been especially apparent in areas such as labor markets and agricultural policy, while in late twentieth-century Germany, for instance, large parts of the social insurance system were for all practical purposes handed over to the social democratic and union organizations, which devoted considerable energy to administering it. However, such group-based trust may, of course, be detrimental to overall trust in the policy. There is no guarantee that if, for example, farmers' organizations get influence over the implementation of subsidies to the agricultural sector, this will increase the trust in this policy for citizens in general.

Some preliminary conclusions

The possible conclusions thus far are as follows. The first is that social capital is mainly produced by a special kind of political institution – i.e. administrative institutions that can be called "universal." This includes a working state under the rule of law, but its principles on fairness, objectivity, impartiality, and equal treatment also apply to other public administrations. What we trust in these institutions is thus not that they will act in our direct personal interests to the extent that we get special favors in relation to other citizens. Trust does not come out of the actual contents; it is based on respect for procedures. The second thing we have determined is that rationalist theory offers no logically acceptable answer to the question of how such institutions can be established. If self-interest governs the actions of people and groups, they will always endeavor to bring about the establishment of institutions that protect their particular interests. Such institutions are by definition not universal; they are particular (or selective). Particular institutions run the gamut from government agencies set up especially to promote the interests of certain groups or individuals to public institutions that are outright corrupt. The police powers in South Africa under apartheid, the courts in the American South during the first decade of the civil rights movement, the British police in Northern Ireland, the German courts of 1933, and the public administration cleansed of ethnic Serbs in the recently formed Croatia of 1991 may serve as examples of such particular institutions.[4] The conclusion is that something other than rational self-interest is required to explain why universal institutions can be established – i.e. some form of social norms and moral ethics.

The second conclusion is that Russell Hardin's analysis of the weakness of universal institutions when it comes to reproducing themselves has much to recommend it. The decisions of government agencies and many other administrative matters are often complicated. Officials must in many cases consider a highly complex system of rules that must be applied to an equally complex reality. Suspicions that universal norms are not being upheld are common, especially in relation to the exercise of power over individuals by the authorities. In this context, the degree of complexity plays a large role. We can, for instance, compare the systems of general child benefit and needs-tested social services. In the former case, distributions by the social insurance office are very rarely questioned (families are entitled to a set amount of child benefit for each child). In the latter case, social workers must consider a wide range of factors related to the family applying for assistance and combine those factors with municipal and state regulations. As a result, even public officials may lose confidence in their own capacity to follow the principles of universalism in their work (Schierenbeck 2002).

The ability of political entrepreneurs to mobilize political support by accusing universal institutions of overt or covert discrimination is not restricted to countries such as Bosnia, Rwanda, Colombia, and Northern Ireland, as the intense debates over affirmative action and quotas reveal. However, there are two utterly different responses to the problem of discrimination and corruption in public administration. One is to accept the logic of the impossibility of universalism and give every group their own institutional devices to remedy discrimination (such as quotas and affirmative action). The problem with this solution is well known – which groups should be counted and how should you determine who belongs to each group (Barry 2000)? The other solution is to put more muscle into the norms and incentives that uphold the ethics of universality of the universal institutions. According to Hardin's analysis, political entrepreneurs do not

---

[4] The first serious incidences of violence in the former Yugoslavia started in ethnic Serb-dominated Krajina area of Croatia in 1991 after the nationalist administration under Tudjman decided to fire all the police and many other local civil servants of Serbian origin. This was an unmistakable signal to the Serbs in the Krajina area that they could expect systematic discrimination in the new Croatia (Scheimann 2002).

choose this line because it does not contribute to their interest in collective mobilization. Instead, their tack is that their own group or category should be given direct influence over the application of policy. Quite simply, they respond to discrimination and corruption by proposing that more discrimination and corruption should be introduced into the system (Lundström 1996). Hardin says that the idea is that the entrepreneurs can mobilize politically around prospects for their own group to gain special advantages. In models that consist of self-interested politicians, organizations, and citizens, it is therefore impossible to find answers to the question of why universal institutions come into being at all and, if they do, how they can survive. The chronic temptation for opportunistic behavior on which these theoretical models are built is a guarantee that all cooperative systems will eventually break down and end in social trap-like situations.

7

Trust and collective memories

We seem to have come to the end of the road in this analysis. We have our thesis about the importance of universal institutions, for which we have found
reasonably good empirical support, but have thus far found no decent explanation of the genesis or survival of such institutions. On the contrary, the
rationalist argument is that such institutions should be impossible and if, for
reasons unknown, they are born despite their impossibility, they should soon
be destroyed by economic and political opportunism. Political, economic,
and other special interests will gradually undermine universal institutions,
either by directly and formally replacing them with partisan institutions
that favor the interests of a special group, or by corrupting them by informal
means so that in reality they work in a partisan fashion. Thus, we cannot
explain the wide variation in the occurrence of universal institutions either.
The argument thus far is that absent the establishment of moral and ethical norms in defense of universal and impartial political institutions, social
capital will wither and the risk that the social trap will close around us will
flourish.

Whatever will be, will be . . . because it was like it was

If it is true that only moral and ethical acts can uphold universal institutions,
those of a logical turn of mind must question whether the only reasonable
explanation for the variation of corruption found among countries and societies is rooted in historically inherited culture. Is it so that Finns, Norwegians,
Swedes (and Chinese living in Hong Kong) will always and forever avoid
the kind of social traps caused by corrupt and discriminatory institutions
because upholding the norms that make universal institutions possible is

embedded in their cultures? Likewise, one might ask if Turks, Romanians, Argentineans, and Nigerians are doomed for eternity to live under corrupt regimes because there is something built into their cultures that precludes the very idea of universal institutions. With reference to African countries, this has been described as neo-patrimonialism, wherein personal, kinship-based and secret transactions with public officials are the rule rather than the exception (Hydén 2000: 22). This can be expressed as the fact that maintaining different equilibria in different societies is embedded in *subjective rationality*. If all officials in a society are known for primarily favoring their families, clans, ethnic groups, or other private contacts, this becomes the normative rationality on the collective level as well. Once such beliefs have taken hold, the subjective rationality says there is no reason for officials or citizens to stop maintaining such corrupt practices (Bardhan 1997). In many African countries, everyday life seems abundant with these kinds of transactions, with police routinely taking bribes from taxi drivers, officials demanding private payment for every kind of service or permit, and local bosses providing protection. At the higher level, demands by politicians and senior officials for kickbacks on every public contract have become part and parcel of the system (Chazan 1999: 188). Corruption becomes a component of everyday culture.

In his study of Italy, Robert Putnam tells about a meeting with a progressive leading regional politician from the south. When the politician heard the results of the study, he expressed his sense of desperation that the region was doomed to being underdeveloped for all time by reason of low social capital and the corruption in its institutions. The politician's despair was a response to Putnam and his research team having traced the cultural legacy of its low social capital back over several centuries, when the differences between southern and northern Italy arose. As the politician understood the analysis – and not without good reason – the game was already over at that point. There simply was not much that could be done about it – the system would be what it would be because, once upon a time, far back in history, it was like it was (Putnam 1993: 188). Clearly, socio-cultural determinism is not just a theoretical puzzle. It is a very real and practical problem for most developing countries and the countries of the former Soviet Union. As Putnam put it, the future of Moscow may come to resemble the prevailing situation in Palermo (1993: 221).

To a certain extent, I believe that Putnam's findings on the significance of cultural legacy resulted from the design of the study. The strength lent to the study by comparing regions of the same country was, of course, that he could keep many factors, such as the constitutional and institutional, constant – but this is also the study's weak spot (cf. Tarrow 1996). Because all the regions Putnam compared worked within the same constitutional framework and were institutionally constructed in the same way with respect to the relationship to central powers and the legal infrastructure, these variables could not constitute an explanation of the differences in the quality of democracy that Putnam so skillfully laid out. One alternative would have been to compare the quality of democracy in a number of regions in different European countries to find out whether differences in how they worked might have something to do with how their constitutional and legal infrastructures were constructed. However, the choice of design for a study like Putnam's is always a win/lose proposition: when you gain something in one area, you lose something else in another. Such an alternative study would, for instance, have had serious problems keeping the party political variable constant, because regions in different countries are controlled by different parties: French social democracy is certainly not the equivalent of Swedish social democracy, for instance. The point I want to get across is not a methodological criticism, but only that in Putnam's study as it was designed, it was built into the analysis that the institutional variables could not explain the variation in the variation of levels of the regions social capital.

In his book *The Multiculturalism of Fear* (2000), political scientist Jacob Levy writes that within political philosophy, we must make a kind of choice between which human conditions must be accepted and which we believe can be changed. Every political theory that is not "foolishly utopian must assume that there are some human limitations and some aspects of the human condition which cannot be overcome, at least not in the foreseeable future" (Levy 2000: 3). The first limitation Levy identifies is that group loyalty is such an inherent human trait. We tend to clothe ourselves in a sense of solidarity with whatever groups, clans, social classes, and other forms of identity may be at hand. According to Levy, however constructed, fleetingly contrived, and imaginary those identities might be according to certain postmodern and relativist theories, they are genuine and palpable to the real people involved. Just because we can successfully argue the thesis that "something" is a "construction," it does not mean that it is within our power to change that "something" as it pleases us. Even if being "Swedish," "a Yankees fan," "Hutu," or "senior citizen" are all social constructions, they are still utterly tangible constructions to the individuals who identify with those identities. They do not lend themselves to reconstruction through retraining programs, be they never so deliberate. Levy presents a plausible argument when he writes that the liberal belief that the problem of ethnic violence could be solved by trying to eliminate ethnic identification by telling people that ethnic identity is just a historically random "construction" is as good as the idea that we could eliminate poverty by declaring material self-interest null and void (Levy 2000: 10). To reconnect to the model in chapter 2 – there is no difference in subjective rationality between someone who, based on a strong ethnic group identity, persecutes another ethnic group because he believes the latter is out to crush his own and someone who attempts to get the highest possible price when selling his condo. Even if the housing market and ethnic self-image can both be called "social constructions," they are still utterly tangible realities to the actors; both types of action may be partially explained by the institutional terms that apply to the actors.

The true nature of humanity and the construction of institutions

Thus, we have the people and we have the institutions. Their repertoires of action vary over time and space, which is what we want to explain. The beliefs and ideological persuasions of Swedes (however they might be defined) are not the same today as they were a hundred years ago. The beliefs that dominate most individuals in Swedish society about things such as family, blood revenge, democracy, equality, and justice differ from those of their sisters and brothers all over the world. And yet we still have the same kinds of variations in political institutions – there is wide variation even within the frameworks of democratic nations. We accept that human beliefs affect institutions, and we accept equally that institutions affect people's beliefs. This is in many respects the truly "big question" of the social sciences and one to which we will probably never arrive at a final answer. The social anthropologists who should know the most about this have not, as far as I can see, arrived at any empirically sound answer (Eriksen 2001; Sahlins 2001; Sandall 2002). However, political theory gives us reason to argue that we should accept people as a given quantity and the institutions as mutable (Barry 2000; Levy 2000). The departure point for this is the normative notion of universalism – i.e. of the basic similarity of all human beings and, by extension, belief in their equal worth and thus their rights to equal treatment in relation to public institutions.[1] The idea that we are culturally different based on some kind of inherent factors (genetic, biological, or some breed of cultural norms that have been grafted onto the cerebral cortex, etc.) is not especially appealing for normative reasons, nor have I found any support for it in neurological research (Kandel, Schwartz, and Jessel 1995).

However, the question of the causal correlation between human belief systems, human actions, and the institutional conditions under which human beings live is exceedingly complicated and there is reason to discuss it in greater detail. If, as evolutionary game theory tells us, agents base their strategies on "history of play," then we need an additional theory that can help us understand how they get this information. A concrete and

---

[1] This equal treatment and impartiality applies only to the public arena, not to the private. Brian Barry (2000) calls it "second-order impartiality."

much-discussed example of the problem of the reach of cultural explanations is found in research on the relationship between Nazism, German
culture, and how to explain the Holocaust.

The question is: Were 6 million Jews exterminated because it was part
of the ethnically German population's inherited and *inherent culture* to
embrace eliminationist anti-Semitism, as Daniel Goldhagen asserts in his
much-noted and discussed book about the Jewish catastrophe during the
Second World War (Goldhagen 1996)? Or should the Holocaust be explained
by the circumstance that both ethnic Germans and their German–Jewish
victims were fostered in authoritarian *bureaucratic institutions* according to
which people followed orders and rules, as Raul Hilberg claimed in his extensive three-volume work on the construction of the German extermination
machine (Hilberg 1985)? Or should the answer be sought in the *ideology* of
Hitler and Nazism, whose intentions, contrary to what many could imagine,
was in fact to exterminate all ethnic Jews, as Lucy Dawidowicz has argued
(Dawidowicz 1975)?

In that case, how could this ideology gain such active and passive support,
specifically in the Germany of the interwar period, that made it possible to
commit murder on an industrial scale during the war? The paradoxical effect
of Goldhagen's culturally explanatory thesis, as Rosenbaum has shown, is
that it strips Adolf Hitler and the other leading Nazis of significance as an
explanation of the Holocaust (Rosenbaum 1998). According to Goldhagen,
if Adolf Hitler had not existed, someone else would have stepped forward
and filled his shoes: "If not Hitler, someone else" is his direct answer to
Rosenbaum; that is, the end result would have essentially been the same
because the culture of eliminationist anti-Semitism had been so powerful in
German culture since the late nineteenth century and the Nazi party and Nazi
leadership were merely its exponents. But if that is so, how can it be reconciled
with Ian Kershaw's comprehensive analysis of the significance of the strategic
and tactical decisions that paved Hitler's road to power (Kershaw 2000)?

Yet another problem with Goldhagen's cultural explanation, as Yehuda
Bauer and others have noted, is that if one had been asked in the 1920s
to identify a European country where anti-Semitism was deeply rooted in
the popular culture and also pervasively violent, the finger would not have
been pointed at Germany, but rather at countries such as Russia, France,
and Romania (Bauer 2000: 122f.). In other words, there were significant
methodological gaps in Goldhagen's culturalist reasoning.[2] One normative
problem Bauer finds important is that the kind of cultural explanations

---

[2] Bauer is kind enough to release Goldhagen from responsibility for this and chooses instead
to blame his teachers at Harvard. I should like to mention the more institutional factor, as
emphasized by Sven Hort: that in a market as overpopulated as the American intellectual
scene, the temptation to exaggerate a thesis in order to be heard above the general din is
sometimes irresistible.

provided by Goldhagen entail a serious risk of racist and/or ethnophobic prejudices against Germans, and by extension of generally racist explanations of historical phenomena like economic underdevelopment, inadequate democracy, and corruption. The product of Goldhagen's attempted explanation is either that the Germans did it because they wanted to do it, or that doing it was built into their historically inherited culture. The problem with the first type of explanation is that it is in reality a tautology – i.e. nothing more than repetition of known data. To say that people act in a certain way because they want or prefer to act that way is not a valid social scientific or historical explanation. The problem with the second type of explanation is that it partially releases individual perpetrators from moral accountability, as it describes them as more or less drugged by the eliminationist anti-Semitic culture or norms established some fifty years before. If a too strong culture is the problem, one can hardly hold individuals responsible for their deeds.[3]

This is not the place to present a more in-depth discussion of every explanation ever presented of the relationship between the German society, Nazism, and the Holocaust. The literature in the field is enormous. Instead, I choose to quote Yehuda Bauer, perhaps the most prominent thinker of the day concerning this phenomenon. After almost three hundred pages of re-analysis of the highly comprehensive and complicated body of research, he arrives at the following conclusion:

> The decisive factor was that the intellectual stratum – the academics, the teachers, the students, the bureaucrats, the doctors, the lawyers, the priests, the engineers – joined the Nazi Party because it promised them future prospects and status. Thanks to the fact that these intellectuals in a rapidly increasing degree came to identify themselves with the regime, it became possible to present the genocide as an inevitable step on the way to an utopian future. When Herr Doktor, Herr Professor . . . came to collaborate in a genocide . . . it became easy to convince the masses that the killing was necessary and to recruit them to execute this. An important role was played by the academics. I return to the question if we actually have learnt anything, if we still aren't producing technically competent barbarians at our universities. (2000: 286)

I must admit that I swallowed more than once the first time I read these lines. What I want to emphasize here is that Bauer is saying two different things. The first is that Nazi sympathizing among the professional and academic communities happened for opportunistic reasons – they were simply hoping for better prospects and higher status (cf. Kershaw 2000: 481). To a certain extent, this naturally had to do with the fact that sympathizers could reduce competition for positions, research grants, and other benefits

---

[3] This criticism of Goldhagen's book deals only with his attempted explanation and construction of theory. The empirical, historical sections of the book constitute a highly impressive research achievement, an opinion that seems to be shared by Yehuda Bauer and Raul Hilberg.

(cf. Friedländer 1999: 92). This took place in an era of severe economic austerity, especially for the academically educated labor force.[4] But as Friedländer and Kershaw assert, the overwhelming majority of non-Jewish German academics, especially those with tenured positions and thus not at risk of competition, were more than willing to be of service to the Nazis in connection with the purges. Those in opposition were exceedingly few.

It should also be added that the academics or lawyers who did protest against the persecution of Jews at that time seem *not* to have taken any personal risks (Müller 1991). It is also a myth that the German lawyers who collaborated in the persecution by administering the legal aspects were only obeying the laws created by the Nazis – i.e. were acting out of what jurisprudence calls legal positivism. First, there were no laws to obey when the purges began in 1933. Secondly, it has been proven that many of the most prominent judges and lawyers in Germany at the time were more than willing to break or bend existing laws in a myriad of ways in the service of Nazi ideology. In his book *Hitler's Justice*, Ingo Müller writes:

> Apart from a small minority of supporters of the [Weimar] republic, no one in the German legal profession endorsed positivism any longer. Carl Schmitt accordingly observed in 1932 that "the era of the legal positivism has come to an end." And professor of constitutional law Ernst Forsthoff avowed in his credo of 1933, The Total State: "Under no circumstances can the state of today draw any sustenance from positivistic thinking." (Müller 1991: 220)

My point is that of all professions in interwar Germany, academics and lawyers should have been the one with the strongest reason to be the most devoted defenders of the universal principles of the rule of law, but such was not the case. Yehuda Bauer also pointed at this lack of a universalist ethic among the academically educated professions. That is, Bauer does *not* say that the results would have been different if the incentives (i.e. the material rewards system for the individuals in those professions) had been changed. Instead, he focuses on the ethical dimension of the customary practices of the professions. Those defined by the regime as "Aryans" in the academic professions had a vested interest in an institutional order that favored them and disfavored a group they saw as competitors. That they would perceive the Jewish population in Germany as a homogeneous group of competitors (and as dishonest ones that always and unquestionably tried to benefit their own group) was however a prerequisite for abandonment of the belief in the German–Jewish population's (and their German–Jewish colleagues') right to

---

[4] The consequence of this in Sweden was that a majority of students in Uppsala and Lund voted in favor of resolutions that wanted to prevent Jewish doctors from Germany from coming to Sweden. Some surely cast their votes for anti-Semitic and xenophobic reasons, but we can reasonably assume that many acted out of pure self-interest.

equal treatment and non-discrimination – i.e. of the importance of uphold-ing the universal institutions. The only question is how could these kinds of ideas enrapture such large, highly educated, and relatively enlightened segments of the German population? What was it, more precisely, that per-suaded them to actively or passively support a policy by which a portion of German citizens, who were their colleagues (and, in many cases, friends), would first be discriminated against, then removed, and finally extermi-nated? If Hitler as an individual and agent played any role in the Holocaust, what was he playing with? What specific assets did he have? There is some-thing missing in Bauer's analysis as well, as we have yet to explain why the intellectual and academic communities in Germany became the willing collaborators of eliminationist anti-Semitism.

This is where notions of the *collective memory* come in. Unlike other countries where anti-Semitism was a prominent feature of society, Germany after 1918 was faced with managing a sweeping and crippling defeat in war and the ensuing and humiliating peace agreement. What the Nazis managed to do, primarily in league with the German military powers, was to establish the myth that much of the blame for the exceedingly costly defeat in the First World War could be laid at the feet of the Jewish population in Germany, who had behaved disloyally and betrayed the German fatherland in its darkest hour – that is, what came to be called the *Dolchstoss*, or "stab-in-the-back" legend (Keil and Kellerhoff 2002). One aspect of the argument was that the blame was put on the social democratic movement, which was thought to be behind the poor morale among large parts of the troops that became a problem for the German war powers in the autumn of 1918 (Kershaw 2000: chapters 3–6). The anti-Semitic undertone of the argument was based on the Jewish heritage of several leading social democratic politicians (Pulzer 1992). This was intensified by the circumstance that several of the leaders of the revolutionary Bavarian Republic in 1918–19 were also part of the German–Jewish segment of the population (Friedländer 1999: 91).

Another of the pillars of the "stab-in-the-back" legend was that Germans of Jewish descent had wriggled out of military service, especially the riskier military operations at the eastern and western fronts (Dawidowicz 1975). To drive the thesis home, the German military leadership initiated a com-prehensive "Jew Census" during the war, meant to prove the betrayal of the war effort by the German–Jewish population. The results were kept secret, probably because the hypothesis could not be confirmed, but the deeply anti-Semitic General Wrisberg leaked false information that was used by anti-Semitic organizations, and not least among them Hitler, as part of his propaganda. By the time an analysis of this bizarre census in early 1920 showed that the percentage of German–Jewish soldiers killed and severely wounded in action was proportional to the group's percentage of the population, beliefs about the perfidy of the Jewish population had already taken firm hold of the public consciousness. Hitler also underlined this false theme in *Mein Kampf* (Friedländer 1999: 88–90) and it was a recurring element of his political arguments (Kershaw 2000: chapter 6). Symptomatically, one of Joseph Goebbels' first decisions after the Nuremburg Laws took effect in 1935 was a decree that the names of fallen German soldiers of Jewish descent should not be inscribed on the memorials to soldiers killed in action in the First World War that many villages and cities in Germany had begun to erect (Friedländer 1999: 315).

There is much to indicate that this mythopoeia resulted in a collective memory among the German population of a "we and they" in which "they" had betrayed the country, and that this collective memory was one of the Nazis' most important assets in the effort to establish the belief, even among the intellectual elite, that the Jewish population should, could, and would be persecuted (Friedländer 1999). To go back to Russell Hardin's thesis on the weakness of universal institutions, such a division into "we" against "they," where "they" are thought to have been given unfair advantages by the existing institutions, was a prerequisite for political entrepreneurs to successfully challenge and dismantle such institutions. The deliberate lie about the cause of the German defeat in 1918 became, as Ian Kershaw argues, one of "Der Führer's" key political assets (Kershaw 2000: chapter 5).

The literature on this problem is vast, of course, and I make no claims here to do anything beyond point out one possible factor that Bauer does not mention – i.e. that something additional was necessary to establish a belief among the leading intellectual stratum that the German–Jewish population legitimately could and should be persecuted and eradicated. There is otherwise no logic in his extensive criticism of Goldhagen's thesis, since we can presume that the corresponding professions in other countries such as France and Russia were no different on this point from their equivalents in Germany. Bauer does not show why the German academically educated professions in particular should differ from corresponding professions in other countries when it came to supporting a severely discriminatory policy against Jews. It is here that the "stab-in-the-back" legend may work as the additional factor we need to explain why the Holocaust was possible.

Interesting in the context is that when it arose, the "stab-in-the-back" legend was not a Nazi product. It was created by the military establishment as a means of denying responsibility for the 1918 defeat. It should be added that the military continued to enjoy high esteem among large parts of the population despite the defeat, and thus the legend gained widespread legitimacy (Keil and Kellerhoff 2002). The Nazi party could thereby benefit from the prestige of military leaders when it chose to establish the myth of the German–Jewish population's treachery in the collective memory of the German people as an explanation for the painful defeat of 1918. I doubt that few researchers in the field other than Goldhagen would deny that the "stab-in-the-back" legend played an important role in the transition of German society from generally ideological anti-Semitism to eliminationist anti-Semitism. How much of a role it played is of course a matter of debate, and we will probably never know with any more precision, as retrospective survey studies cannot be done. My point here is more theoretical than empirical – i.e. to add something more precise than "culture" to the explanatory model of why universal institutions can arise and how they can, as in this case, fall apart. The mendacious "stab-in-the-back" legend was not inherent in or determined by German culture. It was produced by political forces that had a vested interest in its creation and adequate resources to ensure that it was established and widely accepted in German society. The collective memory of the causes of the defeat created by the "stab-in-the-back" legend is thus not a cultural variable of the type we have criticized. It is a political product constructed by actors whose subjective rationality is explainable. Conjuring up the legend was a political and strategic project, which is not to say that the Holocaust was the goal of those responsible for its creation. The point is that Nazis in Germany had access to something that their counterparts in other countries did not – an established myth about who was to blame for the nation's defeat and ensuing misery. Hitler aligned himself with the "stab-in-the-back" legend as an explanation for the 1918 defeat as early in the game as *Mein Kampf*. I quote, albeit reluctantly:

> The general feeling [in the army] was miserable . . . The expeditions were filled with Jews. Almost every clerk was a Jew, and almost every Jew was a clerk . . . When it came to economic life, the situation was even worse. There, the Jews had really become "indispensible." The spider had slowly begun to suck up the people's pores. Through the War Corporations, they had found an instrument by which they, little by little, could finish off the free economy of the nation. (Friedländer 1999: 89)

When Hitler wrote that, he could lean on the status that those militarily responsible for the defeat still enjoyed among large parts of the German population. This status was so high that the research community, who were then as now often political opportunists, dared not examine the empirical grounds for the accusations against the German–Jewish population produced by the military leadership.

The theory of the collective memory and resolution of the rationalist dilemma

One of the difficulties involved in game theoretical analysis is that of knowing the source of actors' beliefs about the identity of other actors, and especially whether they are oriented towards cooperation in solidarity or self-interest and conflict. As shown in chapter two, we cannot establish any solution to the question of how social traps fall out if we do not have these beliefs as input values (cf. Boudon 1996). As I pointed out, mobilizing a group, however just the cause, is a classic social dilemma. In his research on the American civil rights movement, Fred Harris has empirically shown the value of studying variations in the collective memories of the Afro-American population when it comes to explaining why the movement was more successful in some geographical areas than in others (Harris 1999). Naturally, certain such memories of experiences of collective protests can be exceedingly traumatic. We need only remember the Hungarian revolt of 1956 and the massacre at Tiananmen Square in 1989 to cite two examples of failed collective protests.

The problem can be described very simply: The first aspect is naturally what will happen if one protests – i.e. how those in power are going to act. Are they going to prove open to compromise, or will all protest be crushed with massive repression? The memory of earlier, similar events is deeply meaningful here, especially if we consider the impossibility of deciding to forget (Frey 2004; Schiemann 2002). Secondly, the actors must have some understanding of the degree of solidarity they can expect from other actors. For instance, to organize a struggle for the civil rights of a minority group, the actor must have information about what the other actors are going to choose. Once again, there is no point in being the only one to stand up and be counted in solidarity with a group or society that otherwise consists of individuals who are not prepared to sacrifice any of their personal resources to bring about change. On the societal level, this can be described as the fact that "everyone's" actions are dependent on what they believe about everybody else's actions – i.e. on the general beliefs that have been established in the group or society about who can be trusted (Schiemann 2000). To return to the example of the involvement of the academic professions in the purges in Germany, it would certainly have been morally admirable – but useless in that kind of situation – to have been the only ethnic German to have stood up for everyone's rights to equal treatment and the principle of non-discrimination. Andrew Kydd provides an example of this problem in his intriguingly titled paper "Overcoming Mistrust" (2000). Kydd, whose work is grounded in rationalist theory, asserts that to overcome mutual mistrust, actors must establish a "confidence game" by starting to send trust-engendering "signals" to one another. However, Kydd points out that the signals actors send to show that they can be trusted must not be too valuable, as the actors on the receiving end will only utilize what the sender offers without cooperating in return. But nor can they be too cheap, because the recipient will then believe that the sender has laid a trap and that his trust-engendering signals are not sincere. In other words, this is a highly complicated game that produces a scenario in which a group of rationalist actors each waits for the other to make the first move and wherein we can presume a severe risk of misunderstanding in the interpretation of the putative trust-engendering signals (Kydd 2000). Initiating such a game in a culture of misanthropic, corrupt actors seems rather futile. Kydd also ignores the problem that actors cannot rationally decide to forget.

When faced with this problem, rationalist researchers emphasize the significance of *political leaders*. Their role is to use their credibility to create trust among other actors concerning who they should or should not cooperate with (Chong 2000; Johnson 1997). One of the ways they do this is to refer to shared norms and a shared culture distinct to that particular group. The problem with this analysis is that we either end up back in the culture-bound problem set out above – i.e. where our situation is determined by the historically established shared culture – or, as suggested by Robert Bates (1997), where political leaders contrive something that works as social cement for the group in question in order to serve the interests that are the object of their endeavors. That social cement may be all kinds of symbols, rites, myths, etc. In such a case, we end up in the relativist problem in which political leaders are free to "invent" various affiliations, loyalties, and identities for strategic reasons that produce the requisite trust between the actors. According to Bates, there is a link here between rationalist game theory and relativist postmodernism, as the latter emphasizes that things such as affiliation, identity, and history are only social and/or linguistic constructions (Bates 1997).

There are two inherent risks in the relativist argument. The first is that it explains the outcome of all such historical processes after the fact as rational strategies devised by political leaders. They simply create among the population or group the beliefs they need to achieve their ends. Thereby, we have established a sort of functionalist explanation to the historical outcomes we want to explain – the leaders have simply invented what they needed. This becomes research that consists of an endless number of "Just So" stories – i.e. we can declare after the fact that all the game pieces have fallen into their places (Tsebelis 1997). The second risk is that we will end up in total historical relativism, in which case the Holocaust could be seen as a "social construction" invented by the Zionist lobby in the United States to further the interests of the State of Israel. This would put revisionist historians like David Irving in the right – there were no gas chambers. There is a problematic link between the relativist postmodern school of history and the social sciences and the kind of historical revisionism and denial or disparagement of the Holocaust represented by David Irving (Guttenplan 2001: 190f.).

Getting out of this problem is obviously not easy. On the one hand, we can state that rationalist models do not work to explain the enormous variation in institutional design and collective action. Swedes do not engage in corruption because it is not rational for Swedes to engage in corruption, because they have institutions that are effective against corruption – but why these institutions exist or how they have come about cannot be explained inside rationalist theory. Naturally, such an argument brings none of us any new insights or wisdom. On the other hand, the culturally determined models are also highly problematical. Sweden is not a country characterized by corruption because offering or accepting bribes is not inherent in Swedish culture. Or else the Swedish population's "stock" is not such that they are predestined for corruption (Putnam 2002: 309). I am not going to repeat the discussion of the problematical aspects of this type of explanation, but rather simply point out that it can also be seen in the light of Daniel Goldhagen's theoretical débâcle. The conclusion to be drawn is that we need some kind of independent variable that cannot be reduced to simple utility maximization or to the general culture in the society in order to make possible an acceptable explanation for the kind of phenomena we are discussing here. To fill the model presented in chapter 2 with empirical substance, we need something that is not reducible to either self-interest or culture. My argument is that this may be a variant of what has been dubbed the *collective memory*.

The theory of the impact of the collective memory on the actions of social groups was originally launched by French sociologist Maurice Halbwachs in a work from 1951. According to Halbwachs, the collective memory was something that the individuals in social groups embraced in common, but he added that it was the *individuals* and not the group that embraced this mem-ory. The proviso is significant because we have bound ourselves to explana-tions based on the principles of methodological individualism. While the collective memory is an image of past events shared by a limited group of individuals, it is also a variable found on the individual level. That is, it is not the group that remembers something; the carriers of the collective memory are the individuals (Halbwachs 1992). This is meaningful to how individuals are going to act. A classic in the context would be John Gaventa's studies of why workers in certain impoverished coal mining districts in the Appalachian region of the United States, despite their desperate circum-stances, did not organize in unions to fight for better conditions. Gaventa's explanations included the fact that the passive coal miners carried memories of defeats suffered decades before in struggles against the mining companies (Gaventa 1980). The connection to the kind of game theoretical approaches I presented earlier is apparent – the actors shape their expectations of what the other actors might do from these kinds of collective memories. In other words, this is how they get information about the "history of play," and especially about whether the other actors have chosen cooperation or non-cooperation, and thus if they can be trusted or not (Young 1998: 6). This may also be understood as an explanation of how and why the actors in societies and groups develop different "mental maps" that affect how they perceive other actors, including the actors whose job it is to uphold the rules of the game – i.e. the institutions (Denzau and North 1994).

The advantage of the theory of collective memory is that such memories are not necessarily the inevitable product of history or cultural conditions. On the contrary, they are usually the spawn of deliberate and strategic action by political elites in a process wherein the writing of history becomes a weapon in the political struggle (Karlsson 1999; Linderborg 2001). According to one analysis, Milosevic could mobilize the Serbian people to take up arms by using references to events during the Second World War to make it seem credible to the Serbs that the Croats were once again preparing to commit genocide against them (Bates, de Figueiredo, and Weingast 1998). The widespread practice of discrimination against Serbs and the nationalist overtones of the newly formed Croatian state under the leadership of President Franjo Tudjman gave Milosovic all the facts he needed to persuade large parts of the Serbian population of the evil intentions of the Croats (Bennett 1995: 125). The discriminatory actions included the firing of all police in Croatia of Serbian origin, along with the wholesale dismissal of Serbian teachers, doctors, and local officials. When the newly formed Croatian state set up its new army, the government made it clear that only ethnic Croats need apply (Schiemann 2002). For the Serbs living in the new Croatia, these were unmistakable signals that they and their children could count on a future of widespread discrimination in all dealings with authorities, schools, hospitals, etc.

The shots fired at Ådalen in 1931 when the Swedish army killed five demonstrators at a labor conflict is another example. The political fight over the collective memory of this event lasted for decades. Was this a typical reaction from the capitalist state when confronted with the workers' legitimate struggle for better living conditions? Or was it to be interpreted as the outcome of a combination of series of unfortunate circumstances within the military contingent and the irresponsible and illegal action of communist agitators? Or were the shootings the legitimate action of the military faced with a ruthless and violent communist insurrection? In a skillful analysis, historian Roger Johansson showed how representatives of social democracy and LO (the Swedish Trade Union Confederation) began in the early 1980s to reshape their own image of Ådalen from that of a conflict between communist and social democratic policy to a story in which employers and right-wing politicians were given sole blame for that kind of social unrest (Johansson 2001). Sweden in the early 1980s was governed by a non-socialist administration and LO no longer felt any threat from communist factions within the union movement. They thus had an interest in redrawing the picture of what happened so that it could be used for political and union mobilization, but this time in a way that stood in sharp contrast to how LO had formerly viewed the conflict (cf. Nycander 2002).

The central issue in research on collective memories is how societies and groups will remember their pasts. The word "remember" should be interpreted rather broadly here to include everything from how people choose to honor certain historical phenomena through politically resolved ceremonies and memorials (museums, statues, publications) to more experience-based memories or reminders of the past handed down from one generation to the next (Schwartz 2001: 9f.). But there are two variants of research based on the theory of collective memories. The first is based on a relativist, postmodern orientation that emphasizes that history must always be seen as socially constructed by powerful elites. Its main idea is functionalist: That is, views of the past are explained by contemporary needs and interests of those in power. A classic Marxist might say that the historians paid by the ruling class create the beliefs about history upon which the continued reproduction of power depends (Ben-Yehuda 1995: 273).

A relativist would probably express the same idea by saying that the construction of history is shaped by the elites' need for legitimacy. As Foucault put it: "memory is actually a very important factor in struggle . . . If one controls people's memory, one controls their dynamism . . . It is vital to have possession of this memory, to control it, administer it, tell it what is must contain" (Foucault 1975: 25). In this view on the significance of the collective memory, actual historical events and courses play an entirely subordinate role (Coser 1992). As Barry Schwartz has stated, this approach implies a distinct *discontinuity* between the past and the present, to the point where there actually exists no past other than that constructed for us by those in power (Schwartz 1991).

The other approach is the diametrical opposite, of course. It asserts that what actually happened in the past informs our understanding of the present. In this analysis, people's beliefs about the past are deeply embedded in their personal experiences, or how those experiences have been handed down over generations. The memory of the past is in this sense the present and it cannot be changed by the governing elites, no matter how sophisticated their propaganda methods may be (Arthur 1999). In other words, there is a clear *continuity* here between the past and the present (Schwartz 1991). No matter how hard new political leaders in Israel and Palestine (or in Northern Ireland, Bosnia, Rwanda, etc.) tried, they could not overcome the distrust and hate that had arisen between different population groups, especially since it is impossible to command, instruct, or use economic incentives to make people forget. Moreover, as Frey (2004) has argued, the more we try to forget, the more we remember. And the more others tell us to forget an event, the more vivid will our memories of that very event become.

In a seminal paper in this field published in 1991, Schwartz argued that both aspects should be conjoined in a larger theoretical focus, as both could be seen as ends of a continual dimension. That is, neither total continuity or discontinuity between the past and the present exists in reality; rather, each constitutes a sort of stylized archetype – extreme distillations against which empirical analyses can be measured, but which we cannot expect to exist in reality (Schwartz 1991). The ingredients of the collective memory are neither a purely social construction nor historical fact established once and for all, but are rather always found somewhere along the line between those two poles (cf. Stråth 2000). Because historical research cannot be experimental or constitute a complete description of the actual course of events, it will always be possible to discover new elements in the past that compel us to revise our understanding of what actually happened.

However, Schwartz strongly rejects the postmodern relativist point of view that emphasizes only the discontinuity in which cynical political elites manipulate history to further their own interests (Schwartz 2001: ix). He argues that the political powers that be are not usually entirely free to contrive or create collective memories by constructing historical facts. Milosevic did not need to invent the idea that the new Croatian state was going to discriminate against Serbs; all he had to do was point out the measures that Tudjman had in fact taken. There are exceptions; the Jewish census carried out in Germany in 1916 previously discussed is one such case.

History is certainly subjective in that there are no exact criteria for which data individual historians should select or emphasize, but this subjectivity is not total. Even if we cannot "revisit" the past, we can know some things with certainty: Japan attacked Pearl Harbor on December 7, 1941; there were crematoria in Auschwitz; and Swedish communists did use violence before the shootings took place in the Ådalen incident (cf. Ben-Yehuda 1995: 278). How much of this we can and are allowed to know has to do with the existence of independent research that need not comply with the demands of political or economic powers to dominate our thinking about the past. Historian Åsa Linderborg has added an important argument in this context, namely that a relativistic position that goes to the extreme conveys the risk that one does not care to criticize what is apparently false (Linderborg 2001: 38). The relevant question from the relativist position is why should we replace one mythopoeia with another? If one mythopoeia is as good as the next, professional historians at the universities might as well shut up shop and look for work as PR consultants. Demands for intersubjectivity, proof, logic, and openness to critical study are still valid in the writing of history, according to

Linderborg. We can never know with complete certainty, but we can know more and better. It is impossible to reveal mythopoeia from the position that all writing of history is mythopoeia.

An example: the Masada myth

One example of the application of Schwartz's approach is found in Nachman Ben-Yehuda's work on the "Masada Myth" in Israeli politics. In purely physical terms, Masada is the remnants of a rock fortress in the Negev desert in Israel. According to Ben-Yehuda, the myth about what happened in the year 73, constructed from the 1930s onwards by Zionist ideological entrepreneurs, played a pivotal role in the building of the State of Israel, especially in relation to its youth organizations and military forces. Briefly recounted, the myth tells us that after the failed Jewish uprising against Rome in 67, a group of Jewish freedom fighters fled to the Masada fortress, where they entrenched themselves to continue the struggle. They held out against a heavy siege and fierce battles for two or three years. When they finally understood that they could not overcome the military superiority of Rome and that defeat was near, the Jewish freedom fighters chose to commit collective suicide, along with women and children. Thus, almost 1,000 Jewish freedom fighters chose death above slavery and degradation by the Romans.

In Zionist politics, the Masada rocks and the archeological remnants were made into a profane cult center. In Israeli society, Masada symbolized the picture of a heroic fight against superior forces and the need to arm and prepare the Israeli army so that "Masada will never fall again." Officers and soldiers in the Israeli army swore an oath of allegiance at the Masada fortress until the early 1990s (Ben-Yehuda 1995: 147–152). The making of this myth gradually became a formative part of the Israeli identity. The process included mandatory school field trips to Masada, presentation of the myth in textbooks, and widespread media coverage achieved through the periodically vigorous tourism industry. A new country with no history of its own needed to invent one, and clever ideological entrepreneurs could in this case create a history that worked as an ideological cement for the new state (cf. Zerubavel 1995).

As Ben-Yehuda and others have shown, the story is a strategically created and exploited myth. The indisputable facts that exist and that have always been available paint the following picture. The group that committed suicide at Masada was indeed a Jewish group, but it had been forced by the majority of the Jews in Jerusalem to leave the city before it was conquered by the Romans. The Masada group were ejected from Jerusalem because they were thieves and murderers who had preyed on the citizens of the city, including other Jews, in a pattern that we would today call Mafia-like. There is no evidence that the group withstood a siege for more than a short time, nor any evidence that they fought the Romans at all, although there is evidence that other Jewish groups at the time actually did do battle with the superior Roman troops. Available historical evidence shows that before Masada was besieged by the Romans, the Masada group devoted itself to assault, murder, and plunder of nearby Jewish villages. In other words, the story that Masada has to tell is not particularly pleasant or heroic.

Ben-Yehuda's review of how the heroic Masada Myth could be established as a collective memory in Israeli politics is a masterful piece of social science. He shows that the image of the events at Masada as established by Israeli authorities and ideological entrepreneurs is fundamentally untrue. The intriguing thing is how the myth could achieve such an impact, even internationally (the myth is recapitulated in the current edition of the *Swedish National Encyclopedia*, for instance). However, Ben-Yehuda does not argue that the ideological entrepreneurs and government powers invented the myth wholesale. Instead, he shows how skillfully they used *a selection* of the historical facts available to create the myth. The strength of the continuity perspective is that it shows that this was not so much a matter of the fabrication of new facts as it was the omission of existing (and known) historical facts and of ideologically determined interpretations (Ben-Yehuda 1995: 301). It was possible to identify how the Masada Myth was made for precisely the reasons given by Åsa Linderborg.

Studies of collective memories are close to analyses that stress the importance of the political discourse and the political significance of ideas (Berman 1998; Schmidt 2000). Compared with those directions, however, the theory of collective memories as formulated by Barry Schwartz has obvious advantages. The first is that analyses of the significance of ideas contain no working approach to the origins of ideas and why certain ideas or discourses take on more importance than others. This type of analysis easily becomes the target of the kind of cultural explanations that have proven so problematical. The advantage of basing the analysis on the existence of collective memories is that it adds political actors and their resources and strategies to the analysis. Ideas and discourses, like culture, exist, quite simply inherited from history, while collective memories are always produced. Collective memories need not be false – that the Swedish tax administration is not severely tainted by corruption is not a strategically established myth, to take but one example. This image of Swedish administration lives by virtue of individual citizens' concrete experiences of the organization. This approach tells us that trust in public institutions is not determined by the existing culture; it is instead something that is built or destroyed through the real experiences of citizens in their dealings with the institutions and through the image as collective memory that political actors manage to establish.

Again, memories have a few special characteristics that make them particularly interesting in this context. For instance, we cannot rationally decide no longer to remember something (Baddeley 1999; Frey 2004). There is no rational choice to make. Nor can memories be directed into existence via incentives, although they can be the targets of interpretation and reinterpretation. The advantage of the approach to collective memories presented by Schwartz and practiced by Ben-Yehuda is as follows: By having added variables such as political actors and their resources and strategies to the analysis of how the image of institutional trustworthiness is established, we can overcome the kind of historical and cultural determinism that has characterized much of the analysis of social capital in particular and cross-national comparative social science in general. Therein lies the importance of empirical analysis of the genesis of "mental maps" (in the form of collective memories) that must be created in order to use game theoretical models to explain the variation in outcomes of the problem of the social trap. Studies of how nations have risen from the morass of corruption often show that the process involved employing a number of very conspicuous interventions and measures to change the image of how public administrations act. Especially in relation to the tax administration and anti-corruption measures, researchers have stressed the importance of public bodies showing in practice that they were prepared to intervene strongly, even against individuals and firms with close ties to political powers (Berenztein 1996; Stapenhurst and Kpundeh 1999; Thorp 1996).

The Russian tax administration has not been entirely successful, but the year after my visit one could see the following on Russian television: Scenes on news programs reporting raids by the Russian tax police and coverage that in no way tried to conceal the extremely brutal methods that these usually masked police employed. The second element was commercials produced by the tax authority that showed a hospital room in which a surgeon is operating on a patient. The screen suddenly goes black and then a voice and text is shown in which the poor surgeon appeals to Russian citizens to pay their taxes so that the hospital will be able to pay its electric bill so he can continue operating on the poor patient. Whether these have had any effect on willingness to pay taxes in Moscow will have to remain unsaid, however. The point is that while it is indeed difficult and complicated, it is not impossible to "get from Moscow to Stockholm." However, the journey demands not only high ethics and morals on the part of public officials, but also that people perceive the measures to be credible. In all likelihood, the transition from distrust to trustworthiness requires strong signals that the government agency in question has changed (Root 1996).

8

The transition from mistrust to trust

We are facing the following question: In concrete terms, what might be the process that the actors in a society undergo as they make the transition from deep mistrust to trust? That is, once we have ended up in a social trap, how do we get out of it? This has to do with how trust for other actors can be engendered and the legitimacy of public institutions. This is a core issue to be resolved, if societies and groups caught in social traps are not to remain there forever (also known as "steady states"). The problem is that these types of changes are both unusual and difficult to document. Why they are unusual should be apparent by this point. They are difficult to document because ultimately the process is a matter of changes of deep-seated mental or cognitive human beliefs. What might persuade the members of a group that have felt deep mistrust towards another group to start trusting those others? What must come about to make Catholics and Protestants in Northern Ireland, or Muslims, Serbs, and Croats in Bosnia, or Jews and Palestinians in the Middle East, ever change their beliefs about each other? What could make citizens in countries such as Russia and Argentina trust their governments to handle their taxes in a responsible way?

It is no easy task to find good empirical evidence in existing historical material to confirm how these changes in beliefs on who can be reasonably trusted occur. What made Swedes and Danes start seeing each other as brother peoples in the mid-nineteenth century after ten bloody wars, the first in the mid-fifteenth century and the last in 1814 and the source of every conceivable misery (Holmberg 1946)?[1] How did Finland, deeply lacerated

---

[1] The often scorned and ridiculed Scandinavian student movement probably played a critical part (see Holmberg 1946). Its political failure through Sweden's betrayal of Denmark in

by a truly horrible civil war in 1918, leave behind the post-war era political culture of class hatred, vindictiveness, and suspicion and end up as one of the most democratic, economically successful and least corrupt countries in the world?[2] How can the people in countries such as Poland, Hungary, and Russia, which experienced first the moral decay of the communist state and then the ensuing grave corruption, ever come to trust in public administration? For instance, it would be interesting to know what brought about the change in Swedish state administration in the nineteenth century from corruption, purchase of positions, and other irregularities to the kind of legally regulated Weberian bureaucracy that existed by the end of the century. It has been possible to prove that such a change took place (Rothstein 1998b), but we still do not know how it was actually achieved. What did it take for those who held positions to stop demanding payment from their successors? If a bureaucrat has once upon a time paid to get a position, and if he takes it for granted that all other bureaucrats get paid when they leave their positions, something special has to happen to put an end to that activity.

The labor market as a social trap

My choice of empirical illustration has fallen on the subject of labor market relations and specifically the emergence of peaceful and collaborative industrial relations in Sweden in the 1930s that ended as a major part of what

---

1863 when it failed to keep Charles XV's promise to supply troops to defend Denmark from German attack should not detract from the fact that the movement laid the groundwork for a profound change of mentality in Scandinavia. The young intellectuals of both countries promised at a number of much-noted student meetings never again to wage war upon one another, which in all likelihood contributed to the peaceful resolution of the union crisis between Sweden and Norway in 1905. At the Dyböl fortifications in southern Jutland, where Danish military opposition to superior German forces broke down in 1863, there stands an imposing monument to the volunteer Swedes and Norwegians who fought with the Danish army and died in defense of Denmark's freedom.

[2] The importance of Veinö Linna's "crofter trilogy" about the civil war to the success of modern Finland can hardly be overestimated on this point. What Linna succeeded in doing was to make the red faction's insurrection and action comprehensible to the victorious white faction – if not politically, at least on the human level. It was no longer possible to hate the other side or consider them traitors when their motives and actions were made understandable, and in certain situations even defensible, on the human level upon which Linna's novels take place. Linna also depicted the violence from both sides with the same stark realism. Unfortunately, I cannot read Finnish, but Nils-Börje Stormbom's report of the debate in 1950s Finland shows that after the publication of the second volume, Linna engaged in immediate public polemic against the views of established historians on how 1918 should be interpreted. Nils-Börje Stormbom's analysis of the political impact of Linna's writing is masterful. I cannot think of any fictional works that have had greater political impact on the democratic progress of a nation than Linna's (cf. Alapuro 1988: 203).

later became known as "the Swedish Model." The subject has been thoroughly studied, but researchers have failed to solve the theoretical problems of what made the model possible. A brief history: Sweden was not always the land of compromises and negotiations. From the 1890s to the mid-1930s the Swedish economy had the most days of production lost due to industrial disputes of any western industrial nation (Åmark 1992). Class conflicts were intense and sometimes violent. However, during the late 1920s, both sides began to realize that rationalization of production and more orderly relations between organizations could change capitalism from a zero-sum to a positive-sum game (de Geer 1978). Already in the late 1920s the union leadership had identified increased productivity, and not just class struggle, as a major vehicle for improving the conditions of the working class. For example, after arguing against making the National Blue-Collar Union (LO) a more combative organization for attacking employers at the 1926 LO congress, Edvard Johnsson, Secretary General and future chairman, stated that,

> [w]ages – I'm talking about real wages – can, in the long run, only be increased if improved methods of production and economic organization create the necessary conditions . . . To think that the influence of the unions exclusively can decide the wages is as wrong as when the rooster believes that the sun rises because his crowing. If the unions can arrange so that at every point in time, the workers will receive what they are entitled to from the production, then they have fulfilled every reasonable claim. (Quoted in Johansson 1989: 56)

Beginning in 1928, a particularly black year for the Swedish labor market because of the number of lost working days due to industrial disputes, the then Conservative government invited LO and the Swedish Employers' Federation (SAF) to talks about what could be done to achieve a more peaceful labor market. Both parties agreed that both sides stood to win from increased collaboration, and ten years of conferences and investigations, filled with problems and set-backs as both LO and SAF fought against more militant forces within their organizations, eventually led to the famous General Agreement (the Saltsjöbaden Accords) in 1938 (Johansson 1989).

The Swedish labor market of the 1920s was thus characterized by many and sometimes protracted labor conflicts. The parties mistrusted each other deeply as to both content (the struggle about how surplus value should be allocated) and the intentions behind each party's long-term policy. Naturally enough, management found it hard to appreciate the Marxist-inspired argument that their existence was unnecessary and unjust and would come to an end through the forthcoming socialist organization of production. Union leaders believed that management's lack of acknowledgement of them as a legitimate party to negotiations endowed with equal rights was a grave problem (Hansson 1939, cf. Golden 1988).

However, both parties eventually realized that the conflicts – strikes, blockades, boycotts, and lockouts – were terribly costly to their respective organizations. The costs were partially unnecessary and were eventually regarded as irrational because the conflicts, however intense and ideologically charged, always eventually ended with a new agreement between the parties. An obituary published in the Swedish Employers' Federation's magazine *Industria* about the then head of SAF, Hjalmar von Sydow, told how an outraged journalist covering a particularly long and difficult strike asked von Sydow how he thought it would end, whereupon von Sydow calmly replied that it would end as it always did, with a new agreement. What he probably meant was that despite the often tense atmospheres and rhetorical high dudgeon, the parties would sooner or later be compelled to arrive at a compromise. The only question was how long it would take and what it would be allowed to cost the contracting parties. Given that neither party could expect to eliminate the other as an actor and thereafter unilaterally dictate working and pay conditions, the inevitable result was eventual compromise (see, for example, *Industria* 1935: 136). The unions had arrived at the same conclusion. Issue 41 of *Metallarbetaren* (the journal of the powerful Metal Workers' Union) put it this way in 1929:

> The parties are meeting at the negotiating table now, where their strengths will be tested. Each party more or less instinctively understands the relative strengths of the other. If a conflict can be avoided – if there are proven men on both sides of the table, it should be possible – it will not be due to lack of "revolutionary fire," but simply to the fact that it is idiotic to do battle if matters can be settled otherwise.

The question that began forming in the minds of both management and the unions in the 1920s was thus whether, given that there would be an agreement sooner or later, it might not be possible to arrive at such an agreement without the costly consequences of open conflict. It seemed, at least to many of those involved, rather irrational to throw away those costs time and time again when everyone knew that at the end of the day they would be forced to hammer out a compromise settlement. As long as the class struggle raged with no chance of declaring a decided and final winner, labor and management were tied to one another whether they liked it or not. For instance, issue 20 of *Metallarbetaren* in 1928 covered a conflict at a manufacturing company in Marstrand that had gone on for five long years before ending in a settlement by which all workers were re-hired according to the current agreement. Even communist union leaders, and there were many in the movement at that time, soon realized that they would come off badly if they could not present the rank and file with good agreements with the opposition, whom they considered exploiters and believed should be eliminated (cf. Stråth 1982). Protracted and open conflicts were rational only if final victory over the opposition was assured, given the expectation of being able to stand as the victor. For the radical faction of the worker's movement victory would have been tantamount to the introduction of socialism, while for management it would have been to eliminate the unions as a party to negotiations.

The costs of open conflict varied. First, both parties were forced to financially recompense the companies and workers taken out in a conflict. Funds for striking or locked out workers and for companies hit by strikes or taken out in lockouts cost both parties dearly. The financial strains could be substantial, even if the organizations were strong. And throughout the period, the union movement grew ever stronger, reaching more than 600,000 members by the mid-1930s, a factor that management could not ignore.

Second, production stops entailed costs to companies through lower profits and impaired capacity to pay wages. A third factor, noted by historian Maths Isacson, was that the antagonism, bitterness, and mistrust between the parties that followed in the wake of open conflicts could bring high costs in the strains on cooperation between workers and company representatives (i.e. foremen) at local workplaces (Isacson 1987). Production had already become so technically complex by that time that it required dedication, initiative, and personal responsibility from at least part of the labor force. These production factors were generally damaged by the hardnosed mentality and lack of trust that open conflicts engendered (Johansson 1989: chapter 2). In cases where management had used "willing workers" to break an ongoing strike, which was not unusual at the time, tremendous antagonism was created in the workplace that lingered long after the open conflict was over. Especially in relation to the ongoing and often rapid-fire industrial efficiency programs, companies were dependent on union cooperation with management (cf. de Geer 1978).

There are two main ways to reach an agreement with an unwilling opponent. The first is to try and exhaust the opposition's resources while the strike action is in progress and thus weaken its will until it crawls to the cross and agrees to a settlement on the first party's own terms. That strategy can be costly, of course, because it is always possible to misjudge the opposition's resources and to underestimate its willingness to fight and readiness to sacrifice. It is also difficult to predict how conflicts of that type will evolve, as the parties are not privy to precise information about what resources and strategies the opposition has at its disposal.[3] In this case, for instance, it is often uncertain what sympathy actions a union can mobilize from other unions and the extent to which either party can mobilize the political resources of the state in the struggle. Open conflicts in the labor market (as in many other areas) are a strategy laden with heavy risk.

The other way to reach an agreement is to choose to arrange a negotiating system, despite clearly opposing interests as in this case, intended to arrive at a settlement without having to resort to open conflict (cf. Schiller 1988b). This is predicated on the ability of the actors to work with a relatively complicated conceptual model in which they are fully aware that there are clear conflicts of interests, but are equally cognizant that they have a common interest in preventing them from resulting in open warfare (Fossum 2001).

However, it is pointless to be the only player in such a game to refrain from regularly threatening open conflicts aimed at forcing a more favorable agreement, because the reticent actor will equally regularly come out the loser, since he has agreed to a worse settlement than he would otherwise have achieved. If, on the other hand, both parties choose to regularly threaten open conflict, such will occasionally be the result, since the parties cannot maintain credibility in each other's eyes if they back down from such threats, because crying wolf would make the threat worthless the next time the parties sit down to negotiate. Both parties must trust that the other party will not regularly threaten to resort to open conflict in order to get a better agreement. We are dealing with an archetypal social trap here in which the actors, given that they can trustingly cooperate, have much to gain by establishing a negotiating system in which the costs of arriving at an agreement are minimized. But, again, you cannot rationally decide to trust the other because it is impossible to decide to forget being betrayed, even if both parties realize that they would both profit from such a loss of memory.

However, the insight that both parties stood to gain from increased cooperation had also come to many of the leading actors within SAF and LO in the late 1920s. LO leaders had realized that real wage increases could be achieved only through more efficient production, which in turn required the unions to support efficiency programs. They had also begun to understand that wages were dependent on international industrial competitiveness. Open and protracted labor market conflicts stood in the way of both goals (Johansson 1989: 56).

So, what actually was the problem? Why could unions and management, as the rational economic actors they are, not immediately establish

---

[3] This theory on the fundamental unpredictability and thus inherent risk of open conflicts is the core message of von Clausewitz's theory on the nature of war. In other words, this is a general law of unpredictability – i.e. that adherence to the law does not exist in the context of open conflict.

the trusting cooperation by which each had so much to gain? Why did the famous Saltsjöbaden Accords not come until 1938? The answer to that question, as I shall show, was the widespread mistrust between the parties and the difficulties involved in overcoming it. The fight for the collective memory of a particularly traumatic event in Swedish politics, the Ådalen shootings of 1931 in which five people were killed and even more wounded when a military contingent opened fire on unarmed demonstrators, also played a critical role. However, before I get into that, I must digress a moment in order to address the matter of the problem surrounding power and interests in a capitalistically organized labor market. Peace and cooperation are not always better than struggle and conflict. Matters like these should not be determined solely by strategic reasons (prospects of victory). Normative arguments must sometimes prevail.[4]

Power, exploitation, and the logic of organization

As we know, the antagonism between capital and labor can be viewed in a multitude of ways. One is naturally the Marxist view in which the wage earner, regardless of the wage agreement, is generally to be regarded as exploited. It is therefore in the interests of the worker collective to put an end to capitalist exploitation – i.e. to abolish the wage employment system altogether. From such a perspective, any form of cooperation and seeking of paths toward an agreement that do not lead to open conflict are contrary to the long-term interests of wage earners. The notion was widely embraced at the time and called for the establishment of a socialist means of production. The idea was founded on the Marxist doctrine of labor value, which focused on the existence of unwarranted surplus value that accrued to the capitalist, no matter how successful wage earners were as a collective pay negotiating party (Marx 1927).

In this context, we can leave open the question of whether or not the theory of labor value is correct (cf. Elster 1985). The argument is intended to illustrate that the parties that successfully resolve a social dilemma absolutely need not be equal with respect to the balance of power between them or with regard to what they have gained through cooperating. All that is required is for both parties to realize that they have more to lose by resorting to open

---

[4] For instance, I do not believe, as some asserted in Sweden in the winter of 1944, that the Allied Forces should have "stopped at the Rhine" and begun negotiations with the Nazi regime in Berlin. Sadly, war is sometimes preferable to cooperation. The logic of the social trap is based on the premise that the actors are in agreement from the outset that cooperation will benefit everyone, and that is of course not always the case. Normative arguments must also be weighed, not just financial calculations. As the German non-socialist democrats learned to their cost in 1933, there are some actors with whom one should never cooperate.

conflict than by cooperating. As Victor Galaz pointed out, there can be substantial and problematical normative injustices and differences between the parties in the kind of cooperative resolutions of the problem of the social trap written about by Elinor Ostrom, for example. This is of course not just a normative problem, as such imbalances of power can make cooperative resolutions unstable (Galaz 2004).

Just because two parties choose to cooperate, it does not mean that all matters of justice are resolved, especially with reference to the labor market. It is hardly necessary to embrace the Marxist doctrine of labor value to argue that substantial problems exist with respect to democracy and political fairness in a labor market of the kind that resulted from the 1938 Saltsjöbad Accords. One example is the doyen of liberal democracy theory, Robert Dahl, who devoted considerable intellectual energy to the problems of democracy and justice in capitalistically organized working life (Dahl 1989). Dahl's solution to the problem, inspired in part by David P. Ellerman, is a kind of radical corporate democracy. Naturally, there is no reason to believe that developments have come to the end of the road when it comes to finding working solutions to these problems only because the Soviet version of the organization of working life and production was such a stupendous failure (cf. Rothstein 1992d).[5] When the Saltsjöbaden Accords were formally terminated by LO in 1976 by reason of the labor law offensive that the organization had then begun, these problems of power and influence were the central argument (Schiller 1988a). In game theoretical terms, this could be expressed by saying that there are many possible points of equilibrium upon which the parties could agree, depending on how each perceives the strategies and resources of the opposing party.

The logic of organized interests

That which creates a union interest in devising a negotiating model by which open conflicts are avoided is the organizational interest. All other things equal, an interest is stronger if it is organized. However, when it comes to organizational resources there is a crucial difference between the interests of capital owners and wage earners. In the former case, the organizational resource(i.e. the company) is created as a direct consequence of the logic of the production system. The situation is not the same with respect to the wage

---

[5] There is reason here to mention the Vienna Congress of 1815 when the victorious powers met to bury the French revolution's promises of liberty, equality, and fraternity once and for all. Prince Metternich and his peers believed that events had proven that such democratic demands led only to tyranny, persecution, lawlessness, and war. However, it was to be only thirty-three years, in 1848, before the forces of democracy once again caused a commotion in Europe.

earners' interest, in that they must themselves create, pay for, and maintain unions outside the logic of the production system (Offe and Wiesenthal 1980). Put simply, there are unionized and non-unionized industries and companies and the degree of union organization varies widely among countries and industries.

My point here is to show that union leaders must always look out for two interests simultaneously – the workers' interest in better working conditions and the interest in preserving and strengthening the union organization. To initiate a bold and costly struggle for better working conditions (or to crush the capitalist system of exploitation, in the idiom of the Swedish labor market in the 1920s and the 1970s alike) may entail significant risks to the continued strength, or perhaps even survival, of the union. To understand what drives unions, we must include both types of interest in the analysis. As Alan Cawson asserted, the class interest is expressed via organizations, but the logic of organization will in reality shape that interest (Cawson 1986: 87). LO leaders were extremely hesitant to get involved in major conflicts as of the turn of the twentieth century and thereafter, because of fear of what the conflicts might cost the organization in the form of lost membership and revenues, along with the very real risk to the entire organizational structure (Nycander 2002; Westerståhl 1945).

This hesitation was shared by others, including German union leaders who did not rally round Rosa Luxemburg's war cry that the unions should use mass strikes as a political weapon. Instead, German union leaders prevented the social democratic party from adopting such a strategy in 1904 (Looker 1972; Marks 1989). Contrary to what is claimed by Marx and Engels in the *Communist Manifesto*, the proletariat were not in the least propertyless, but indeed had something to lose – i.e. their often hard-built organization. But this was not solely a union issue – the SAF president Hjalmar von Sydow expressed it thus in 1928: "Labor struggles cost an incredible amount of money, and of course those who handle the money and have to acquire it become inclined towards a peaceful policy by the very nature of the circumstances" (Socialdepartementet 1929: 76).

The classic debate on cooperation or conflict in the European labor movement took place in 1899 at the German social democratic party congress, between the revolutionary Rosa Luxemburg and the reformist Eduard Bernstein. Luxemburg's argument against Bernstein's reformist policy of cooperation was that while workers should certainly be organized in order to achieve partial improvements in wages and working conditions, the entire point of that kind of organization was to prove that the reformist policy of cooperation was unfeasible and wrong and that the movement should instead use mass strikes to confront the capitalist society and take power. The problem with Luxemburg's analysis was the question she never answered:

Why should individual wage earners give up their resources to support a union that does not produce results in the form of better wages and working conditions? Let us look at that logic from the perspective of union leaders. To motivate the organization, they must reach an agreement with management that contains some kind of improvement in wages and working conditions. Such agreements will always be criticized by some union members for not being favorable enough, thus compelling union leaders to accept responsibility for and defend the agreement, which by extension means they must arrive at a standpoint by which there is such a thing as a fair agreement between labor and management organizations (Olofsson 1979).

Therewith, the logic of organization has kicked in and fundamentally changed the conditions of the struggle between the social classes. The weapon – the organization of workers – that Marx, Lenin, and Luxemburg (and countless others) had hoped would be the lever that overturned capitalism ("Workers of the World, Unite") instead became the proof that it was not only necessary but possible to reach fair agreements with the capitalist opposition (Olofsson 1979; Rothstein 1987). To quote one of the most prominent architects of the Saltsjöbad policy on the LO side, Sigfrid Hansson, when asked whether the union movement wanted consensus or conflict:

> It is certainly true that labor unions have taken on the nature of *fighting organizations*, and that the union movement as part of the socialist movement has accepted the class struggle. But on the other hand, the organizations and the movement have always understood and accepted reality when it came to their immediate and for the moment most important task, that of progressively improving the position of workers in the labor market. Clear-sighted and responsible union members have understood that with respect to the wage policy, as with practical politics in general, we must adjust our actions to the "law of least resistance." (Socialdepartementet 1929: 39)

Hansson then pointed out that the Swedish union movement had actually been strongly oriented towards achieving consensus – e.g. through the development of the negotiation and settlement system – and that involvement in the labor peace conference did not entail any kind of reorientation. He blamed the problems on prejudice and lack of good will on the part of the opposition, especially its unwillingness to acknowledge the unions as an equal party. In later writings especially, he noted that the Saltsjöbad Accords were in reality only a codification and continuance of the negotiating models that had emerged at the local level and thus was not a new or foreign step for the Swedish union movement (Hansson 1939, 1942).

According to the logic of organization, union leaders must work with dual utility functions in their calculations, unlike the model actors upon whom economic theory is usually based (cf. chapter 2). As there are several different utility functions, there is no easy way to rank the preferences, as the values and interests the actors embrace cannot be weighed and compared using a uniform scale. For instance, how should a radical union leader of that time have weighed the value of ending capitalism against the value of strengthening the union, when the latter could be achieved only by closing an agreement with, and thus legitimizing, the opposition that the union wanted to abolish?

Creating trust between the combatants in the class struggle

In the late 1920s, ideas emerged in Sweden and other western countries on how societies could establish labor markets with significantly fewer open conflicts. The terms used for that concept were *labor peace* and *Mondism*, the latter after the English executive (Sir Alfred Mond) who originally launched the idea on the larger, international scale. The minority government led by the right-wing party that governed Sweden after the 1928 election invited the negotiating parties in the labor market to a national Labor Peace Conference in the autumn of the same year. The initiative garnered widespread coverage in the press and assembled no fewer than 350 participants and spectators who represented the majority of the organizations then existing in the Swedish labor market. It needs hardly be pointed out that representatives of communist and syndicalist union factions were not present. They regarded the decision of LO leadership to accept the invitation as "an abandonment of the class struggle and sacrifice of the freedom of workers." They asked themselves: "could the exploiters abolish exploitation without abolishing themselves?" (Casparsson 1966: 49). That same year, Sven Lindroth, leader of the Moscow-oriented communist party, published a book with the evocative title *Mondism or Class Struggle: Union Party Truce or a United Proletarian Front against the Capitalist Offensive?*[6]

It is noteworthy that when the governing administration discussed the arrangement of the conference with LO and SAF, they agreed that neither organization's chairman would give the opening address on behalf of his organization. The decision was made so that "questions of status" would not "come to the forefront and impede an open exchange of opinions." Instead, they agreed that the opening addresses would be given by people of lower formal rank in the organizations (Casparsson 1966: 48). The Labor Peace Conference was consequently begun with a number of rather conciliatory and cooperation-oriented speeches on the first day, not least among

---

[6] In Swedish: *Mondism eller klasskamp? Facklig borgfred eller proletär enhetsfront mot kapitalets offensiv?*

them one by Sigrid Hansson, whose many hats included that of editor of LO magazine *Fackföreningsrörelsen.* What both parties stood to gain by moving away from open conflicts and towards cooperation seemed clear to all speakers. The minister of social affairs underlined the notion in his speech, but also emphasized that success would be predicated on the parties meeting each other in a *new spirit,* wherein each was prepared to disavow "preconceived opinions and ingrained mistrust" (Socialdepartementet 1929: 17). The day after, one of the main actors in the drama, SAF president Hjalmar von Sydow, was considerably more pessimistic. While he saw the tremendous advantages of more cooperative relations, his doubts were deep-rooted *in the following*:

> I am remembering the preaching on these matters among workers for the last twenty or thirty years. The unions have never failed to pack pamphlets and press coverage with the old, worn-out Marxist theories that all profits of labor should belong to the workers, etc. The employer, the representative of capitalism, plunders and exploits the workers. He is on a par with those who unlawfully seize the property of another. Year after year, in press coverage and pamphlets, all of this has been drummed into the minds of workers and it is no wonder that it had results. (Socialdepartementet 1929: 74)

Obviously, both main actors were implying that the opposition's *mental maps* were going to be the major stumbling block to resolving the social trap inherent in costly conflicts. Most union speakers, as well as von Sydow, mentioned the beliefs about the opposition that had long since been instilled in the minds of their respective members. As von Sydow claimed, if one subscribed to Marxist theories, then employers were no better than common thieves with whom one did not open a trusting collaboration. However, he also noted in his speech that this sort of Marxist rhetoric had been toned down in recent years (Johansson 1989: 71). Meanwhile, union representatives repeatedly mentioned the lack of respect from management and unwillingness to acknowledge the unions as an equal and legitimate party to negotiations. According to LO chairman Arvid Thorberg, this had so often created such "mistrust" and "bad feeling" between the parties that relatively minor differences of opinion had led to extremely costly open conflicts. However, he admitted that the union movement had often employed "more than one exaggeration" in its propaganda, but also emphasized the remnants of the old "patriarchal rule" that lived on in the attitudes of many employers (1989: 117).

The Labor Peace Conference ended with a statement by cabinet minister Sven Lübeck that the government intended to create a labor peace committee whose task would be to put forward proposals and measures to promote "consensus and labor peace" and to which LO and SAF would each appoint five representatives. The government also intended to appoint an appropriate number of *impartial* committee members. The notion was backed by von Sydow, Thorberg, and unanimously by the entire conference by acclamation. The final words in the minutes of the conference are those of the chairman of LO and are worthy of quotation:

> I ask that labor also be allowed to give to the chairman our respectful thanks for the initiative taken. It is my sincere hope that this meeting will contribute to understanding on both sides that we are, in purely human terms, rather like one another. We must now practically address our differences and the difficult problems that exist for both of us in order to arrive at a felicitous outcome for all. Please allow me to extend our sincere thanks. (1989: 144)

It is difficult in hindsight to estimate more precisely the importance of this conference. Histories of the rise of the Swedish Model do not usually accord it any great significance (for an exception, see Johansson 1989), probably because things such as trust, mentalities, and collective memories have not been core issues for the Swedish historians, sociologists, and political scientists who have analyzed the period. Their analyses have instead focused on the more material and interest-oriented aspects, which is peculiar for several other reasons.

Looking at the date, it is noteworthy that the Labor Peace Conference was held barely six months after the Swedish labor and union movement had gathered for one of the largest manifestations in its history, the protests against the Labor Court established by the non-socialist parties and the liberal minority government, as well as the law on collective agreements. Far in excess of one hundred thousand workers came together in various demonstrations against the "compulsion laws" upon which they believed the Labor Court was built and their criticism of the liberal administration was harsh (Casparsson 1966: 37–40).

There is also reason to mention the bitterness towards the Liberal Party for having forced the social democratic minority government to resign in 1926. That came about in relation to matters of conflict management in the labor market surrounding the so-called "Stripa Directive"[7] and the bitter memory still preyed on the minds of many Social Democratic politicians and union officials, as well as many communists and syndicalists activists who at that time played a not insignificant role in labor disputes (cf. Golden 1988). However, the minister of social affairs in the new right-wing government, Sven Lübeck, the very man who had issued the invitations to the

---

[7] A ruling by the National Unemployment Commission in 1926 that deprived unemployed workers of economic assistance if they did not accept work at a mine that was put under union blockade. This conflict caused great bitterness within the labor movement and forced the social democratic minority government to resign.

conference and acted as its host, had by reason of his efforts as a mediator in many labor conflicts come to enjoy the "respect and esteem" of many union leaders (Casparsson 1966: 46). In his history of the Swedish union movement, Westerståhl writes the following about the significance of the labor peace conference in the prevailing political situation:

> Considering how the labor peace conference had been organized, it was obvious that it was not intended to lead to any immediate or specific results. Instead, its effects would become manifest in the long-run. Naturally, it was by itself important that the very spirit of cooperation and mutual understanding in this way was brought to the fore. The great positive interests most newspapers, not least the Social Democratic ones, gave the conference, contributed to shed light on a new and often unnoticed part of the relations between employers and workers. As a sign of this changed attitude it is noteworthy that *Industria* in 1929 published a number of articles in which the fundamental principles in the relations between unions and employers were reconsidered and in which a new spirit of understanding and appreciation was put forward. (Westerståhl 1945: 196, trans. by author)

Westerståhl adds that one reason for the positive reception of the Labor Peace Conference by both sides was that a couple of protracted conflicts within the paper pulp and mining industries had "to great costs for both parties, ended in a status quo" (1945: 190). Note that labor conflicts at that time had direct consequences in an entirely different way than they do now upon many individuals outside the conflict through the frequent occurrence of sympathy blockades and boycotts, which could at times have a grave impact on the "public sense of justice," because they affected people and companies that did not consider themselves parties to the conflict.

In his history of the genesis of the Saltsjöbad Accords, the prominent union official Ragnar Casparsson writes that while much of the criticism of union actions as "black-mail and mischievousness blockades" was exaggerated, it was still impossible to "deny the existence of union actions that broke the law, which in its turn could be brought back to the fact that union leaders lacked the courage or the will power [to] demand from unions and individuals the respect for rules and regulations which put the rights to make decisions about strikes and blockades in the hands of the national union boards" (Casparsson 1966: 129). Leading individuals on both sides thus understood that the conflicts were unnecessarily costly and that their main result was to damage the reputations of the organizations.

The new social democratic party leader Per-Albin Hansson also supported the efforts of LO towards labor peace. That the strategy worked became a central element of his internal plan for driving out the forces within party leadership that were more oriented towards the class struggle

(Isaksson 2000). As Bengt Schüllerqvist has shown, Hansson believed that the strategy also required a rhetoric other than the Marxist one that had predominated within the party up to that point – "class struggle could be interpreted to mean civil war" and that was something with which Hansson's new "people's home strategy" must not be associated in any way (Schüllerqvist 1992: 121–124). That one of the foremost LO architects of the efforts towards labor peace, Sigfrid Hansson, was the party leader's brother probably played a not insignificant role in this context.

The collapse and its consequences

The labor peace committee, the concrete result of the Labor Peace Conference, began its work in early 1929. The committee was made up of leading representatives from labor and management and a number of members appointed by the government, including a chairman defined as "impartial." The committee issued two reports, but as Ragnar Casparsson writes, they were overtaken by the considerable alarm caused by the events in Ådalen in May 1931. Despite the objections of LO leadership, the delegates to the LO congress in the autumn of 1931 decided that the organization should withdraw from the labor peace committee because of what happened in Ådalen. The argument was that LO could of course not cooperate with a party that acted in such a way that a conflict escalated to the point that the military opened fire on striking workers with lethal results. LO also protested against the ensuing "persecution of the union movement" by the management-allied press in the discussions following the events in Ådalen (Casparsson 1966: 56). The spokesman for the Building and Woodworkers' Union expressed it thus at the LO congress:

> There can be no resonance for the idea of cooperation between management and labor when the former recommend the use of bayonets against workers. I hope that the congress will repudiate the notion and agree that this humbug should be put to an end. (Quoted from Johansson 1989: 114)

That statement was followed by several similar ones by delegates to the congress. There were manifestations and protests all over the country against the actions of the military in Ådalen. It would be no exaggeration to claim that union members' mistrust of employers reached an "all-time low" after the tragedy (Johansson 2001). According to one social democratic opinion writer who was closely affiliated with the cooperation-oriented Per-Albin Hansson wing, not only were five people killed in Ådalen, so was the nascent will to reach consensus. Until May 26, and thus for almost ten days, there was a nearly total work stoppage throughout Ådalen as well as spontaneous strikes in many other places around the country. Protesters demanded that the military and strikebreakers be ejected from Ådalen and that LO initiate strong protest actions such as a general strike (Isaksson 2000: 105).

But not everyone regretted the occurrence. Within the more Moscow-connected of the two communist parties, which wanted to bring about a general strike wave as a response to the events, there was an eventual call to account because of the party's inability to create new "Ådalens" (Schüllerqvist 1992: 129–135). To the communist faction of the labor movement, the events in Ådalen were a kind of confirmation that their analyses of the situation of the working class and choice of strategy were right. This begs the question of how it was possible to get from that point to opening the negotiations that led to the Saltsjöbad Accords only five years later. How did the parties make the transition from the deepest mistrust to the kind of internationally unique trusting cooperation that the Saltsjöbad Accords and what later became known as "the Swedish Model" entailed?

The battle for collective memory: round-trip to Ådalen

What actually happened in Ådalen in May 1931? This is not the place for a detailed account or a new explanation, for which I refer the reader to the comprehensive literature on the subject cited here. Instead, I would like to underline the importance of the rapidly ensuing battle within the labor movement as to what *collective memory* the events in Ådalen would produce. Essentially, two clashing "worldviews" were established to interpret the meaning of what had happened (Isaksson 2000: 108). The first, promoted by the communists, syndicalists, and the more class struggle-oriented wing of social democracy led by Arthur Engström and Zäta Höglund, was aimed at creating a picture of Ådalen as an example of the archetypal capitalist state action in response to the demands of the working class for their legitimate rights. Out of the shots fired in Ådalen, along with a number of similar, earlier events, these political entrepreneurs wanted to establish an image of a relentless bourgeois state that in unholy alliance with the capitalist class would stop at nothing when it came to preserving the privileges of the class society (Nycander 2002: 54–60). Innocent workers who wanted only to claim their civil rights had fallen victim to assault of the military and capital.

The message was clear: only continued, unrelenting class struggle against the bourgeois state remained – all thoughts of consensus and cooperation should be abandoned. The communist slogan was unequivocal: "Three years of Mondism – five workers murdered" (Johansson 2001: 100). A communist MP asserted in the *Riksdag* that workers should create their own armed police, since the Ådalen events had proved the impossibility of confronting employers and their strikebreakers without weapons in hand (Nycander 2002: 55).

The theme that the violent acts of the military had proved that cooperation with management was meaningless recurred even in the much-publicized funeral ceremonies, which were molded into a show of power by the local communists who had led the fateful demonstration. In the introduction to the eulogy, the communist officiant Axel Nordström stated that "the bullets that killed our comrades also killed our illusions of consensus and reconciliation with our class enemy – the bourgeois class – and the rotten system that claimed their lives". (quoted from Johansson 2001: 169)

The second line within the labor movement, represented by the wing surrounding Per-Albin Hansson and party secretary Gustav Möller of the social democratic party and LO leadership, gave an entirely different inter-pretation of the events. The outcome was not at all the logical consequence of demands by the working class for their rights, but rather of both parties acting in precisely the manner that the labor peace policy was intended to avoid. First, they believed that while it was certainly wrong to use the mili-tary in such situations, they saw the action more as the result of a series of unfortunate circumstances and the police force's lack of experience with sim-ilar situations.[8] Secondly, they blamed the communist leaders of the strikes and demonstrations, whom they believed had acted both irresponsibly and illegally, the former by fomenting the outraged and partially revolutionary atmosphere in Ådalen and the latter by breaking into company premises and openly assaulting several strikebreakers.

Thirdly, management had behaved in precisely the provocative manner that the labor peace contingent wanted to avoid by hiring strikebreakers, which was of course the clearest possible signal to the union that they had not been acknowledged as a legitimate party to negotiations endowed with full and equal rights (Isaksson 2000; Schüllerqvist 1992). The power of a union is invested in its ability control the supply of labor, so there is no graver threat to the organization than that used by the employers in Ådalen.

The battle between the two wings of the labor movement over which col-lective memory of Ådalen would dominate was intense and bitter. As Roger Johansson showed, it is still in progress today to a certain extent. Throughout the postwar era, the social democratic party in particular was interpreting and reinterpreting the meaning of Ådalen according to which way the pre-vailing political winds were blowing (Johansson 2001). The contemporary

---

[8] The military command on site had interpreted the demonstration as a military attack that had to be stopped and not as what it actually was – i.e. a demonstration by admittedly agitated but unarmed individuals. One reason for the military's action was that they believed the final destination of the procession was the strikebreakers' camp. As the latter were armed, the military predicted a serious conflict if the procession were not stopped (Nycander 2002: 53).

struggle between social democrats and communists was expressed not only in how the events should be interpreted, but also in how the funeral ceremonies should be arranged. As time went on, the infighting went all the way down to what should be inscribed on the memorials and how the graves should be arranged. As Johansson writes, two very different pictures emerged in the eulogies given by communists versus those delivered by LO representatives. The speeches seemed to be political manifestos and were given prominent coverage in the party press on each side. The LO representative's speech was even reprinted in its entirety as an appendix to LO's printed annual report in 1931, which was a unique action. According to Johansson, the image reproduced by the communists was that Ådalen was a matter of "a life-and-death struggle on clearly defined fronts" while that given by LO leadership emphasized that the events in Ådalen were unique and therefore could not be generalized to the rest of the labor market (Johansson 2001: 172). The battle for the collective memory of Ådalen would prove decisive to the future of political developments in Sweden.

According to Anders Isaksson's biography of Per-Albin Hansson, the future "father of his country" was metaphorically born at the precise moment he found out what had happened in Ådalen. By keeping a cool head in the extremely tense situation that instantly arose, Hansson succeeded not only at finally defeating the internal, more class struggle-oriented party opposition, but also at gaining widespread support in public opinion for his cooperation-oriented political rhetoric (the "people's home" policy). The internal party opposition's description of the Ådalen incident was difficult to differentiate from that promoted by both communist parties and the syndicalists (Isaksson 2000: 162). If that policy direction had won out within social democracy, and there was a great deal to indicate that such could have been the case, the labor peace policy would in all likelihood not have become the predominant party, and later union, line. Therewith, according to Isaksson, Hansson would probably not have won the internal party fight and succeeded at establishing his "people's home" strategy.

The policy of confrontation, which initially enjoyed the greatest support, did not emerge victorious. Instead, the collective memory of Ådalen that Hansson promoted became paramount, not only within the labor movement but also within much of bourgeois opinion. According to Roger Johansson's comprehensive analysis of Ådalen in Swedish politics, the Hansson picture became hegemonic until the leftist wave of the 1970s (Johansson 2001: 447–449). Isaksson's conclusion after detailed analysis of the course of events was that it was in choosing which political interpretation should be given to Ådalen that Hansson, in the critical situation that had arisen, demonstrated the "strategic mastery" that led to his later political victories, both inside and outside the party (Isaksson 2000: 173). In game theoretic parlance, in a critical moment he shifted the "tipping point" into a new equilibrium (Schelling 1960; cf. Tarrow 2004). What Hansson did was put himself on the side of the law – the side of universalism – when he publicly also condemned the violence and other assaults perpetrated on the strikebreakers at Ådalen and elsewhere around the country. The resentment that that those involved felt towards the strike-breakers did not, according to Hansson, give them the right to resort to physical violence, not even against strikebreakers. Even those deserving of contempt "can demand protection of their personal safety, and the law of 'might makes right' has no place in a civilized society," he argued. If people condemned the violence of the other side, they could not defend their own group's right to take the law into their own hands (Isaksson 2000: 176f.). It should be added that Ådalen was far from the only time violence broke out during a strike. On the contrary, in the wake of the crisis and many con-flicts, violence had become an increasingly common element in the Swedish labor market of the day. Demonstrating workers were wounded by police bullets in Sweden even in the summer months after the Ådalen incident. Vio-lence against strikebreakers (or "willing workers" as they were also called) had become legion within large factions of the union movement and had garnered a great deal of press coverage. The attention-getting exposé that same year of a conspiracy among non-socialist forces in Stockholm and ele-ments within the police and the military to establish an armed protective corps, referred to as the "Munck Corps," should also be noted in the context (Johansson 2001: 130).

How serious was this escalating violence and increasing lawlessness in the Swedish labor market? That is naturally difficult to estimate, but Sweden was not an isolated island even then. Close to home, the situation had degen-erated alarmingly, including in Finland where the fascist Lappo movement, known for its use of violence against labor, had burgeoned. The Finnish civil war of 1918 with its horrifying aftermath in the form of the white faction's concentration camps and violence against the red faction was probably still fresh in the minds of Finns and Swedes alike.

Germany was another nearby "hot spot" where political violence per-petrated as murder and assault had long been rife. Reports of violence in Germany against union leaders and activists were common, especially in the union press. A review of all the issues of the powerful Metal Union's biweekly journal *Metallarbetaren* in the 1930s showed that while the famous "horse-trading"[9] and its ensuing new economic policy was given minimal coverage, reports on political violence in Germany against union activists

---

[9] The political deal between the social democrats and the Farmers' Party in 1993 that laid the ground for the "new" economic policy to combat unemployment.

were very common. Of the forty-nine issues of *Metallarbetaren* published in 1933, half contained articles of that kind, often featuring very detailed descriptions of how union leaders were imprisoned, beaten, and killed by the Nazis. In other words, there was no dearth of examples that, even in the proximity of Sweden, violence in the labor market could spin out of control and threaten democracy and the actual existence of the union movement.

Hansson's and Möller's views on the struggle between union and employer interests was that the former could not and should not convert the universal right to personal protection against assault into a particular institution that protected only union interests. Therewith, in his polemic against the leftist wing of the party and communist agitators, Hansson made a clear distinction between the unions' interest in laws that protected their monopoly over the supply of labor on the one hand and the interest in preserving universalism in state institutions on the other. According to Hansson, the parties' fight to protect their respective interests would have to be fought within the frameworks established by democracy and the rule of law and he was thus prepared to criticize the phenomena coming out of the unions that had come to be understood by widespread non-socialist and liberal opinion as exaggerations and arbitrariness (Isaksson 2000: 178). However, he believed that employers would eventually realize that they had more to gain by acknowledging the unions as legitimate partners and accordingly refrain from using strikebreakers. It should be added that after right-wing leader Arvid Lindman stepped forward in defense of the armed bourgeois guards in Stockholm (the Munck Corps), Hansson could present himself as the foremost champion of the notion that violence and lawlessness could not be allowed to triumph in Swedish politics of the day.

Based on the theory of the collective memory, the Ådalen incident is highly significant to modern Swedish political history. On the one hand, the analyses of Anders Isaksson and Roger Johansson, for example, show the great importance the various parties attached to gaining acceptance for their particular version of history. This was in truth a "fight for the history." On the other hand, their analyses also show that the collective memory could not in this case be fabricated at will based on the actual historical course of events, from a purely strategic and power political perspective. The actors certainly devoted considerable political and other resources to getting their image and interpretation of the events to prevail in the minds of the public. However, the question of who would win the battle for the collective memory of Ådalen in 1931 was not solely a matter of who had the most power and resources.

This is clearly evident in the light of the non-socialist faction's (including SAF and the right-wing party, which was then by far the most economically, and perhaps also politically, powerful force in the country) colossal failure at gaining general acceptance for their version of the Ådalen incident. Their ploys to that end included describing the shots fired by the soldiers as a necessary response to a communist-organized attack on the military. SAF and the right wing were absolutely unwilling to acknowledge that the military behaved improperly and that the management side of the conflict had been exceptionally provocative. Instead, they chose to emphasize that it was the duty of the state to defend, at any price, the strikebreakers' (the "willing workers'") right to trespass blockaded workplaces. However, the initial attempts of the non-socialist press to put all the blame on the demonstrators broke down quickly, for the simple reason that they had their facts wrong. The demonstrators did not, as claimed in prominent articles in some non-socialist newspapers, shoot first. The demonstrators did not open fire on the military at all, as no one in the procession was carrying a firearm (Johansson 2001: 100–118). This could be proved, as could the fact that demonstrators were obviously headed for the strikebreakers. The Hansson–Möller line won the fight against the right wing and SAF in part because they chose to stick to the facts of the case.

Roger Johansson's conclusion, which is supported by Anders Isaksson's analysis, is that the victorious Hansson–Möller line meant that an image was established in the dominant collective memory by which the cause of the tragic degeneration of the conflict was ultimately to be found in irresponsible communist agitation and the bourgeois "class egotistical" policy of not acknowledging the unions as legitimate negotiating partners. According to Johansson's analysis, the lesson gleaned from the Ådalen incident that Hansson managed to establish in Swedish politics was that self-interested action was dangerous and that all citizens had a responsibility for finding compromises that were favorable for the development of society (Johansson 2001: 452). That is, according to Gustav Möller and Per-Albin Hansson, without trusting cooperation between the parties in the labor market the social trap would snap shut, not only around the Swedish labor market, but around all of Swedish society.

Once again, I must emphasize that this should not be taken as an argument that Hansson's interpretation of the events was in fact historically accurate from any kind of objective perspective. The point of this analysis is empirical rather than normative, to the extent that it is meant to serve as evidence of the actual input values (mental maps) the parties had upon which to base their actions in the strategic game prior to the Saltsjöbad Accords. After Ådalen, union representatives knew that a government led by Hansson was prepared to support them, but only to a certain point, which stopped at any breach of the universal norms of democracy and the rule of law. Those on the management side knew the same after Ådalen – Hansson and Möller's line had become that which game theory usually calls *general knowledge*. The employers knew there was a limit to how far the unions could push a government led by Hansson and Möller when it came to the rules that would apply. They knew that when faced with a choice between union interests and the principle of the rule of law, Hansson and Möller would defend the latter.

Finally, management also knew, and this was particularly important to them, that Hansson and Möller were prepared to take on a tough fight, not only with syndicalists and communists, but also with an internal party faction that claimed the opposite. Hansson and Möller had set down the rules of the game in such a way that they had established what game theoretical literature considers extraordinarily difficult to achieve – a *credible commitment* to the impartiality of political institutions (see chapter 5). One important aspect of that commitment was the undertaking to wage a fierce battle against communist and syndicalist influences within the union movement (Schüllerqvist 1992).

The Saltsjöbad Accords: the hidden agenda of trust

Many researchers who have studied the text of this famous agreement have been struck by its lack of content as to material stipulations. The Accords are first and foremost a formal regulation of the negotiating process between the parties (Edlund *et al.* 1989). However, the aspect to which the actors involved constantly referred was the new "spirit" embodied in the agreement. According to Bertil Kugelberg, who held a central position at SAF and was the president of the organization from 1947 to 1966, the impact of the agreement on relations between the parties could not be overestimated – he believed that it was a means of resolving conflicts between the parties "through wise restraint rather than violence." Like many others, he emphasized the tremendous change the agreement brought about towards achieving a "more peaceful atmosphere" in the Swedish labor market (Kugelberg 1989: 93f.). After the agreement was reached, Prime Minister Hansson stated in the *Riksdag* that its chief virtue was the "new spirit" that had sprung up between the parties (Lower House, 1939-01-18). The editor of the principal management-side newspaper, Axel Brunius, believed that the central aspect was the "mental reorientation" that the Accords represented. When negotiations were begun in 1936, Brunius had warned against extravagant hopes, for not even the most detailed agreement could guarantee labor peace, but he had similar reservations about attempts to deal with the issue legislatively. All that could be hoped for, according to Brunius, was that an agreement might bolster trust between the parties. The crux of the matter was whether both organizations could refrain from tactical maneuvers and smoke screens and instead behave honestly and in a trust-inspiring manner (*Industria* 1936: 176).

In order to grasp why this trust was so important, we must understand how complex the game can get when it comes to wage negotiations. Bertil Kugelberg's memoirs give us a glimpse into the tactical problems in these games of negotiation (Kugelberg 1986, see also the interview in *Arbetsgivaren* 1977: 32). When an agreement is to be reached, the parties usually meet with their "large" delegations, and their various positions are put on the table. Naturally, disagreement ensues and in order to arrive at the compromise necessary to avoid open conflict, negotiations usually have to be held among only a few or only the individual leaders of each party. These "ironing out" sessions can be tough and a finished draft agreement can be reached only if both parties elect to compromise. The difficult part is that the draft agreement, which the leaders of both parties have compromised into existence, must be ratified by each organization's negotiating committees. This is often the moment of truth for the leaders of the organizations, as they must then show their own what skilled negotiators they have been. They must defend the concessions they have made and, it stands to reason, emphasize the concessions to which they have convinced the opposition to agree.

The outcomes to this situation vary. Both parties may gain the approval of their respective committees, after which the agreement is set. Or the committees on both sides may reject the draft agreement, whereupon negotiations must be resumed and an attempt made to arrive at something more acceptable. Finally, the agreement may be ratified by one side but rejected by the other, which is the most difficult of the three situations, as it means that the leaders of the organizations must meet again in a situation where the party who has managed to gain acceptance of the concessions he agreed to finds out that they were not good enough and that the opposition is demanding further concessions in order to reach an agreement. The party whose committee has accepted the draft, perhaps after gut-wrenching discussions about why he ever agreed to concessions x, y, and z, has to go back to his committee and explain that the concessions were not enough. This is hardly a desirable situation, as the upshot for the leader is loss of face and status before his own.

The problem is that neither leader can control whether the other will choose to bluff when it comes to reporting what happened when he tried to garner the negotiating committee's support for the compromise. One party may quite simply take the negotiated compromise to his committee and tell them they should absolutely not agree to it, then go back to the opposing party and aver that the committee had refused to accept the compromise upon which they had agreed, despite his assiduous efforts to persuade them.

Of course, that kind of bluff can, as Kugelberg describes it, be a very useful strategy to extract even greater concessions from the opponent (Kugelberg 1986: 107). The problem is that if one or both parties suspects that the other is using those kinds of tactics, the game of negotiations is in danger of degenerating into precisely the kind of open conflict the players want to avoid. It is this complication in the game of wage negotiations that makes trust in the opposition critical. If one actor believes that the other is going to bluff when it comes to the seriousness of his attempt to gain acceptance of the compromise among his own group, the reasonable strategy would be for the first actor also to use the same tactics. The outcome of the problem becomes that even if there are very large collectives on both sides, the purely interpersonal trust between the leaders plays a vital role.

The process that led to the agreement has also been described by those who were involved in a way that many historians have found difficult to deal with. I am thinking primarily of testimony about the importance that interpersonal trust between the negotiators on both sides seems to have had (Casparsson 1966; Hansson 1939; Kugelberg 1986). Naturally, it is difficult to analyze the significance of "soft" factors such as interpersonal trust in more materialistic and interest-based histories (Åmark 1992; cf. Swenson 2002). But seen in light of the theory of the social trap, trust falls perfectly into place and becomes a make-or-break factor. As Bertil Kugelberg wrote in his memoirs: "The importance of the Saltsjöbad negotiations cannot be overestimated. Exaggerated beliefs about the opposition's malicious atti-tude evaporated.We also found that – alongside the natural antagonisms – the parties had common interests in a number of respects, which could very well be promoted through coordinated actions" (Kugelberg 1985: 52).

Meanwhile, the issue is whether this does not leave us with an explana-tion that identifies the purely personal factors among the actors involved as the deciding factor when attempting to explain how it was at all possible to go from Ådalen to Saltsjöbaden. The question we must ask is where this trust between the parties came from, and then we can refer only to the spe-cial Swedish culture oriented towards compromise and consensus. Have we gone full circle to arrive back at a purely culturally determined explanation? There is good reason to linger awhile yet with this problem – i.e. to study whether there is something particular that distinguished Sweden from other countries with respect to labor market relations in that era.

There is some anecdotal information which indicates that such might be the case. For instance, in his history of the genesis of the Saltsjöbad Accords, Ragnar Casparsson describes the surprise that the opposing parties in the Swedish labor market engendered on a joint trip to France just prior to the birth of the Accords. Their French hosts on both sides of the labor fence could not for the life of them understand that the leaders of LO and SAF traveled together, dined together, met under the same roof, and could on the whole conduct joint discussions in a civilized manner. They had never seen the like of it and could apparently not really understand how any of it was possible. Nor could the French understand that their Swedish guests could base their deliberations on public wage trend statistics accepted by both parties, as it was taken for granted in France that such material was never reliable and was always manipulated (Casparsson 1966: 214–218).

Skogsindustriarbetaren magazine (1939: 17) printed a similar story about a group of French union leaders on a junket to the LO school at Brunnsvik, who could not believe their eyes when they discovered that the school had invited Gustaf Söderlund, the president of SAF, to be a guest lecturer to the union classes.[10] The idea that there would be any point whatsoever in listening to the other side had apparently never crossed their minds. Even the management-side magazine jested good-naturedly about foreign observers of Sweden who marveled over the Swedish spirit of consensus (*Industria* 1938: 84). The question that must be asked is as follows: Was there, as these events imply, something special about labor market relations even prior to the Saltsjöbad Agreement that distinguished Sweden from other countries?

Political institutions and the capacity for trust

The answer to the question of whether there was a distinctive quality to labor relations that separated Sweden from other countries early on is a clear and unequivocal "yes." The capacity for dialog between the parties that resulted in the Saltsjöbad Accords can be found in how, early in the twentieth century, the Swedish state institutionalized arenas in which the parties continually met to shape and implement Swedish labor market policy. Contrary to that which emerges from accepted studies of the rise of the Swedish Model, the transition from the conflict and mistrust of the 1920s to the cooperation and the spirit of consensus of the latter 1930s was not a sudden change. Leading representatives of both parties had begun to cooperate and engage in continuous dialog on an array of intricate issues, on both the local and national levels, and those patterns of cooperation had usually been arranged through state-sponsored initiatives.

In broad outline, the story played out as follows. At an early stage, the Swedish state sought dialog between labor movement organizations surrounding the matter of how what had been dubbed the "worker question" could be resolved. The problem identified was that while this new class had

---

[10] This had begun in 1935, probably at the urging of Sigfrid Hansson, and it was in these lectures, which were widely distributed by SAF, that the outlines of the Saltsjöbad Accords were introduced.

certainly developed widespread internal solidarity, it was isolated from the rest of society. In 1912, a state commission of inquiry that had recommended giving unions a voice in public administrative bodies related to the labor market described the problem as being that:

> The sense of solidarity, while certainly commendable, that has emerged within the working masses, is restricted to themselves and they seem unwilling to extend it to the entire society for which they share responsibility . . . Herein lies an apparent social danger, that must in the interests of all be eliminated. Government author-ities everywhere are thus facing the difficult task of ameliorating the antagonisms of interests, smoothing conflicts of interest, and mending the rents that open in the social fabric. (Quoted from Rothstein 1992a: 93)

It would be greedy to ask for clearer evidence that the Swedish state was early to see the dangers of the social trap with respect to labor market relations. The results of those ideas showed up quickly. As early as 1902 when the conser-vative government established the country's first social insurance program, it requested the participation of the union movement in implementing the reform. The government wanted to attach a "worker insurance council" to the agency that would be responsible for the reform, which would consist of five representatives from each side. The council was never established, not for lack of will but rather because no acceptable technical election method for appointing such representatives could be found. However, that kind of corporatively composed body soon became a common element of Swedish politics.

On the local level, local employment offices were set up starting in 1902, in which each party was given an equal number of seats on the boards of directors and which were led (again) by an impartial chairman, usually a higher-ranking municipal official or a judge from the local court system. This may seem today to be a rather simple measure, but at the time power over the employment offices was a highly politically charged arena by reason of the frequent local labor conflicts. The party that had control over the distribution of work naturally had the upper hand in that regard – unions could exploit the power to block the employers and the employers could, if they controlled the employment offices, recruit "willing workers" and blacklist strike leaders from employment in general.

In Germany and many other countries (including Denmark and Norway), control over the employment office system had become an issue fraught with conflict between the parties, but the matter played out in a completely different way in Sweden (cf. Schiller 1967: 9–36).

For instance, when the City of Stockholm studied whether it should estab-lish public employment offices in the late 1890s, those involved immediately noted the negative experiences from Germany, where employment offices had become a weapon in the class struggle. It is difficult to discover the source of the notion that this knotty issue should be taken away from the opposing interests and made into a public concern, but it gained rapid acceptance in Sweden. By 1907, all larger cities in the country had set up bipartisan public employment offices. These municipal employment offices were established according to a uniform design throughout the country, which was based on the principle that they should be impartial and remain neutral towards conflicts between the parties.

Starting in 1907, state subsidies were paid to the employment offices provided they were organized as above. It is interesting in the context that leading representatives of both social democracy and SAF were initially skeptical about these establishments. SAF had far-reaching plans to introduce the system that prevailed in much of Germany, where the employers had taken control over the employment offices and used them as a very effective instrument against the unions (Schiller 1967: 9–36). Hjalmar Branting spoke out in the *Riksdag* in 1903 against the bill to support the system of state subsidies because he felt there was a risk that the employment offices would be exploited by management to recruit strikebreakers. A couple of years later their fears had been allayed and local representatives of both parties took part in several employment office conferences organized by the National Board of Trade, starting in 1906. The chairmen of both SAF and LO attended one of the larger conferences in 1912.

There is reason to ponder the temporal logic of this development, as it began before all adult males were enfranchised (in 1909) and many years before parliamentary democracy was secured (in 1917). Representatives of employers and unions had thus, prior to that point, begun continually cooperating on an issue that was sensitive to both parties, on the national level as well, but especially on the local level. Particularly surprising is that this cooperation, as far as can be judged, seems to have proceeded in a relatively frictionless manner. There are no reports of any local antagonism, and the five contemporary reports of proceedings from various employment offices that I have reviewed (Uppsala, Stockholm, Malmö, Göteborg, Helsingborg) contained no notes indicating conflicts about anything other than trivialities.

At the behest of the cabinet offices, the National Board for Social Affairs conducted a study of the employment office system, on which it submitted its report in 1916. The report stated "there have been no objections from any direction to the organizational principles upon which public employment offices are based." The National Board for Social Affairs also stated that the strong development of the employment offices was the outcome of the corporative principle of organization and the trust accorded the system by both management and labor organizations "which in our country have fortunately refrained from using job referrals as a weapon in the social struggle, which in Germany has to a degree distorted the entire issue of employment offices" (1916: 94). The report continued:

> Despite the sharp social and political antagonisms that in other areas of society could make themselves felt between members of the management and labor camps, the same individuals on employment office boards have, in the experience of the National Board for Social Affairs, always loyally cooperated in the interests of objectivity. (Quoted in Rothstein 1992a: 94)

There is reason to linger a moment with this assessment. What the National Board of Social Affairs said was that "the same individuals" who outside the public institutions could be involved in serious conflicts changed their behavior when asked to act within the frameworks of those institutions. Their sometimes intense and doubtless bitter struggle of interests was *transformed* by the institutional conditions into cooperation towards a common goal. It would be difficult to find clearer evidence that human actions are influenced by institutional conditions and not the inherent, culturally determined norms of the people involved. This also dovetails nicely with Elinor Ostrom's findings on how local actors can manage the difficult social dilemma of conservation of natural resources. The institutional conditions proved capable of reshaping the actions of the actors from the point where they considered only their own short-term economic interests (which thus meant that the social trap was a foregone conclusion) to that where they began discussing how they could work together to find cooperative solutions (Ostrom 1990: 138).

This type of corporative institution spread rapidly within the Swedish state administration. The establishment in 1912 of the National Board for Social Affairs is perhaps the clearest example. As a civil service department, the National Board for Social Affairs was entirely different from what it is today, in that the agency was responsible primarily for issues related to the labor market. When the department was established, two "social delegates" were attached as members of the national civil service board and those delegates were the chairmen of SAF and LO. The board met regularly and was involved in laying the foundations of Swedish social and labor market policy. Among other things, the board discussed a far-reaching proposal on legislation intended to increase labor peace as early as 1915. Judging by the minutes of the meeting, the discussions seem to have been held under exceedingly orderly and constructive conditions. When the National Board for Social Affairs assessed the value of the construction in an opinion submitted to the cabinet offices, its report was highly favorable and stated that the board had successfully avoided many problems related to sensitive issues via the opportunity to engage in confidential and informal talks and that this had "smoothed out the antagonism of interests" in the area (Rothstein 1992a: 94f.). Thus, during the National Board for Social Affairs' first few years, the chairmen of SAF and LO met almost every week to discuss their common affairs, along with the civil servants on the board.

Among the other bodies given an equivalent construction during that area was the Labor Council, which was established in 1919 and mandated to deal with matters related to the implementation of the eight-hour working day. It was composed of two members each from SAF and LO and three civil servants with judicial competence. In other words, the Council had the nature of a court, roughly the same construction given to the Labor Court in 1929. It was constructed in that way because the eight-hour day was not implemented in Sweden in the same way as in most other countries – i.e. through direct statutory provisions that regulated working hours in detail. Instead, a very general law was enacted, what we would today call a "framework law," and application of the law was devolved to the Labor Council, which allowed working-hours regulations to be adjusted to the conditions prevailing in different industries. When the issue of the law on the eight-hour day was brought up in the *Riksdag* in 1930, SAF chairman Hjalmar von Sydow, who had himself sat on the Council, delivered a highly positive statement about the work of the Labor Council. His contribution to the debate in the Riksdag is worthy of quotation:

> Provided that the employer and workers agree, the Labor Council has the right to grant a dispensation from the application of the law with no restriction other than that the permitted working hours may not be unreasonable. This is the highest relief available to the employer under the law and it is very often applied. Not a single meeting of the Labor Council is held at which a dispensation is not granted on the basis of this statute. There are important branches of industry here in Sweden that have boomed in recent years and which would never have been able to do so without these dispensations. (Upper House 1930, no. 22: 14f.)

The quotation indicates a couple of important things. First, that von Sydow, despite belonging to the old school of more patriarchal employer representatives, had extensive and positive experience within this type of state institution of reaching consensus with union representatives on matters of great importance but also a complex and sensitive nature. Secondly, there seems to have been something special, even for the actors of the day, about how people in Sweden in particular were able to arrange institutional conditions so that trusting cooperation could be established between opposing parties. It should be added that there were several such corporatively composed institutions in Sweden at the time, but it seems unnecessary to describe them all in order to underpin the following two conclusions of this analysis.

First, the type of cooperative patterns in the Swedish labor market expressed by the Saltsjöbad Accords should not be seen only as a radical break with a previous praxis of confrontation. The occurrence of many and protracted labor market conflicts have blinded Swedish historians to the reality that in parallel with those struggles there was also extensive coopera-tion between the parties in corporatively institutionalized forms (Johansson 1989; Lundh 2002). In other words, both parties had experience (memory) of both trustful cooperation and intense conflicts, and of the other party being trustworthy and deceitful. The idea that even glaring conflicts of interests could be resolved without open conflict did not suddenly enter the minds of the actors one fine day in 1936 in the beautiful Saltsjöbaden Hotel. There was a long and meaningful praxis (and memories) on which to fall back. This praxis of cooperation need not be explained by the notion that there was something in the special Swedish culture (the temperament, the landscape, etc.) that gave rise to a few special prerequisites. Nor are we compelled to surrender to explanations that revolve around the dispositions and strate-gies of individuals. The policy of cooperation may be regarded as the result of the political institutions that had been established at an early stage within this area.

Second, these institutions did not come about through the initiative of the parties, but rather as an expression of the Swedish state's attempt to manage the "worker question." It is noteworthy that the organized working class was considered a legitimate party to the Swedish before the principles of parliamentary democracy were accepted. In that respect, the Swedish state differed considerably from the French, German, and British states, for exam-ple, not to mention the Russian state. The Swedish state appears to have been considerably more open than the others to consider and cooperate with the organized labor movement. It was not as authoritarian as the German state, which pushed the German labor movement back into ghetto-like isolation from the rest of society, from which position it became, despite its vigor, an easy victim for the burgeoning Nazi movement (Birnbaum 1988).

The Swedish labor movement was early to accept the notion that there might be a need for people in responsible positions who were not bound to either side, but could instead act impartially and objectively, which applied to the chairmen of local employment offices and members of the Labor Council, as well as in the rapidly accepted Labor Court. The idea that conflicts of interest could be resolved in accordance with certain universal principles that could be applied by public officials who put a high value on objectivity and impartiality thus became something that was not only accepted early on, but also regarded as an asset by the faction of the labor movement that later supported the principles of the Saltsjöbad Accords.

Pierre Birnbaum, Colin Crouch, and Gerhard Lembruch are among those who have asserted that established corporative networks of institutionalized trust between the state and the representatives of special interests create a sort of "mental map" in the minds of those involved that shows how social conflicts should be resolved (Birnbaum 1988; Crouch 1993; Lembruch 1991). When a society is faced with managing a new situation, the outcomes vary depending on the patterns states establish early in the process. When choosing their working strategies, the actors use what I would call here a "collective memory" of how equivalent matters were resolved (or not resolved) in the past. In Sweden, the institutionalized patterns that created forums for dialog and cooperation between the opposing sides in the labor market were established early in the game, and they worked. In the period immediately prior to the breakthrough of democracy, the country was governed in part by an enlightened civil service corps oriented towards safeguarding the best interests of the state. It would certainly be too much to claim that this corps welcomed the new social force of the labor movement but, once it was a fact, the officials understood that the labor movement could not, as in Germany, be excluded from political influence. Instead, the Swedish state attempted to devise forms of cooperation that both parties could accept in order to attempt to reconcile the interests of the labor movement with what it perceived as the public interest in social peace. The means to that end chosen by the Swedish state were institutions in which open conflicts could be transformed into dialog.

On the difficult art of sending signals about trust

Thus, even before the Saltsjöbad Accords, there existed a clear "collective memory" among the actors that cooperation towards common interests was possible within the framework of impartially arranged institutions. But, as shown in chapter 6, such institutions are notoriously unstable, because each party can always change them to its own advantage. In a situation characterized by extensive antagonisms of interests, producing the trust that impartial institutions will remain impartial is, according to our theoretical assumptions, very difficult. Accordingly, it probably required something more than just the "collective memory" noted above for this to work, especially since history gives no guarantees about the future. For theoretical reasons, we should return to the meaning of Per-Albin Hansson's choice of strategy after the Ådalen incident.

His unequivocal defense of the principles of the rule of law, his criticism of union violence against strikebreakers, and his policy that the state should not help the unions towards a law against strikebreaking that protected their interests alone sent a clear signal to the business organizations concerning his views on the role of state institutions with respect to the position of each party and conflicts in the labor market. Unlike the communists, but also unlike large factions of his own party, he took the position that the state and its laws would not be reshaped with his help to unilaterally favor the LO side (Nycander 2002: 56ff.). He declared forthrightly in the *Riksdag* that the state he was to lead would not become a unilateral instrument in the service of the unions. He remarked in the *Riksdag* that "the union movement, like other powers in society, must subordinate itself to the public interest and adjust itself to the public sense of justice" (Lower House, 1935:4: 12). However, words alone do not always inspire trust. What made the signal credible to SAF should have been that he did not hesitate to take up the fight for that position within his own party and his own movement (Isaksson 2000).

The signal to the management side was thus transmitted: under Hansson's leadership, state institutions would remain universal with respect to the parties' position in the labor market and would not be changed into particular institutions to the benefit of the special interest group most closely aligned with his party.[11] The Ådalen incident may thus to a certain extent be said to have been the prerequisite for the Saltsjöbad Accords, in that it gave Hansson (and LO leadership) the opportunity to establish a position on the matter of state impartiality that could be perceived by the opposition as *trustworthy*. That policy was to apply in the Swedish labor market until the labor law offensive that LO and SAF began four decades later (Nycander 2002: 299ff.). That Hansson's signal was understood very clearly by one of the leading actors on the management side, SAF president Gustav Söderlund, is evident in two much-noted speeches he gave at the LO school in 1935 – i.e. in conjunction with the opening of the Saltsjöbad negotiations.

First, he used two of Hansson's principles as his own main points. The first was that management must unconditionally acknowledge the unions as legitimate opponents. He went so far as to say that what the unions had achieved thus far for their members was "a great deed" and that the unions had "become, in the large companies of our era, necessary bodies for

[11] Undoubtedly, the social democratic and LO policy of starting a relentless battle against the communists within the union movement also played a central role as a signal to the management side. The stubbornly fought contests against the communists were, for instance, reported extensively in the SAF magazine *Industria* (e.g. 1933: 201, 244, 296, 375f.; 1934: 329).

cooperation between management and labor" (*Industria* 1935: 331). While there was no getting around the antagonism between capital and labor, it was to Söderlund as natural as the antagonism between buyer and seller concerning the price of goods in any market. He believed, however, that those antagonisms were best resolved by means of orderly negotiations, as open conflicts were not worth the cost to either party.

The second of Hansson's principles that Söderlund made his own was the matter of state impartiality. He recounted in detail many of the failed attempts to secure labor peace in other countries through the compelling power of the state. His conclusion was that such measures could not be taken without favoring one of the two parties. He then added:

> If each party, on matters about which it feels most hard pressed, seeks to obtain the intervention of the state to escape the difficulties, all will soon be mired in a system where liberty is progressively constricted to the benefit of state compulsion. We must not believe that either party can, over the long-term, enjoy the state's help and protection of its interests and still retain its liberty in other areas. It is high time that this is clearly understood by both sides. (*Industria* 1935: 339)

Per-Albin Hansson's signal, which in this case was ardently amplified by his brother Sigfrid in the LO magazine, had obviously been understood by the opposition. However, it should also be noted that Söderlund here perhaps also gave us the solution to the riddle of how impartial institutions can rise and survive – *the element of uncertainty and risk*. If the actors in a game like this are secure in the knowledge that they enjoy superior political power, it is naturally in their interests to abandon the principles of impartiality and universalism and attempt to change the rules of the game so that they always benefit their own party. But if they are not entirely sure of always being in such a favorable position, the choice of impartial and universal institutions may be preferable.

We can thus conclude that if we want to "move from Moscow to Stockholm" three things are needed. First, the deliberate action of the state and its leaders is crucial. Social trust comes from above and is destroyed from above. Simply put, they must be able to send trustworthy signals that they will guarantee and respect the impartiality of the relevant public institutions. Admittedly, the supply of such leaders is an unsolved problem. A second conclusion is the importance of institutions that allow for deliberation and communication, as was the case with the corporatist institutions in the Swedish case. Thirdly, we must probably recognize that universal institutions will not be the first choice of any political group or agent. But given insecurity about the future, such institutions may come about as a choice of a second order. Given that agents cannot always be sure that they will be able to dominate and turn the practice of public institutions to their own advantage, it may be in their own interest to opt for universal institutions. For political parties, there might be the risk of being voted out of office. For unions and employers, there might be the risk of losing their political influence of those who have the power of public institutions. For public servants, there might be the risk of being audited. For the civil servants who run the audit bureau, without some reference to ethics and norms, there is no solution to the problem from Moscow.

9

The conditions of trust and the capacity for dialog

There are many different ways to understand the project of political science. One is that political science encompasses the use of newer and more refined methods to mine reality for improved – in the sense of truer – pictures of how the political aspects of society work. Another is that it should be regarded more as a philosophical cultural achievement that carries on the discussion of political government that, as we know it, was started nearly 2,500 years ago by Plato, Aristotle, and their contemporaries. In the latter case, the achievement consists of, like the stubborn peasant, plowing these fields again and again to keep them fertile for new generations so that the classical insights into the problems and opportunities of political government do not disappear into the dustbin of history. Certainly, now and then undergrowth of a new kind must also be cleared away (cf. Barry 2000). By plowing these furrows over and over again we make it possible for new insights to grow, on isolated occasions in history, about how humanity should avoid falling into new disastrous wars of "all against all" or the authoritarian Leviathan state – the two alternatives given us by Thomas Hobbes.

The division within the discipline between these alternative understandings of the political science project is often doctrinaire. Those devoted to the normative issues are, at best, ignorant of the advances of empirical research. The eternal questions are the same, wholly apart from them. And researchers within empirically oriented political science look askance upon the work of the political philosophers in the attempt to provide scientifically tenable answers to normative questions.

As for me, I would like to see the two projects unified – that is, an approach in which we can use the progressively more refined study methods at our disposal to try and answer the normative questions on how good government might be achieved. Such a discussion must inevitably begin with a normative discourse on what we mean by "good government" – and, by extension, a good society. I believe that questions of political philosophy must be the point of departure for the analysis. If not, empirical research may run amok, not least through inadequate concern for research ethics. In a small country such as Sweden, the study of political power on the terms of those in political power is not without its problems. Alternatively, political science research may become a technically refined showpiece devoid of philosophical and social meaning. At the same time, a political philosophy on how the good society might be achieved is meaningless if it is not engaged in direct dialog with empirical research on what we actually know, or can know, about the effects of various kinds of political institutions (Rothstein 1998a). There is reason to echo Yehuda Bauer's fears that we are at risk of producing "technically competent barbarians at our universities" (Bauer 2000: 286, cf. Rothstein 2004).

A government is in form nothing other than a set of political institutions and we are now in a position to gather empirical knowledge about the impact of such institutions on people's lives. Forging a link between normative and empirical research should be an obvious task. In my opinion, the main line of political philosophy, both classical and modern, should not be understood as a discussion solely of political ideals and individual virtues that various thinkers have believed people or their political leaders should embrace. Instead, it should be regarded as a continuing analysis of the relationship between the concrete design of the government – i.e. its actual institutions – and the normative ideals that those institutions in fact produce in the society.

The conceivable variations in the institutional design of a democratic government are nearly endless. It is easy to point out at least ten basic elements of democratic constitutions that can fundamentally differ. A democratic government may contain a unicameral or bicameral system, majority or proportional elections, parliamentarianism or presidential governance, judicial review with or without a constitutional court, federalism or a unitary state, strong or weak local government, a merit-based or politically recruited civil service, the use of various forms of referenda, independent central banks or not, etc. Thus, there are at least 2^{10} (that is, 1,024) currently known ways in which a country can organize the democratic machinery. As there are in reality even more important elements to a democratic government, and because there are many intermediate forms of the ten basic elements, the possible variants in the design of a democracy are in reality many more than 1,024.

One inevitable conclusion from this intellectual experiment is that, contrary to that occasionally claimed in debate, it is impossible to empirically prove what kind of democratic government is to be preferred, for one simple reason: The number of countries that have been democratic for any length of time is considerably fewer than 1,024 (plus). This should inspire not insignificant humility before the political science project. There are real limits to our ability to engineer in any mechanical fashion the ideal form of democracy. That which we can do is look at one or two of the basic elements listed above in comparative empirical studies. I have focused on just one of them here – the role played by the nature of public administration in producing or destroying the supply of social capital in a society. The orientation of public administration is, however, not independent of the other basic elements and this must be kept in mind when drawing conclusions from a study such as this.

The temptation of Syracuse

The classics of political philosophy lend themselves to many different readings. However, it is apparent that much of their discussion of nearly 2,500 years ago had particularly to do with the relationship between the institutional design of the government in different societies and the social norms the institutions engendered among the citizenry. In many respects, Plato's arguments in *The Republic* are a comparative study of the effects of the institutional design of a number of governments. He is particularly intriguing in the *Laws*, when in the guise of the "Athenian Stranger" he discusses with Cleinias of Crete and Megillus of Sparta the constitutions of those states. Plato argues that the state is needed not only as a protector against hostile attack, but also to create internal peace and "good will" among the citizens – i.e. probably that which has been defined here as *social capital*. Plato goes so far as to argue that internal peace and good will are the highest human goods. The best sort of legislator, says this "Athenian Stranger," is one who can draft laws that produce "concord" and inner harmony in the society.

Plato also refers to the need for laws that exist for the common good. "Laws that exists only for the interest of certain people, we call party laws and not citizens' laws, and we argue that it is empty speech when these are mentioned as justice." According to Plato, it is therefore crucial that the highest offices are given to individuals known for being the most law-abiding (cit. in Malnes and Midgaard 1993: 39). Plato believed that the chief threat to political stability was the strong orientation of groups towards driving through ordinances that favored their selfish interests (Sabine 1963: 45). Once a regime had become corrupt, said Plato, there was little that could be done to recreate the good government (Lilla 2001: 194).

Aristotle was equally clear that the construction of the institutions (the laws) of a society could not be regarded solely from the contractual angle, wherein the citizens are protected from one another and where the intent is to ease their financial transactions. On the contrary, the argument in the *Politics* is that the duty of the institutions is to help create morally good citizens. One of his points is that the good moral intentions of the citizens are not enough to cause them to act morally in fact. The tasks of law include persuading citizens that a sufficient number of other citizens are also acting morally. Once again, there is not much point in being the only one to behave ethically in an otherwise thoroughly corrupt society (George 1993: 21ff.). We can say that Aristotle, Plato, and their contemporaries regarded all the various state formations they could observe and about which they possessed historical knowledge as a sort of laboratory for the study of the relationship between the design of political institutions and the social formation of norms in the society. By varying the design of government, it was also possible to create both "virtuous" and "vicious" citizens.

It is not entirely unproblematic for researchers to influence and participate in the political discussion of the design of government. In *The Reckless Mind* (2001), Mark Lilla analyzes why a number of important twentieth-century European intellectuals chose to lend themselves to the defense of totalitarian regimes which they knew were engaged in egregious persecution and oppression of their citizens. The group includes not only Nazi collaborators Martin Heidegger and Carl Schmitt, but also some of the intellectual heroes of postmodernism and the particularistic anti-enlightenment project such as Michel Foucault and Jacques Derrida (Lilla 2001; cf. Windschuttle 1997). The list of prominent intellectuals who have chosen to stand on the side of despots throughout history is embarrassingly and painfully long.

However, Mark Lilla also recounts Plato's travels to Syracuse on Sicily. One of Plato's students had become acquainted with the new ruler of Syracuse and vouched that he was not yet another in a long line of corrupt and/or opportunistic tyrants, but rather a new kind of sovereign who wanted to be taught directly by the great philosopher himself concerning how the good government should be designed. Not surprisingly, things went astray as usual and Plato returned to Athens disappointed. However, his disappointment was not directed at the ruler of Syracuse or his former student who had enticed him there. According to Lilla, Plato became most irritated about his own naïveté, that is, about his belief that it was possible to persuade a sovereign power of the importance of restraint in the exercise of his power. Given his experiences and the insights that followed, he should have known better. Plato's fury over his own naïveté is also a warning for contemporary intellectuals who may feel tempted to make such a "journey to Syracuse." The argument and the primacy of reliable evidence have limited effect outside the walls of the academic seminary.

On the meaning of not being able to know everything about the future

This study began with a normative problem: How societies should avoid ending up in the kind of situations that can be characterized as "social traps." That these are highly likely is beyond all doubt – whether we begin with familiar theories of human behavior or with empirical realities. Opportunism is a universal human trait and rationality will often fail us because we cannot rationally decide to forget treacherous behavior. We can morally forgive such behavior, which means we will not take to retaliation and revenge, but that does not imply that we will forget.

In common with anthropologist Thomas Hylland Eriksen and biologist Dag O. Hessen, we have asked ourselves if, given the existence of egoism as one potential human characteristic, we can end up in a society where nobody wants to live (Eriksen and Hessen 2000: 209). The conclusion I have drawn is that we can avoid such social traps only if we can produce adequate stock of social capital. The primary answer has been the design of political institutions. The variation in the supply of social capital that we can confirm exists among different societies is not the product of people's involvement in voluntary associations or their original access to social networks, which has been one of the predominant theories in this approach. Social networks are a component of social capital and therefore cannot reasonably be considered also a component of the explanation for it. Instead, we have found that the crucial determinant of the supply of social capital is the supply of universal or impartial political institutions, particularly on the policy implementation side. Should this finding prove resilient in future empirical analyses, I believe that political science will have delivered an important result with respect to its fundamental question of the relationship between government and social conditions, as well as to the more applied aspects of the discipline.

With this result in hand, it is necessary to go further and ask why such institutions occur to such a varying degree in different countries, and in different eras in the same countries. We have rejected explanations that refer to the people themselves possessing, just because they happen to have been born in certain societies, some kind of inherited, inherent qualities that endow them with unequal capacity to produce social capital through establishing universal institutions. Normative universalism – i.e. that human beings are essentially the same and have their fundamental traits in common – has been a central point of departure in this analysis. The varied supply of social capital and universal institutions must be explained in some way other than with references to things such as "stock," whether understood in the cultural or biological sense (cf. Eriksen and Hessen 2000: 207).

I have also argued that rationalist theory offers no possible explanation of how such institutions can arise, or why they can survive. In a premise where the actors, in the form of political special interest groups, always act based on self-interest, they would always prefer to create particularistic institutions – i.e. institutions that directly benefit their own social, economic, or cultural group. Established, strong financial interests – firms or industry organizations, for example – would always prefer laws and regulations that favor their interests rather than those that make it possible for new stake-holders to compete on equal terms in the best interests of the consumer. The ethnic or social groups that constituted the majority in the society would always create and uphold laws that protected their particular interests rather than acting according to the principles of universalism. Nevertheless, universal institutions, which according to the results presented here are the wellsprings of social capital, do arise and sometimes work for a very long time. How is this possible?

One answer is that at certain times, in certain situations, and in certain countries, there have existed particularly good, wise, and sagacious political leaders who have understood the importance of establishing universal political institutions (cf. Myhrman 1994). We should not rule out that this is the case, of course, but if so, we do not have much of a general explanation to offer. Another answer, the conclusion of the preceding chapter, has to do with the degree of uncertainty. George Tsebelis has argued that, given the existence of utility maximizing actors, we can only imagine the possibility of creating universal institutions under the kind of "veil of ignorance" upon which John Rawls' celebrated theory of justice is based (Tsebelis 1990: 117). That is, provided that we cannot know in advance or be entirely certain about how things are going to turn out for us (or the group we represent), universal institutions are preferable to particular institutions as a second-order choice. According to Rawls, the morally right action when facing the issue of which principles of distribution shall apply is to attempt to imagine that we are in a situation in which we do not know who we are (rich or poor, Muslim or Christian, socialist or liberal, man or woman, healthy or sick . . .). According to Rawls' theory, rationally acting individuals will then create just institutions (Rawls 1971).

This solves Rawls' problem of finding a basis for a non-utilitarian theory of justice but not the concrete political problem, for the simple reason that we cannot presume that we are dealing with actors who are ready for this morally conditioned quick-change number (if it is even possible to execute from a psychological point of view). Logical minds are compelled to ask why actors who are engaged in an economic, political, or cultural struggle of interests (with the often dubious methods employed) would suddenly, when faced with the task of setting rules for that struggle of interests, be converted into morally upstanding individuals who choose to ignore their interests and resources when designing the regulatory system. And those who have done any research into the political logic of corporatism never cease to be amazed at the studied combination of artfulness and shamelessness with which special interest groups can claim that their particular proposals for rules and institutions do not primarily benefit themselves, but rather the public interest.

One alternative, if we want to base our thinking on the kind of actors that exist here in the world, is to begin with the concept that game theory calls "imperfect information" – i.e. that in matters related to the future, actors must often act in the presence of significant uncertainty. To connect back to the discussion in chapter 8, the leadership of LO realized that they were not sure that they would emerge the victors in all (or perhaps even the majority) of the labor conflicts that would occur in the increasing tension in the labor market and in society in general. They lacked information about an array of important things, such as the opposition's resources and fighting morale, the future economic and political situation, and their own group's willingness to sacrifice and capacity for united action. Given all of that uncertainty, it may have been rational to accept the kind of universal institutions the state was offering in the form of the Labor Court to resolve disputes on collective agreements and to create similar regulations through the Saltsjöbad Accords in order to arrive at agreements at a reasonable cost. In this context, we can designate the actors' decision to establish universal institutions as a choice of the *logic of the strategic game of the second order*. Provided that the choice to adopt particular institutions that favor only the group's own interests is associated with substantial risk because of all the uncertainty that exists, there is a rationality to be found in endeavoring to establish universal and impartial institutions as the "second best" alternative.

Thereby, we have found a theoretical solution to the problem of the peculiar idealism that has distinguished the attempts of the rationalist school to explain the rise of universal institutions (see chapter 6). The genesis of universal institutions need not be explained by the existence of a special kind of actor endowed with specially high morals who is able to act in special moments of insight and power. Instead, we can make use of the theoretical insights that have emerged from evolutionary game theory, and in particular of research on the informational problems of actors in sequential strategic situations (cf. Young 1998). If we do not have perfect information about the future (which is, of course, the usual case), it may be an entirely rational strategy to choose to try and establish impartial and universal institutions, rather than institutions that benefit only us. The rationalist school's problems in finding any explanation for the rise of universal and impartial institutions are caused by their unrealistic assumptions that the actors are in possession of perfect information about the future.

The idea of *the logic of the strategic game of the second order* presumes that the actors actually understand that there are tangible risks involved in trying to establish particular institutions, and naturally that may often be the case. Even long before the Saltsjöbad Accords, Swedish employers accepted the system of collective agreements which was based on viewing the unions as legitimate negotiating partners. In that respect, they differed from employers in many other countries. The root of that difference may have been that SAF held other norms and values than their counterparts abroad, but it might also have been due to differences in their assessments of the future. SAF president Hjalmar von Sydow spoke out on the matter in a 1932 speech. When he joined SAF in 1903, the question was, according to him, open:

> but I believe the board of directors of the employers' confederation has always believed that workers should have the right to organize. On the other hand, the employers' association for the metal trades initially advocated the opposite opinion. After the failed general strike of 1909, we probably heard voices that said, "Seize the opportunity and crush the workers' organizations!" We could very well have done so; it would not have been difficult, but it would have served no purpose. We could have crushed the unions for the moment, but they would have risen again soon enough and then the bitter memory would have lingered on. (*Industria* 1932: 235)

As I interpret von Sydow, the choice of strategy – i.e. to acknowledge the unions as the legitimate representatives of workers – was conditioned by two factors: One, SAF was not at all sure that it would have been possible to definitively "crush" the unions, and two, since new negotiations would inevitably be held, SAF wanted to make sure that the opposition did not view it with bitterness and suspicion. The unions' "collective memory" of management as an opponent was a factor that SAF had to include in its calculations. Von Sydow understood that it is not easy to negotiate with an opponent who believes you (once again) intend to destroy him.

One proposed alternative is that universal and impartial institutions may rise if we have a situation in which the actors are compelled to publicly justify their positions. Some political philosophers have argued that the very nature of democratic transparency, in which actors must defend their positions in open debate, makes it difficult to morally vindicate a policy based solely on benefiting a special interest group (see Rothstein 1998a: 141). However, I have become less persuaded that this effect is especially strong. We can never be entirely sure that the actors will not behave deceitfully to the extent that what they claim to be a universal and impartial institution will in actuality have a particular effect to the personal advantage of those proposing it. As said, we should never underestimate the inventiveness of political actors when it comes to this form of art. As George Tsebelis has asserted, the choice of institutions is the sophisticated actor's equivalent to the unsophisticated actor's choice of political action programs. This is so because while political action programs can be reformed or abolished, institutions generally have considerably more long-term effects on the direction of development (Tsebelis 1990: 132).

Behaving deceitfully in the context of negotiations on how institutions should be designed has its own particular risks, however. One is that there is a great deal to indicate that this business of trusting another actor is what Olof Petersson has called a kind of "barrier norm" (Petersson 1996: 74ff.). According to Petersson, there are two types of norms. First there are the "balance norms" – the civil servant should comply with the norm of being efficient, but that endeavor must be balanced against the norm of being "responsive" to the opinions of citizens. The second type are "barrier norms" – that is, they are absolute. Either the official complies with the principle of the rule of law in the exercise of her office, or she does not. Trust in other specific actors when it comes to their ability to manage certain tasks may in many cases be of the same absolute nature – i.e. it is an "either/or" situation.

Of course, people may feel more or less trust in a wide variety of actors and for "other people" in general. But when it comes to actors with whom they are negotiating on serious matters – e.g. the design of institutions – it is reasonable to believe that they either trust or do not trust them. The following may serve as an example. There is good reason to presume that SAF knew that LO knew that SAF knew . . . that it was meaningless to come to the negotiations in Saltsjöbaden on a new framework agreement if the intent was to use deceitful behavior to try and trick the opposition into an agreement that would unilaterally benefit only the trickster's side. Such action would not only have impeded the negotiations, it would probably have stripped them of meaning. In other words, uncertainty about the outcome is not enough to enable the creation of universal and impartial institutions. Some kind of basic trust in the opposition's actions is also necessary.

The capacity for trust and the meaning of honesty in society

There are, as we have shown, many advantages to having access to social capital, not least when it comes to being perceived as a trustworthy individual. In her comprehensive analysis of the social meaning of trust, Barbara Misztal formulated the notion as that "above all, trust, by keeping our mind open to all evidence, secures communication and dialog" (Misztal 1996: 10). She puts her finger on an essential point in the discussion of trust – i.e. that in the discussion of how actors with partially conflicting interests should be able to design universal and impartial regulatory systems, they must trust each other when it comes to the forthrightness of the discussion. It is meaningless to enter into the kind of complex negotiations and discussions intended to result in a universal and impartial regulatory system if one is convinced that the other side is fundamentally untrustworthy (Rose-Ackerman 2004). As we have shown, such regulatory systems are often of a rather complicated nature. And if they are to have the kind of legitimacy that makes them robust, they should be designed by the actors involved according to the specific conditions at hand. Social traps are alike in theory, but the concrete design of institutional solutions can produce very large variations (Warren 1999). For instance, creating institutions that prevent the depletion of fishing waters is different from devising regulations that reduce open conflicts in the labor market, which is different from building institutions that make it possible for different ethnic and religious groups to live in peace with one another. Opportunities to force working universal and impartial institutions on actors from above or from the outside seem rather limited (Ostrom 1990).

This means that uncertainty about the future is not enough to equip actors in a social dilemma with what they need to establish universal and impartial institutions. The actors must also believe that the other actors involved will come to the negotiating table with honest intentions. I refer here to the type of decision processes that are usually referred to as "deliberative" (Mulhberger 2001; Warren 1999). "Deliberation" means that those involved are prepared from the outset not to be obdurate in their opinions but are rather willing, in light of objective arguments and evidence, to deliberate their positions. If the first party instead presumes that the other actors will systematically lie, if he believes that they lack respect for him as a negotiating partner endowed with equal rights, that they are not prepared to listen to and deliberate the worth of his arguments, and that they are unwilling to accept objective reasons for changing their original opinions, it is meaningless to begin talks about how a regulatory system might be constructed (Mackie 1998).

There is thus a clear connection between social capital and what has come to be called *deliberative* democracy. Barbara Misztal pointed out that if we have no trust in the other side, we will not be prepared to listen and consider their arguments either. Instead, we will presume that their argument is basically nothing more than the outcome of a cynical power game aimed at tricking us into accepting a regulatory system that is disadvantageous to us. We believe that the other side's true opinions will be concealed behind seductive rhetorical maneuvers. If we also presume that our opponent is going to present false or deceptive evidence to support his opinions, any further communication becomes meaningless. The kind of moral reasoning prescribed by deliberative democracy "falls between impartiality, which requires something like altruism, and prudence, which demands no more than enlightened self-interest" write two of the prominent advocates of the theory, Amy Gutmann and Dennis Thompson (Gutmann and Thompson 1996: 2). Enlightened self-interest may consist of refraining from the attempt to establish rules that benefit only ourselves and refraining from trying to corrupt existing regulatory systems, precisely because we understand that we in fact cannot always know everything about the future.

This leaves us with the following advice to my Russian friend. Changing the people's understanding of public institutions may demand very strong signals from above showing citizens and civil servants beyond "reasonable doubt" that from now on there is a "new game in town." Even if most citizens and bureaucrats realize that they would gain from honestly paying their taxes and refrain from corruption, they cannot rationally decide to erase memories about each other's past deceitful behavior, unless they get convincing evidence that change has really occurred. Secondly, trustworthy institutions can produce the social capital necessary for establishing conditional consent. Such institutions should not only be about due process and the rule of law. In all likelihood, they must also be geared towards increasing equality of opportunity. And lastly, in the long run, trustworthiness can be achieved only through sincere dialog and effective participation.

Bibliography

Acheson, James A. and Jack Knight 2000. "Distribution Fights, Coordination Games, and Lobster Management." *Comparative Studies in Society and History* 42: 209–238

Alapuro, Risto 1988. *State and Revolution in Finland.* Berkeley: University of California Press

Åmark, Klas 1992. "Social Democracy and the Trade Union Movement: Solidarity and the Politics of Self-Interest," in Klaus Misgeld, Karl Molin, and Klas Åmark (eds.), *Creating Social Democracy: A Century of the Social Democratic Labor Party in Sweden.* University Park: Pennsylvania University Press: 56–77

Arias, Enrique Desmond 2002. "The Trouble with Social Capital: Networks and Criminality in Rio de Janeiro." Boston: Annual Meeting of the American Political Science Association

Arthur, Paul 1999. "Trust-Building in Northern Ireland: The Role of Memory," in Lorraine Waterhouse and Halla Beloff (eds.), *Trust in Public Life.* Edinburgh: Edinburgh University Press: 42–52

Axelrod, Robert 1987. *The Complexity of Cooperation.* Princeton: Princeton University Press

Baddeley, Alan D. 1999. *Essentials of Human Memory.* Hove: Psychology Press

Banfield, Edward C. 1958. *The Moral Basis of a Backward Society.* New York: Free Press

Bardhan, Pranab 1997. "Corruption and Development: A Review of the Issues." *Journal of Economic Literature* 35: 1320–1346

Barker, D. G. 1992. *The European Value Study 1981–1990.* Tilburg: Gordon Cook Foundation of European Values Group

Baron, Stephen, John Field, and Tom Schuller (eds.) 2000. *Social Capital: Critical Perspectives.* Oxford: Oxford University Press

Barro, Robert 2001. "Democracy and the Rule of Law," in Douglass C. North, William Summerfield, and Barry Weingast (eds.), *Governing for Prosperity.* New Haven: Yale University Press: 209–232

Barry, Brian 2000. *Culture and Equality.* Oxford: Oxford University Press

Basu, Kushik 1998. "The Role of Norms and Law in Economics: An Essay on Political Economy." Ithaca, NY: Department of Economics, Cornell University

Bates, Robert H. 1997. "Rational Choice and Political Culture." *APSA-CP: Newsletter of the APSA Organized Section in Comparative Politics* 8: 5–6

Bates, Robert H., Rui J. P. de Figueiredo, Jr., and Barry R. Weingast 1998. "The Politics of Interpretation: Rationality, Culture, and Transition." *Politics & Society* 26: 221–256

Bauer, Yehuda 2000. *Rethinking the Holocaust.* New Haven: Yale University Press

Bendor, Jonathan and Dilip Mookherjee 1987. "Institutional Structure and the Logic of Ongoing Collective Action." *American Political Science Review* 81: 137–156

Bendor, Jonathan and Piotr Swistak 1997. "The Evolutionary Stability of Cooperation." *American Political Science Review* 91: 290–307

2000. "The Impossibility of a Pure Homo Economicus." Washington, DC: Annual Meeting of the American Political Science Association

Ben-Ner, Avner and Louis Putterman (eds.) 1998. *Economics, Values and Organizations.* Cambridge: Cambridge University Press

Bennett, Christopher 1995. *Yugoslavia's Bloody Collapse: Causes, Course and Consequences.* London: Hurst & Co.

Bennich-Björkman, Li 1997. *Organizing Innovative Research: The Inner Life of University Departments.* New York: Pergamon

Ben-Yehuda, Nachman 1995. *The Masada Myth: Collective Memory and Mythmaking in Israel.* Madison: University of Wisconsin Press

Berenztein, Sergio 1996. "Rebuilding State Capacity in Contemporary Latin America: The Politics of Taxation in Argentina and Mexico," in William C. Smith and Roberto P. Korzeniewicz (eds.), *Politics, Social Change and Economic Restructuring in Latin America.* Boulder, CO: Lynne Rienner: 229–248

Berman, Sheri 1997. "Civil Society and the Collapse of the Weimar Republic." *World Politics* 49: 401–429

1998. *The Social Democratic Moment: Ideas and Politics in the Making of Interwar Europe.* Cambridge, MA: Harvard University Press

Biel, Anders and Tommy Gärling 1995. "The Role of Uncertainty in Resource Dilemmas." *Journal of Environmental Psychology* 15: 221–233

Birnbaum, Pierre 1988. *States and Collective Interests.* Cambridge: Cambridge University Press

Bjereld, Ulf, Marie Demker, and Jonas Hinnfors 1999. *Varför vetenskap.* Lund: Studentlitteratur

Blomkvist, Hans 1988. *The Soft State: Housing Reform and State Capacity in Urban India.* Dissertation, Uppsala: Uppsala University Press

2001. "Stat och förvaltning i u-länder," in Bo Rothstein (ed.), *Politik som organisation.* Stockholm: SNS: 215–252

Bonadeo, Alfredo 1973. *Corruption, Conflict, and Power in the Works and Times of Niccolò Machiavelli.* Berkeley: University of California Press

Boudon, Raymond 1996. "The 'Cognitivist Model': A Generalised 'Rational Choice Model.'" *Rationality and Society* 8: 123–150

Bowles, Samuel and Herbert Gintis 2002. "Behavioural Science – Homo Reciprocans." *Nature* 414 (6868): 125

Brehm, John and Scott Gates 1997. *Working, Shirking, and Sabotage: Bureaucratic Response to a Democratic Public.* Ann Arbor: University of Michigan Press

Brodin, Anna 2000. *Getting Politics Right: Democracy Promotion as a New Conflict Issue in Foreign Aid Policy.* Göteborg: Department of Political Science, Göteborg University

Brown, Vivienne 1994. *Adam Smith's Discourse.* London: Routledge

Busch, Zetterberg, Karin 1996. *Det civila samhället och välfärdsstaten.* Stockholm: City University Press

Casparsson, Ragnar 1966. *Saltsjöbadsavtalet i historisk belysning.* Stockholm: Tiden

Cawson, Alan 1986. *Corporatism and Political Theory.* Oxford: Blackwell

Chazan, Naomi (ed.) 1999. *Politics and Society in Contemporary Africa.* Boulder, CO: Lynne Rienner

Choe, Yonyok 1997. *How to Manage Free and Fair Elections: A Comparison of Korea, Sweden and the United Kingdom.* Dissertation, Göteborg: Department of Political Science, Göteborg University

Chong, Dennis 2000. *Rational Lives: Norms and Values in Politics and Society.* New York: Cambridge University Press

Claiborn, M. P. and P. S. Martin 2000. "Trusting and Joining? An Empirical Test of the Reciprocal Nature of Social Capital." *Political Behavior* 22: 267–291

Cohen, Jean L. and Andrew Arato 1993. *Civil Society and Political Theory.* Cambridge, MA: MIT Press

Coser, Lewis A. 1992. *Introduction to Maurice Halbwachs, "On Collective Memory."* Chicago: University of Chicago Press

Crouch, Colin 1993. *Industrial Relations and European State Traditions.* Oxford: Clarendon Press

Dagger, Richard 1997. *Civic Virtues*. Oxford: Oxford University Press

Dahl, Robert A. 1989. *Democracy and Its Critics*. New Haven: Yale University Press

Darwall, Stephen 1999. "Sympathetic Liberalism: Recent Work on Adam Smith." *Philosophy and Public Affairs* 28: 139–164

Dasgupta, Partha 1988. "Trust as Commodity," in Diego Gambetta (ed.), *Trust: Making and Breaking Cooperative Relations*. New York and Oxford: Basil Blackwell, 240–256

Dawes, Robin M. and David M. Messick 2000. "Social Dilemmas." *International Journal of Psychology* 35: 11–116

Dawes, Robin M. and Richard H. Thaler 1988. "Anomalies: Cooperation." *Journal of Economic Perspectives* 2: 187–197

Dawidowicz, Lucy 1975. *The War Against the Jews*. London: Wiedenfeld & Nicolson

de Geer, Hans 1978. *Rationaliseringsrörelsen i Sverige*. Stockholm: SNS Förlag

de Soto, Hernando 2001. *The Mystery of Capital*. London: Bantam Press

Delhey, Jan and Kenneth Newton 2003. "Who Trusts? The Origins of Social Trust in Seven Societies." *European Societies* 5: 93–137

2004. "Social Trust: Global Pattern or Nordic Exceptionalism." Working Paper, Wissenschaftszentrum für Socialforschung, Berlin

della Porta, Donatella 2000. "Social Capital, Beliefs in Government, and Political Corruption," in Susan J. Pharr and Robert D. Putnam (eds.), *Disaffected Democracies*. Princeton: Princeton University Press

della Porta, Donatella and Yves Mény (eds.) 1997. *Democracy and Corruption in Europe*. London: Pinter

della Porta, Donatella and Alberto Vannucci 1999. *Corrupt Exchanges: Actors, Resources, and Mechanisms of Political Corruption*. New York: Aldine de Gruyter

Denzau, Arthur T. and Douglass C. North 1994. "Shared Mental Models: Ideologies and Institutions." *Kyklos* 47: 3–31

Diamond, Jared 2004. "Twilight at Easter." *The New York Review of Books* 51(5)

Dowding, Keith and Desmond King (eds.) 1995. *Preferences, Institutions and Rational Choice*. Oxford: Clarendon Press

Durlauf, Steven N. 2002. "Bowling Alone: A Review Essay." *Journal of Economic Behavior & Organization* 47: 259–273

Easterly, William 2001. *The Elusive Quest for Growth: Economists' Adventures and Misadventures in the Tropics*. Cambridge, MA: MIT Press

Edlund, Sten, Anders L. Johansson, Rudolf Meidner, Klaus Misgeld, and Stig W Nilsson (eds.) 1989. *Saltsjöbadsavtalet 50 år: Forskare och parter begrundar en epok*. Stockholm: Arbetslivscentrum

Eidelson, Roy. J. and Judy. I. Eidelson 2003. "Dangerous Ideas: Five Beliefs that Propel Groups toward Conflict." *American Psychologist* 58: 182–192

Eisenstadt, Schmuel N. 1968. "Social Institutions," in D. I. Sills (ed.), *International Encyclopedia of the Social Sciences*. New York: Macmillan and Free Press

Eklund, Klas 1992. *Vår ekonomi: en introduktion till samhällsekonomin*. Stockholm: Tiden

Ekman, Bo 2002. "Smit inte från förtroendekrisen." Stockholm: *Dagens Nyheter.* A4

Elster, Jon 1983. *Sour Grapes: Studies in the Subversion of Rationality*. Cambridge: Cambridge University Press

1985. *Making Sense of Marx*. Cambridge: Cambridge University Press

1989a. *The Cement of Society.* Cambridge: Cambridge University Press

1989b. *Nuts and Bolts for the Social Sciences*. Cambridge: Cambridge University Press

1991. "Rationality and Social Norms." *Archives Europennées de Sociologie* 31: 233–256

1998. *Deliberative Democracy*. Cambridge: Cambridge University Press

2000a. "Rational Choice History: A Case of Excessive Ambition." *American Political Science Review* 94: 685–695

2000b. "Rationality, Economy, Society," in Stephen Turner (ed.), *Cambridge Companion to Weber*. New York: Cambridge University Press, 205–211

Encarnación, Omar G. 2003. *The Myth of Civil Society: Social Capital and Democratic Consolidation in Spain and Brazil*. New York: Palgrave Macmillan

Engwall, Lars 1998. "Farväl till den rationella osynliga handen!," in Barbara Czarniawska (ed.), *Organisationsteori på svenska*. Malmö: Liber, 116–126

Eriksen, Thomas Hylland 2001. *Small Places, Large Issues: An Introduction to Social and Cultural Anthropology*. London: Pluto

Eriksen, Thomas Hylland and Dag O. Hessen 2000. *Egoism*. Stockholm: Nya Doxa

Eriksson, Lina 2005. *Economic Man: The Last Man Standing?* Dissertation, Göteborg: Department of Political Science, Göteborg University

Erlander, Tage 1976. *1955–1960*. Stockholm: Tiden

Esaiasson, Peter and Sören Holmberg 1996. *Representation from Above: Members of Parliament and Representative Democracy in Sweden*. Aldershot: Dartmouth

Falaschetti, Dino and Gary Miller 2001. "Constraining the Leviathan: Moral Hazard and Credible Commitment in Constitutional Design." *Journal of Theoretical Politics* 13: 389–411

Fehr, Ernst and Urs Fischbacher 2002. "Why Social Preferences Matter: The Impact of Non-Selfish Motives on Competition, Cooperation and Incentives." *Economic Journal* 112: C1–33

Fehr, E., U. Fischbacher, and S. Gachter 2002. "Strong Reciprocity, Human Cooperation, and the Enforcement of Social Norms." *Human Nature* 13: 1–25

Fossum, John 2001. *Labor Relations: Development, Structure, Processes.* New York and London: McGraw-Hill/Irwin

Foucault, Michel 1975. "Film and Popular Memory: An Interview with Michel Foucault." *Radical Philosophy* 11: 25–26

Frank, Björn and Günter G. Schulze 2000. "Does Economics Make Citizens Corrupt?" *Journal of Economic Behavior and Organization* 43: 101–113

Frank, Robert H., Thomas D. Gilovich, and Dennis T. Regan 1993. "Does Studying Economics Inhibit Cooperation?" *Journal of Economic Perspectives* 7: 159–171

    1996. "Do Economists Make Bad Citizens?" *Journal of Economic Perspectives* 10: 187–192

Frey, Bruno S. 2004. "'Just Forget It.' Memory Distortion and Bounded Rationality." Working Paper, Zurich: Institute for Empirical Research in Economics, University of Zurich

Friedländer, Saul 1999. *Nazi Germany and the Jews, 1: The Years of Prosecution.* London: Phoenix

Fritzell, Johan and Olle Lundberg 1994. *Vardagens villkor: Levnadsförhållanden i Sverige under tre decennier.* Stockholm: Brombergs

Fukuyama, Francis 1995. *Trust: The Social Virtues and the Creation of Prosperity.* New York: Free Press

Galaz, Victor 2004. "Stealing from the Poor? Game Theory and the Politics of Water Markets in Chile." *Environmental Politics* 13: 414–437

Gambetta, Diego (ed.) 1988. *Trust: Making and Breaking Cooperative Relations.* New York and Oxford: Basil Blackwell

    1993. *The Sicilian Mafia: The Business of Private Protection.* Cambridge, MA: Harvard University Press

Garme, Cecilia 2001. *Newcomers To Power: How to Sit on Someone Else's Throne. Socialists Conquer France in 1981, Non-Socialists Conquer Sweden in 1976.* Uppsala: Uppsala University Press

Gaskin, Katherine and Justin Davis Smith 1995. *A New Civic Europe? A Study of the Extent and Role of Volunteering.* London: The Volunteer Center

Gaventa, John 1980. *Power and Powerlessness: Quiescence and Rebellion in an Appalachian Valley.* Oxford: Clarendon Press

George, Robert P. 1993. *Making Men Moral: Civil Liberties and Public Morality.* Oxford: Oxford University Press

Giddens, Anthony 1984. *The Constitutions of Society*. Cambridge: Polity
   Press
Glaeser, Edward L., David I. Laibson, José A. Scheinkman, and Christine L.
   Soutter 2000. "Measuring Trust." *Quarterly Journal of Economics* 115:
   811–846
Glaeser, Edward, Jose Scheinkman, and Andrei Shleifer 2002. "The Injustice
   of Inequality." Cambridge, MA: National Bureau of Economic Research
Goertzel, Ted 1994. "Belief in Conspiracy Theories." *Political Psychology* 15:
   731–742
Golden, Miriam A. 1988. "Historical Memory and Ideological Orientation
   in the Italian Workers' Movement." *Politics & Society* 16: 1–34
   2003. "Electoral Connections: The Effects of the Personal Vote on Polit-
   ical Patronage, Bureaucracy and Legislation in Postwar Italy." *British
   Journal of Political Science* 33: 189–212
Goldhagen, Daniel J. 1996. *Hitler's Willing Executioners*. New York: Knopf
Goldstein, Judith and Robert O. Keohane (eds.) 1993. *Ideas and Foreign
   Policy: Beliefs, Institutions and Political Change*. Ithaca, NY: Cornell
   University Press
Goodin, Robert (ed.) 1995. *The Theory of Institutional Design*. Cambridge:
   Cambridge University Press
   1997. "On Constitutional Design." Oslo: ARENA, Oslo University
Goul Andersen, Jørgen 1995. "Samfundsind og egennytte." *Politica* 25
   1998. *Borgerne og Lovene*. Århus: Aarhus Universitetsforlag
Goul Andersen, Jørgen and Jens Hoff 1996. *The Scandinavian Welfare States*.
   London: Macmillan
Granberg, Donald and Sören Holmberg 1988. *The Political System Matters*.
   Cambridge: Cambridge University Press
Granovetter, Mark 1985. "Economic Action and Social Structure: The
   Problem of Embeddedness." *American Journal of Sociology* 91: 481–
   510
   1988. "The Sociological and Economic Approaches to Labor Market
   Analysis: A Social Structural View," in George Farkas and Paula
   England (eds.), *Industries, Firms and Jobs*. New York: Aldine de Gruyter:
   187–216
Granqvist, Roland 1987. *Privata och kollektiva val*. Lund: Arkiv
Griswold, Charles L., Jr. 1999. *Adam Smith and the Virtues of Enlightenment*.
   New York: Cambridge University Press
Grootaert, Christiaan and Thierry van Bastelaer 2001. "Understanding and
   Measuring Social Capital: A Synthesis of Findings and Recommenda-
   tions from the Social Capital Initiative." Washington, DC: World Bank
Gross, Jan T. 2001. *Neighbors: The Destruction of the Jewish Community in
   Jebwabne, Poland*. Princeton: Princeton University Press

Gunnarsson, Christer and Mauricio Rojas 1995. *Tillväxt stagnation, kaos: en institutionell studie av underutvecklingens orsaker och utvecklingens möjligheter.* Stockholm: SNS
Gutmann, Amy and Dennis Thompson 1996. *Democracy and Disagreement.* Cambridge, MA: Belknap Press
Guttenplan, D. D. 2001. *Förintelsen inför rätta.* Stockholm: PAN – Norstedts
Gärling, Tommy 1999. "Value Priorities, Social Value Orientations and Cooperation In Social Dilemmas." *British Journal of Social Psychology* 38: 397–408
Hage, Jerald and Barbara Foley Meeker 1988. *Social Causality.* Boston: Unwin Hyman
Halbwachs, Maurice 1992. *On Collective Memory,* ed., trans. and with an introduction by Lewis A. Coser. Chicago: University of Chicago Press
Hall, Peter A. 1986. *Governing the Economy: The Politics of State Intervention in Britain and France.* New York: Oxford University Press
    1999. "Social Capital in Britain." *British Journal of Political Science* 29: 417–464
    2003. "Aligning Ontology and Methodology in Comparative Politics," in James Mahoney and Dietrich Rueschemeyer (eds.), *Comparative Historical Analysis in the Social Sciences.* New York: Cambridge University Press: 373–407
Hansson, Sigfrid 1939. *Från Mackmyra till Saltsjöbaden.* Stockholm: Kooperativa förbundet
    1942. *Den svenska fackföreningsrörelsen.* Stockholm: Tiden
Hardin, Garrett 1968. "The Tragedy of the Commons." *Science* 612: 1243–1268
Hardin, Russell 1995. *One for All: The Logic of Group Conflict.* Princeton: Princeton University Press
    1998. "Trust in Government," in Valerie Braithwaite and Margaret Levi (eds.), *Trust & Governance.* New York: Russell Sage Foundation: 9–27
    1999. "Do we Want Trust in Government?," in Mark E. Warren (ed.), *Democracy & Trust.* New York: Cambridge University Press: 22–41
    2001. "Conceptions and Explanations of Trust," in Karen S. Cook (ed.), *Trust in Society.* New York: Russell Sage Foundation: 3–40
    2002. *Trust and Trustworthiness.* New York: Russell Sage Foundation
Harris, Fredrick C. 1999. "'I Shall Never Forget It': Collective Memory, Micromobilization, and Black Political Activism in the 1960s." New York: Russell Sage Foundation
Hattam, Victoria Charlotte 1993. *Labor Visions and State Power: The Origins of Business Unionism in the United States.* Princeton: Princeton University Press

Hechter, Michael 1992. "The Insufficiency of Game Theory for the Res-
olution of Real-World Collective Action Problems." *Rationality and
Society* 4: 33–40
Hecksher, Gunnar 1952. *Svensk statsförvaltning i arbete.* Stockholm: SNS
Förlag
Hedlund, Stefan 1997. "The Russian Economy: A Case of Pathological
Institutions?" Uppsala: Department of East European Studies, Uppsala
University
1999. *Russia's Market Economy: A Bad Case of Predatory Capitalism.*
London: UCL
Hedström, Peter and Richard Swedberg 1998. "Social Mechanisms: An
Introductory Essay," in Peter Hedström and Richard Swedberg (eds.),
Social Mechanisms: An Analytical Approach to Social Theory. New York:
Cambridge University Press: 1–31
Helliwell, John F. 2003. "How's Life? Combining Individual and National
Variables to Explain Subjective Well-Being." *Economic Modelling* 20:
331– 360
Hermansson, Jörgen 1990. *Spelteorins nytta: Om rationalitet i politik och
vetenskap.* Uppsala: Statsvetenskapliga föreningen
Herreros, Francisco 2004. *The Problem of Forming Social Capital: Why Trust?*
New York: Palgrave Macmillan
Hilberg, Raul 1985. *The Destruction of the European Jews.* New York: Holmes
& Meier
Hodess, Robin, Jessie Banfield, and Toby Wolfe 2001. "Global Corruption
Report 2001." Berlin: Transparency International
Holmberg, Åke 1946. *Skandinavismen i Sverige vid 1800-talets mitt.*
Göteborg: Göteborg University
Holmberg, Sören 1999. "Down and Down We Go: Political Trust in Sweden,"
in Pippa Norris (ed.), *Critical Citizens.* Oxford: Oxford University Press:
103–122
2000. *Välja parti.* Stockholm: Norstedts
Holmberg, Sören and Lennart Weibull 1997. "Förtroendets Fall," in Sören
Holmberg and Lennart Weibull (eds.), *Ett missnöjt folk?,* Göteborg:
SOM-institutet, Göteborg University: 79–102
Holmberg, Sören and Lennart Weibull (eds.) 2002. *Det våras för politiken:
SOM-undersökningen 2001.* Göteborg: SOM-institutet, Göteborg
University
2004. *Ju mer vi är tillsammans. SOM-undersökningen 2003.* Göteborg:
SOM-institutet, Göteborg University
Hope, Kempe Ronald and Bonrwell C. Chikulo (eds.) 1999. *Corruption and
Development in Africa: Lessons from Country Case-Studies.* New York:
St. Martin's Press

Hydén, Göran 2000. "The Governance Challenge in Africa," in Göran Hyden, Dele Olowy, and Hastings W. O. Okoth-Ogendo (eds.), *African Perspectives on Governance*. Trenton, NJ: African World Press: 5–32

Häll, Lars 1994. *Föreningslivet i Sverige*. Stockholm: Statistiska Centralbyrån

Inglehart, Ronald 1997. *Modernization and Postmodernization: Cultural, Economic and Political Change in 43 Countries*. Princeton: Princeton University Press

1999. "Trust, Well-Being and Democracy," in Mark E. Warren (ed.), *Democracy & Trust*. New York: Cambridge University Press: 88–120

Isacson, Maths 1987. *Verkstadsarbete under 1900-talet: Hedemora Verkstäder före 1950*. Lund: Arkiv

Isaksson, Anders 2000. *Per Albin – IV: Landsfadern*. Stockholm: Wahlström & Widstrand

Jamieson, Alison 2000. *The Antimafia: Italy's Fight against Organized Crime*. Basingstoke and New York: Macmillan/St. Martin's Press

Jeppsson Grassman, Eva and Lars Svedberg 1999. "Medborgarskapets gestaltningar. Insatser i och utanför föreningslivet," in Demokratiutredningen (ed.), *Civilsamhället (SOU 1999: 84)*. Stockholm: Fakta Info: 121–180

Johansson, Anders L. 1989. *Tillväxt och klassamarbete*. Stockholm: Tiden

Johansson, Roger 2001. *Kampen om historien. Ådalen 1931: Sociala konflikter, historiemedvetande och historiebruk 1931–2000*. Stockholm: Hjalmarsson & Högberg Förlag

Johnson, James 1997. "Symbol and Strategy in Comparative Political Analysis." *APSA-CP: Newsletter of the APSA Organized Section in Comparative Politics* 8: 6–8

Jones, Bryan D. 1999. "Bounded Rationality." *Annual Review of Political Science* 2: 297–321

Kandel, E. R., J. H. Schwartz, and T. M. Jessel 1995. *Essentials of Neural Science and Behavior*. Norwalk, CT: Appleton & Lange

Karklins, Rasma 2002. "Typology of Post-Communist Corruption." *Problems of Post-Communism* 49: 22–32

Karlsson, Klas-Göran 1999. *Historia som vapen*. Stockholm: Natur och Kultur

Katzenstein, Peter J. 1985. *Small States in World Markets: Industrial Policy in Europe*. Ithaca, NY: Cornell University Press

Kaufman, Stuart J. 2001. *Modern Hatreds: The Symbolic Politics of Ethnic War*. Ithaca, NY: Cornell University Press

Keil, Lars Broder and Sven Felix Kellerhoff 2002. *Deutsche Legende: wom "Dolchstoss" und anderen Mythen der Geschische*. Berlin: Links

Kershaw, Ian 2000. *Hitler. 1889–1936: Hubris.* London: Penguin

Knack, Stephen and Philip Keefer 1997. "Does Social Capital Have an Economic Payoff? A Cross-Country Investigation." *Quarterly Journal of Economics* 112: 1251–1288

Kollock, P. 1997. "Transforming Social Dilemmas: Group Identity and Cooperation," in P. Danielson (ed.), *Modeling Rational and Moral Agents.* Oxford: Oxford University Press: 186–210

  1998. "Social Dilemmas: The Anatomy of Cooperation." *Annual Review of Sociology* 24: 183–214

Kornai, János 2000. "Hidden in an Envelope: Gratitude Payments to Medical Doctors in Hungary." Working Paper, Collegium Budapest Institute for Advanced Study

Kornai, János, Bo Rothstein, and Susan Rose-Ackerman 2004. *Creating Social Trust in Post-Socialist Transition.* New York: Palgrave Macmillan

Kramer, Roderick M. and Tom R. Tyler (eds.) 1996. *Trust in Organizations: Frontiers of Theory and Research.* London: Sage

Krastev, Ivan and Georgy Ganev 2004. "The Missing Incentive: Corruption, Anticorruption and Reelection," in Susan Rose-Ackerman and János Kornai (eds.), *Building a Trustworthy State in Post-Socialist Transition.* New York: Palgrave Macmillan: 150–172

Krishna, Anirudh 2002. *Active Social Capital: Tracing the Roots of Development and Democracy.* New York: Columbia University Press

Kuenzi, Michelle 2004. "Social Capital, Political Trust, and Ethnicity in West Africa." Chicago: Annual Meeting of the American Political Science Association

Kugelberg, Bertil (ed.) 1985. *Fred eller fejd: Personliga minnen och anteckningar.* Stockholm: SAF

  1986. *Från en central utsiktspunkt.* Stockholm: Norstedts

  1989. "Kommentarer," in Sten Edlund, Anders L. Johansson, Rudolf Meidner, Klaus Misgeld, and Stig W. Nilsson (eds.), *Saltsjöbadsavtalet 50 år: Forskare och parter begrundar en epok.* Stockholm: Arbetslivscentrum: 92– 98

Kuhnle, Stein and Per Selle 1992. *Government and Voluntary Associations.* Aldershot: Avebury

Kumlin, Staffan 2004. *The Personal and the Political: How Personal Welfare State Experiences Affect Political Trust and Ideology.* New York: Palgrave Macmillan

  2005. "Making and Breaking Social Capital: The Impact of Welfare State Institutions." *Comparative Political Studies,* forthcoming

Kydd, Andrew 2000. "Overcoming Mistrust." *Rationality and Society* 12: 397–424

La Porta, Rafael, Florencio Lopez-de-Silanes, Andrei Shleifer, and Robert
W. Vishny 1997. "Trust in Large Organizations." *American Economic
Review* 87: 333–338
1999. "The Quality of Government." *Journal of Law, Economics and Orga-
nization* 15: 222–279
Laurin, Urban 1986. *På heder och samvete: skattefuskets orsaker och utbred-
ning.* Stockholm: Norstedt
Ledyard, John O. 1995. "Public Goods: A Survey of Experimental Research,"
in John H. Kagel and Alvin E. Roth (eds.), *The Handbook of Experi-
mental Economics.* Princeton: Princeton University Press: 311–369
Lembruch, Gerhard 1991. "The Organization of Society, Administrative
Strategies and Policy Networks," in Roland Czada and Adrienne
Windhoff-Héretier (eds.), *Political Choice: Institutions, Rules and the
Limits of Rationality.* Boulder, CO: Westview Press: 86–107
Letki, Natalia 2003. "What Makes Citizens Trustworthy? Individual Commu-
nity and Structural Determinants of Honesty and Law-Abidingness."
Working Paper, Nuffield College, Oxford University
Levi, Margaret 1988. *Of Rule and Revenue.* Berkeley: University of California
Press
1990. "A Logic of Institutional Change," in Karen Schweers Cook and
Margaret Levi (eds.), *The Limits of Rationality.* Chicago: University of
Chicago Press: 401–433
1991. "Are There Limits to Rationality?" *Archives Européennes de Sociologie*
32: 130–141
1996. "Social and Unsocial Capital: A Review Essay of Robert Putnam's
Making Democracy Work." *Politics & Society* 24: 45–55
1997. "A Model, a Method, and a Map: Rational Choice in Comparative
and Historical Analysis," in Mark I. Lichbach and Alan S. Zuckerman
(eds.), *Comparative Politics: Rationality, Culture and Structure.* New
York: Cambridge University Press: 19–42
1998a. *Consent, Dissent, and Patriotism.* New York: Cambridge University
Press
1998b. "A State of Trust," in Valerie Braithwaite and Margaret Levi (eds.),
Trust & Governance. New York: Russell Sage Foundation: 77–101
Lewin, Leif 1980. *Governing Trade Unions in Sweden.* Cambridge, MA:
Harvard University Press
1991. *Self-Interest and Public Interest in Western Politics.* Oxford: Oxford
University Press
1992. "The Rise and Decline of Corporatism." *European Journal of Political
Research* 26: 59–79
Levy, Jacob T. 2000. *The Multiculturalism of Fear.* New York: Oxford
University Press

Lichbach, Mark I. 1995. *The Rebel's Dilemma.* Ann Arbor: University of
    Michigan Press
    1997. *The Co-operator's Dilemma.* Ann Arbor: University of Michigan
    Press
Lichbach, Mark I. and Alan s. Zuckerman 1998. "Research Tradition and
    Theory in Comparative Politics: An Introduction," in Mark I. Lichbach
    and Alan S. Zuckerman (eds.), *Comparative Politics: Rationality, Culture
    and Structure.* New York: Cambridge University Press: 3–37
Lilla, Mark 2001. *The Reckless Mind.* New York: The New York Review of
    Books
Lind, E. A. and Tom R. Tyler 1997. *The Social Psychology of Procedural Justice.*
    New York: Plenum
Linderborg, Åsa 2001. *Socialdemokraterna skriver historia: Historieskrivning
    som ideologisk maktresurs 1892–2000.* Stockholm: Atlas Akademi
Lindvall, Johannes 2004. *The Politics of Purpose: Swedish Economic Policy
    after the Golden Age.* Dissertation, Department of Political Science,
    Göteborg: Göteborg University
Lipsky, Michael 1980. *Street-Level Bureaucracy: Dilemmas of the Individual
    in Public Services.* New York: Russell Sage Foundation
Little, Daniel 1991. *Varieties of Social Explanation.* Boulder, CO: Westview
    Press
Loewenstein, George, Matthew Rabin, and Colin Camerer 2004. *Advances
    in Behavioral Economics.* New York: Russell Sage Foundation
Lohmann, Susanne 2003. "Why Do Institutions Matter: An Audience Cost
    Theory of Institutional Commitment." *Governance* 16: 95–110
Looker, Robert 1972. "Introduction," in Robert Looker (ed.), *Rosa
    Luxemburg: Selected Political Writings.* London: Jonathan Cape:
    3–17
Lundh, Christer 2002. *Spelets regler: institutioner och lönebildning på den
    svenska arbetsmarknaden 1850–2000.* Stockholm: SNS Förlag
Lundquist, Lennart J. 1996. *Byråkratisk etik.* Lund: Studentlitteratur 2000.
    Democratins väktare: åmbetsmännen och vårt offentliga etos. Lund: Stu-
    dentlitteratur
Lundquist, Lennart J. 2001. "Games Real Farmers Play." *Local Environment*
    6: 407–419
Lundström, Mats 1996. *Jämställdhet eller sexistisk rättvisa?* Stockholm: SNS
    Förlag
Lundström, Tommy and Filip Wijkström 1997. *The Nonprofit Sector in
    Sweden.* Manchester: Manchester University Press
Lustick, Ian S. 1997. "Culture and the Wager of Rational Choice." *APSA-
    CP: Newsletter of the APSA Organized Section in Comparative Politics* 8:
    11–13

MacDonald, Paul K. 2003. "Useful Fiction or Miracle Maker: The Competing Epistemological Foundations of Rational Choice Theory." *American Political Science Review* 97: 551–565

Mackie, Gerry 1998. "All Men Are Liars: Is Democracy Meaningless?," in Jon Elster (ed.), *Deliberative Democracy*. New York: Cambridge University Press: 69–96

MacMullen, Ramsay 1988. *Corruption and the Decline of Rome*. New Haven: Yale University Press

Malnes, Raino and Knut Midgaard 1993. *De politiska idéerna historia*. Lund: Studentlittaratur

Mantzavinos, C., Douglass C. North, and Syed Shariq 2002. "Learning, Change and Economic Performance." Boston: Annual Meeting of the American Political Science Association

March, James B. and Johan P. Olsen 1989. *Rediscovering Institutions: The Organizational Basis of Politics*. New York: Basic Books

Margolis, Howard 1982. *Selfishness, Altruism, and Rationality: A Theory of Social Choice*. Cambridge: Cambridge University Press

Marks, Gary 1989. *Unions in Politics: Britain, Germany, and the United States in the Nineteenth and early Twentieth Centuries*. Princeton: Princeton University Press

Marwell, Gerald and Robyn Dawes 1981. "Economists Free Ride, Does Anyone Else?" *Journal of Public Economics* 15: 295–310

Marx, Karl 1927. *Value, Price and Profit*. Chicago: C. Kerr

McAdam, Doug, Sidney G. Tarrow, and Charles Tilly 2001. *Dynamics of Contention*. Cambridge: Cambridge University Press

Mettler, Suzanne and Joe Soss 2004. "The Consequences of Public Policy for Democratic Citizenship: Bridging Policy and Mass Politics." *Perspectives on Politics* 2: 55–74

Micheletti, Michele 1995. *Civil Society and State Relations in Sweden*. Aldershot: Avebury

Milgrom, Paul R., Douglass C. North, and Barry R. Weingast 1990. "The Role of Institutions in the Revival of Trade: The Medieval Law Merchant, Private Judges and the Champagne Fairs." *Economics and Politics* 2: 1–23

Miller, Gary J. 1992. *Managerial Dilemmas: The Political Economy of Hierachy*. Cambridge: Cambridge University Press

Miller, Gary and Thomas Hammond 1994. "Why Politics is More Fundamental Than Economics: Incentive-Compatible Mechanisms are not Credible." *Journal of Theoretical Politics* 6: 5–26

Milner, Henry and Eskil Wadensjö (eds.) 2001. *Gösta Rehn, the Swedish Model and Labour Market Policies: International and National Perspectives*. Aldershot: Ashgate

Misztal, Barbara A. 1996. *Trust in Modern Societies.* Cambridge: Polity Press
Molander, Per 1994. *Aqvedukten vid Zaghouan.* Stockholm: Atlantis
Morrow, James D. 1994. *Game Theory for Political Scientists.* Princeton: Princeton University Press
Mulhberger, Peter 2001. "Social Capital and Deliberative Theory." San Francisco: Annual Meeting of the American Political Science Association
Müller, Ingo 1991. *Hitler's Justice: The Courts in the Third Reich.* London: Tauris
Myhrman, Johan 1994. *Hur Sverige blev rikt.* Stockholm: SNS Forlag
Nalbandian, John 1991. *Professionalism in Local Government: Transformations in the Roles, Responsibilities, and Values of City Managers.* San Francisco: Jossey-Bass
Naurin, Daniel 2001. *Den demokratiske lobbyisten.* Umeå: Borea
Nelander, Sven and Viveka Lindgren 1994. "Röster om facket och jobbet: Facklig aktivitet och fackligt arbete." Stockholm: Landsorganisationen
Newton, Kenneth 1999a. "Social and Political Trust in Established Democracies," in Pippa Norris (ed.), *Critical Citizens: Global Support for Democratic Government.* New York: Oxford University Press: 323–351
   1999b. "Social Capital and Democracy in Modern Europe," in Jan W. van Deth, Marco Maraffi, Kenneth Newton, and Paul F. Whiteley (eds.), *Social Capital and European Democracy.* London: Routledge
Nilsson, Lennart (ed.) 2002. *Flernivådemokrati i förändring.* SOM Institute Report 27. Göteborg: Göteborg University
Norén, Ylva 2000. "Explaining Variation in Political Trust in Sweden." Copenhagen: European Consortium for Political Research Joint Session of Workshops
   2002. *Svenskars politiska förtroende.* Göteborg: Department of Political Science, Göteborg University
North, Douglass C. 1990. *Institutions, Institutional Change and Economic Performance.* Cambridge: Cambridge University Press
   1998. "Where Have we Been and Where are we Going?," in Avner Ben-Ner and Louis Putterman (eds.), *Economics, Values and Organization.* Cambridge: Cambridge University Press: 491–508
North, Douglass C., William Summerfield, and Barry R. Weingast 2000. "Order, Disorder, and Economic Change: Latin America versus North America," in Bruce Bueno De Mesquita and Hilton R. Root (eds.), *Governing for Prosperity.* New Haven: Yale University Press: 17–59
Nycander, Svante 2002. *Makten över arbetsmarknaden: Ett perspektiv på Sveriges 1900-tal.* Stockholm: SNS Förlag

Öberg, Per-Ola 1994. *Särintresse och allmänintresse: Korporatismens ansikten.* Stockholm: Norstedts

OECD 1999. *Public Sector Corruption: An International Survey of Prevention Measures.* Paris: OECD

Offe, Claus 1999. "How Can we Trust our Fellow Citizens?," in Mark E. Warren (ed.), *Democracy & Trust.* Cambridge: Cambridge University Press: 42–87

2004. "Political Corruption. Conceptual and Practical Issues," in Susan Rose-Ackerman and János Kornai (eds.), *Building a Trustworthy State in Post-Socialist Transition.* New York: Palgrave Macmillan: 77–99

Offe, Claus and Helmuth Wiesenthal 1980. "Two Logics of Collective Action," in Maurice Zeitlin (ed.), *Political Power and Social Theory.* Greenwich: JAI Press: 3–33

Olofsson, Gunnar 1979. *Mellan klass och stat.* Lund: Arkiv

Olson, Mancur Jr.. 1996. "Big Bills Left on the Sidewalk: Why Some Nations are Rich, and Others Poor." *Journal of Economic Perspectives* 10: 3–22

Olsson, Sven E. 1993. *Social Policy and Welfare State in Sweden.* Lund: Arkiv

Oskarsson, Sven 2003. *The Fate of Organized Labor: Explaining Unionization, Wage Inequality, and Strikes across Time and Space.* Dissertation, Department of Government, Uppsala: Uppsala University

Ostrom, Elinor 1990. *Governing the Commons: The Evolution of Institutions for Collective Action.* New York: Cambridge University Press

1998. "A Behavioral Approach to the Rational Choice Theory of Collective Action." *American Political Science Review* 92: 1–23

1999. "Coping with Tragedies of the Commons." *Annual Review of Political Science* 2: 493–535

Ostrom, Elinor and T. K. Ahn 2001. "A Social Science Perspective on Social Capital: Social Capital and Collective Action." Exeter: Social Capital: Interdisciplinary Perspectives

Paldam, Martin and Gert Tinggaard Svendsen 2000. "Missing Social Capital and the Transition in Eastern Europe." Departmentof Economics, Aarhus University, www.martin.paldam.dk

Parks, C. D. and A. D. Vu 1994. "Social Dilemma Behavior of Individuals from Highly Individualist and Collectivist Cultures." *Journal of Conflict Resolution* 38: 708–718

Pasotti, Eleonora 2001. "Clients to Citizens: Public Opinion Mobilization in Naples." San Francisco: Annual Meeting of American Political Science Association

Patterson, Orlando 1999. "Liberty against the Democratic State: On the Historical and Contemporary Sources of American Distrust," in Mark

E. Warren (ed.), *Democracy & Trust*. Cambridge: Cambridge University Press: 151–207

Perlinski, Marek 1990. "Livet utanför fabriksgrindarna och kontorsdörren," in Rune Åberg (ed.), *Industrisamhälle i omvandling*. Stockholm: Carlssons: 106–133

Peterson, Scott 2000. *Me Against My Brother: At War in Somalia, Sudan, and Rwanda*. London: Routledge

Petersson, Olof 1996. *Rättsstaten: Frihet, rättssäkerhet och maktdelning i dagens politik*. Stockholm: Publica

Petersson, Olof, Anders Westholm, and Göran Blomkvist (eds.) 1987. *Medborgarnas makt*. Stockholm: Carlssons

Pettersson, Thorleif 1992. "Välfärd, värderingsförändringar och folkrörelseengagemang," in Sigbert Axelsson and Thorleif Pettersson (eds.), *Mot denna framtid*. Stockholm: Carlssons: 172–230

Pettersson, Thorleif and Kalle Geyer 1992. *Värderingsförändringar i Sverige: Den svenska modellen, individualismen och rättvisan*. Stockholm: Brevskolan

Pinker, Steven 1997. *How the Mind Works*. New York: W. W. Norton

Platt, John 1973. "Social Traps." *American Psychologist* 28: 641–651

Portes, Alejandro 2000. "The Two Meanings of Social Capital." *Sociological Forum* 15: 1–12

Pulzer, Peter G. J. 1992. *Jews and the German State: The Political History of a Minority 1848–1933*. Oxford: Blackwell

Putnam, Robert D. 1993. *Making Democracy Work: Civic Traditions in Modern Italy*. Princeton: Princeton University Press
2000. *Bowling Alone: The Collapse and Revival of American Community*. New York: Simon & Schuster

Putnam, Robert D. (ed.) 2002. *Democracy in Flux: Social Capital in Contemporary Societies*. New York: Oxford University Press

Rawls, John 1971. *A Theory of Justice*. Oxford: Oxford University Press

Ringmar, Erik 1996. *Identity, Interest and Action: A Cultural Explanation of Sweden's Intervention in the Thirty Years' War*. Cambridge: Cambridge University Press

Rodrik, Dani 1999. "Institutions For High-Quality Growth: What They Are and How to Acquire Them." *International Monetary Fund: Conference on Second Generation Reform*, Washington, DC

Rojas, Mauricio 2004. *Historia de la crisis Argentina*. Madrid: Cadal

Root, Hilton R. 1996. *Small Countries, Big Lessons: Governance and the Rise of East Asia*. Hong Kong: Oxford University Press

Rose-Ackerman, Susan 1999. *Corruption and Government: Causes, Consequences, and Reform*. Cambridge: Cambridge University Press

2001. "Trust, Honesty and Corruption: Reflections on the State-Building Process." *Archives Européennes de Sociologie* 42: 526–551

2004. "Public Participation in Consolidating Democracies: Hungary and Poland," in János Kornai and Susan Rose-Ackerman (eds.), *Building a Trustworthy State in Post-Socialist Transition*. New York: Palgrave Macmillan: 9–28

Rosenbaum, Ron 1998. *Explaining Hitler: The Search for the Origins of his Evil*. New York: Random House

Ross, Marc Howard 1998. "Culture and Identity in Comparative Analysis," in Mark I. Lichbach and Alan S. Zuckerman (eds.), *Comparative Politics: Rationality, Culture and Structure*. New York: Cambridge University Press: 87–117

Rother, Larry 1999. "Where Taxes Aren't So Certain," *New York Times*: 4:3

Rothstein, Bo 1987. "Corporatism and Reformism: The Social Democratic Institutionalization of Class Conflict." *Acta Sociologica* 30: 295–311

1992a. *Den korporativa staten: Intresseorganisationer och statsförvaltning i svensk politik*. Stockholm: Norstedts

1992b. "Explaining Swedish Corporatism: The Formative Moment." *Scandinavian Political Studies* 13: 131–149

1992c. "Labor-Market Institutions and Working-Class Strength," in Sven Steinmo, Kathleen Thelen, and Frank Longstreth (eds.), *Structuring Politics: Historical Institutionalism in a Comparative Perspective*. Cambridge: Cambridge University Press: 33–56

1992d. "Social Justice and State Capacity" *Politics & Society* 20: 101–126

1996a. "Political Institutions: An Overview," in Robert E. Goodin and Hans-Dieter Klingemann (eds.), *A New Handbook for Political Science*. Oxford: Oxford University Press: 104–125

1996b. *The Social Democratic State: The Swedish Model and the Bureaucratic Problem of Social Reforms*. Pittsburgh: University of Pittsburgh Press

1996c. "Är insikter i ekonomi effektiva?" *Ekonomisk Debatt* 46: 33–38

1998a. *Just Institutions Matter: The Moral and Political Logic of the Universal Welfare State*. Cambridge: Cambridge University Press

1998b. "State Building and Capitalism: The Rise of the Swedish Bureaucracy." *Scandinavian Political Studies* 21: 287–306

1999. "Förtroende för andra och förtroende för politiska institutioner," in Sören Holmberg and Lennart Weibull (eds.), *Ljusnande framtid*. Göteborg: SOM-institutet, Göteborg University: 387–397

2000a. "Det sociala kapitalet i den socialdemokratiska staten: Den svenska modellen och det civila samhället." *Arkiv för studier i arbetarrörelsens historia*, 79: 1–55

2000b. "Trust, Social Dilemmas and Collective Memories." *Journal of Theoretical Politics* 12: 477–503

2001. "The Universal Welfare State as a Social Dilemma." *Rationality and Society* 14: 190–214

2002. "Sweden: Social Capital in the Social Democratic State," in Robert D. Putnam (ed.), *Democracies in Flux: The Evolution of Social Capital in Contemporary Society*. Oxford: Oxford University Press: 289–333

2004. "Is Political Science Producing Technically Competent Barbarians?" *European Political Science* 1: 1–15

Rothstein, Bo and Sven Steinmo 2002. "Restructuring Politics: Institutional Analysis and the Challenges of Modern Welfare States," in Bo Rothstein and Sven Steinmo (eds.), *Restructuring the Welfare State: Political Institutions and Policy Change*. New York: Palgrave Macmillan: 1–31

Rothstein, Bo and Dietlind Stolle 2002. "How Political Institutions Create and Destroy Social Capital: An Institutional Theory of Generalized Trust." San Francisco: Annual Meeting of the American Political Science Association

2003. "Social Capital, Impartiality, and the Welfare State: An Institutional Approach," in Marc Hooghe and Dietlind Stolle (eds.), *Generating Social Capital: The Role of Voluntary Associations, Institutions and Government Policy*. New York: Palgrave Macmillan: 191–210

Sabine, George H. 1963. *A History of Political Ideas*. London: George. G. Harrap

Sahlins, Marshall 2001. *Culture in Practice: Selected Essays*. New York: Zone Press

Salamon, Lester and Helmut Anheier 1994. *The Emerging Sector: An Overview*. Baltimore: Johns Hopkins Institute for Policy Studies

Sally, David 1995. "Conversation and Cooperation in Social Dilemmas: A Metaanalysis of Experiments from 1958 to 1992." *Rationality and Society* 7: 58–92

Sandall, Roger 2002. *The Culture Cult: Designer Tribalism and Other Essays*. Oxford: Westview Press

Sayer, Andrew 1992. *Method in Social Science*. London: Routledge

SCB, Statiska Centralbyrån 1997. "Välfärd och ojämlikhet i ett 20-årsperspektiv." Stockholm: Statistics Sweden

Scharpf, Fritz W. 1997. *Games Real Actors Play: Actor-Centered Institutionalism in Policy Research*. Boulder, CO: Westview Press

Schelling, Thomas C. 1960. *The Strategy of Conflict*. Cambridge, MA: Harvard University Press

1996. *Social Mechanisms and Social Dynamics*. Stockholm: Department of Sociology

Schiemann, John W. 2000. "Meeting Halfway Between Rochester and Frankfurt: Generative Salience, Focal Points, and Strategic Interaction." *American Journal of Political Science* 44: 1–16

2002. "History and Emotions. Beliefs and Mental Models: Toward a Hermeneutics of Rational Choice." Boston: Annual Meeting of the American Political Science Association

Schierenbeck, Isabell 2002. "Vem bryr sig om regelverket? Om frontlinjebyråkrater, handlingsutrymme och förvaltningsdemokratisk legitimitet," in Jon Pierre and Bo Rothstein (eds.), *Välfärdsstat i otakt: Om politikens oväntade, oavsiktliga och oönskade effekter.* Lund: Studentlitteratur: 102–120

Schiller, Bernt 1967. *Storstrejken 1909: förhistoria och orsaker.* Dissertation, Göteborg: Göteborg University

1988a. *"Det förödande 70-talet": SAF och medbestämmandet 1965–1982.* Stockholm: Arbetsmiljöfonden: Allmänna Förlaget

1988b. *Samarbete eller konflikt.* Stockholm: Arbetsmiljöfonden: Allmänna Förlaget

Schmidt, Vivien A. 2000. "Values and Discourses in the Politics of Adjustment," in Fritz W. Scharpf and Viven A Schmidt (eds.), *Welfare and Work in the Open Economy: From Vulnerability to Competitiveness.* Oxford: Oxford University Press: 229–309

Scholz, John T. 1998. "Trust, Taxes and Compliance," in Valerie Braithwaite and Margaret Levi (eds.), *Trust & Governance.* New York: Russell Sage Foundation: 135–166

Scholz, John T. and Mark Lubell 1998. "Trust and Taxpaying: Testing the Heuristic Approach to Collective Action." *American Journal of Political Science* 42: 398–417

Schüllerqvist, Bengt 1992. *Från kosackval till kohandel: SAPs väg till makten.* Stockholm: Tiden

Schwartz, Barry 1991. "Social Change and Collective Memory: The Democratization of George Washington." *American Sociological Review* 56: 221–236

2001. *Abraham Lincoln and the Forge of National Memory.* Chicago: University of Chicago Press

Selle, Per 1998. "The Transformation of the Voluntary Sector in Norway: A Decline of Social Capital?," in Jan van Deth, Marco Maraffi, Ken Newton, and Paul F. Whiteley (eds.), *Social Capital and European Democracy.* London: Routledge: 97–121

Selle, Per and Bjarne Øymyr 1995. *Frivillig organisering og demokrati.* Oslo: Samlaget

Shapiro, Ian and Alexander Wendt 1992. "The Difference that Realism Makes." *Politics and Society* 20: 197–223

Shleifer, Andrei and Robert W. Vishny 1998. *The Grabbing Hand: Government Pathologies and Their Cures.* Cambridge, MA: Harvard University Press

Sitkin, Sim B. and Stickel Darryl 1996. "The Road to Hell: The Dynamics of Distrust in an Era of Quality," in Roderick M. Kramer and Tom R. Tyler (eds.), *Trust in Organizations: Frontiers of Theory and Research.* London: Sage: 196–215

Socialdepartementet, Kungl (Swedish Ministry of Social Affairs). 1929. "Arbetsfredskonferensen i Stockholm 1 december 1928." Stockholm: Socialdepartementet

Soss, Joe 2000. *Unwanted Claims: The Politics of Participation in the US Welfare System.* Ann Arbor: University of Michigan Press

SOU, Statens Offentliga Utredningar 1996, "Folkbildningen: en utvärdering." Stockholm: Fritzes Offentliga Publikationer
2000. "Domarutnämningar och domstolsledning: frågor om utnämning av högre domare och domstolschefens roll (SOU 2000: 99)." Stockholm: Fritzes Offentliga Publikationer

Stapenhurst, Rick and Sahr J. Kpundeh 1999. "Curbing Corruption: Toward a Model for Building National Integrity." Washington, DC: World Bank, Economic Development Institute

Steinmo, Sven 2003. "Bucking the Trend? The Welfare State in the Global Economy: The Swedish Case." *New Political Economy* 8: 46–67

Steinmo, Sven and Kathleen Thelen 1992. "Historical Institutionalism in Comparative Politics," in Sven Steinmo, Kathleen Thelen, and Frank Longstreth (eds.), *Structuring Politics: Historical Institutionalism in Comparative Analysis.* New York: Cambridge University Press: 1–32

Stensöta, Helena 2004. *Den empatiska staten: Jämställdhetens inverkan på daghem och polis 1950–2000.* Dissertation, Department of Political Science, Göteborg: Göteborg University

Stinchcombe, Arthur 1992. "Simmel Systematized." *Theory and Society* 21: 183–202

Stolle, Dietlind 2000a. "Clubs and Congregations: The Benefit of Joining Organizations," in Karen S. Cook (ed.), *Trust in Society.* New York: Russell Sage Foundation: 202–244
2000b. "Communities, Citizens and Local Government. Generalized Trust and the Impact of Regional Settings: A Study of Three Regions in Sweden." Bergen: LOS Centre, Workshop, Investigating Social Capital
2003. "The Sources of Social Capital," in Marc Hooghe and Dietlind Stolle (eds.), *Generating Social Capital: Civil Society and Institutions in a Comparative Perspective.* New York: Palgrave Macmillan: 18–40

Streeck, Wolfgang and Philippe C. Schmitter 1985. "Community, Market,
State – and Associations? The Prospective Contribution of Interest
Governance to Social Order," in Wolfgang Streck and Philippe C.
Schmitter (eds.), *Private Interest Government: Beyond Market and State*.
London: Sage: 1–29

Stråth, Bo 1982. *Varvsarbetare i två varvsstäder: en historisk studie av verk-
stadsklubbarna vid varven i Göteborg och Malmö*. Göteborg: Svenska
Varv

Stråth, Bo (ed.) 2000. *Myth and Memory in the Construction of Community*.
Brussels: Peter Lang

Svallfors, Stefan 1996. *Välfärdsstatens moraliska ekonomi*. Umeå: Borea
Förlag

1997. "Worlds of Welfare and Attitudes to Redistribution: A Comparison
of Eight Western Nations." *European Sociological Review* 13: 283–304

Svensson, Torsten 1994. *Socialdemokratins dominans*. Uppsala: Almqvist &
Wiksell

1996. *Novemberrevolutionen: Om rationalitet och makt i beslutet att avre-
glera kreditmarknaden 1985*. Stockholm: Fritze

Swank, Duane 2002. *Global Capital, Political Institutions, and Policy Change
in Developed Welfare States*. New York: Cambridge University Press

Swenson, Peter 2002. *Capitalists against Markets: The Making of Labor Markets and Welfare States in the United States and Sweden*. New York:
Oxford University Press

Swidler, Ann 2001a. "Cultural Repertoires and Cultural Logics: Can They
be Reconciled?" Anaheim, CA: Annual Meeting of the American Sociological Assocation

2001b. *Talk of Love: How Culture Matters*. Chicago: University of Chicago
Press

Sztompka, Piotr 1998. "Trust, Distrust and Two Paradoxes of Democracy."
European Journal of Social Theory 1: 19–32

Tarrow, Sidney 1996. "Making Social Science Work Across Space and Time:
A Critical Reflection on Robert Putnam's *Making Democracy Work*."
Americal Political Science Review 90: 389–397

2004. "Bridging the Quantitative–Qualitative Divide," in Henry E. Brady
and David Collier (eds.), *Rethinking Social Inquiry*. Lanham: Rowman
& Littlefield: 171–181

Temple, Jonathan and Paul Johnson 1998. "Social Capability and Economic
Growth." *Quarterly Journal of Economics* 113: 965–980

Teorell, Jan 1998. *Demokrati eller fåtalsvälde: Om beslutsfattande i partior-
ganisationer*. Dissertation, Uppsala: Uppsala University

Thelen, Kathleen 1999. "Historical Institutionalism in Comparative Perspective." *Annual Review of Political Science* 2: 369–404

Thorp, Rosemary 1996. "The Reform of the Tax Administration in Peru," in
    Antonia Silva (ed.), *Implementing Policy Innovations in Latin America*.
    Washington, DC: Inter-American Development Bank: 34–51
Torpe, Lars 2000. "Democratic Community as Social Capital." Department
    of Economics, Politics and Public Administration, Aalborg: Aalborg
    University
Tsebelis, George 1990. *Nested Games: Rational Choice in a Comparative Per-
    spective*. New York: Cambridge University Press
    1997. "Rational Choice and Culture." *APSA-CP: Newsletter of the APSA
    Organized Section in Comparative Politics* 8: 15–17
Turner, Mark 2001. *Cognitive Dimensions of Social Science*. Oxford: Oxford
    University Press
Tyler, Tom R. 1992. *Why People Obey the Law*. New Haven: Yale University
    Press
    1998. "Trust and Democratic Governance," in Valerie Braithwaite and
    Margaret Levi (eds.), *Trust & Governance*. New York: Russell Sage
    Foundation: 269–314
UNDP 2002. *Human Development Report 2002: Deepening Democracy in a
    Fragmented World*. New York: United Nations Development Program,
    Oxford University Press
Uslaner, Eric M. 1999. "Democracy and Social Capital," in Mark E. Warren
    (ed.), *Democracy & Trust*. New York: Cambridge University Press: 121–
    150
    2002. *The Moral Foundation of Trust*. New York: Cambridge University
    Press
    2004. "Trust and Corruption," in Johan Graf Lambsdorf, Markus Taube,
    and Matthias Schramm (eds.), *Corruption in the New Institutional Eco-
    nomics*. London: Routledge: 139–151
van Deth, Jan W., Marco Maraffi, Ken Newton, and Paul F Whiteley (eds.)
    1999. *Social Capital and European Democracy*. London: Routledge
van Lange, Paul A., Wim Liebrand, David A. Messick, and Henk Wilke
    2000. "Social Dilemmas: The State of the Art," in Wim Liebrands,
    David Messick, and Henk Wilke (eds.), *Social Dilemmas: Theoretical
    Issues and Research Findings*. London: Pergamon Press: 1–37
Viviano, Frank 2001. *Blood Washes Blood: A True Story of Love, Murder, and
    Redemption under the Sicilian Sun*. New York: Pocket Books
Warren, Mark E. 1999. "Democratic Theory and Trust," in Mark E. Warren
    (ed.), *Democracy & Trust*. New York: Cambridge University Press: 310–
    345
Weibull, Lennart 1995. "Det ytliga oförnuftet," *Svenska Dagbladet*,
    November 11

Weingast, Barry R. 1993. "Constitutions as Governance Structures: The Political Foundations of Secure Markets." *Journal of Institutional and Theoretical Economics* 149: 286–311

1997. "The Political Foundations of Democracy and the Rule of Law." *American Political Science Review* 91: 245–263

Werhane, Patricia 1994. *Adam Smith and his Legacy for Modern Capitalism.* Oxford: Oxford University Press

Westerståhl, Jörgen 1945. *Svensk fackföreningsrörelse: organisationsproblem, verksamhetsformer, förhållande till staten* Stockholm: Tiden

Wheen, Francis 2000. *Karl Marx.* London: Fourth Estate.

Whiteley, Paul F. 1999. "The Origins of Social Capital," in Jan W. van Deth, Marco Maraffi, Kenneth Newton, and Paul F Whiteley (eds.), *Social Capital and European Democracy.* London: Routledge: 25–45

Windschuttle, Keith 1997. *The Killing of History: How Literary Critics and Social Theorists are Murdering our Past.* New York: Free Press

Wolfe, Alan 1989. *Whose Keeper? Social Science and Moral Obligation.* Berkeley: University of California Press

Wollebaek, Dag and Per Selle 2002. "Does Participation in Voluntary Associations Contribute to Social Capital? The Impact of Intensity, Scope, and Type." *Nonprofit and Voluntary Sector Quarterly* 31: 32–61

Wollebæck, Dag, Per Selle, and Håkon Lorentzen 2001. *Frivillig insats: Sosial integrasjon, demokrati og økonomi.* Oslo: Fagbogforlaget

Woolcock, Michael and Deepa Narayan 2000. "Social Capital: Implications for Development Theory, Research and Policy." *The World Bank Research Observer* 15: 225–249

Wuthnow, Robert 1998. "The Foundations of Trust." College Park, Maryland: Institute for Philosophy & Public Policy

Yamagishi, Toshio 2001. "Trust as a Form of Social Intelligence," in Karen S. Cook (ed.), *Trust in Society.* New York: Russell Sage Foundation: 121–147

Young, H. Peyton 1998. *Individual Strategy and Social Structure: An Evolutionary Theory of Institutions.* Princeton: Princeton University Press

Zakaria, Fareed 2003. *The Future of Freedom: Illiberal Democracy at Home and Abroad.* New York: W. W. Norton

Zerubavel, Yael 1995. *Recovered Roots: Collective Memory and the Making of Israeli National Tradition.* Chicago: University of Chicago Press

Zetterberg, Hans and Carl-John Ljungberg 1997. *Vårt land, den svenska socialstaten.* Stockholm: City University Press

Ziegler, Rolf 1998. "Trust and the Reliability of Expectations." *Rationality and Society* 10: 427–450

Index

240

0463X71